DUE DATE

# EDUCATION, GLOBALIZATION AND THE NATION STATE

*Also by Andy Green and from the same publishers*

EDUCATION AND STATE FORMATION

# Education, Globalization and the Nation State

Andy Green
*Reader in Education*
*Institute of Education*
*University of London*

First published in Great Britain 1997 by
**MACMILLAN PRESS LTD**
Houndmills, Basingstoke, Hampshire RG21 6XS and London
Companies and representatives throughout the world

A catalogue record for this book is available from the British Library.

ISBN 0–333–68315–3 hardcover
ISBN 0–333–68316–1 paperback

---

 First published in the United States of America 1997 by
**ST. MARTIN'S PRESS, INC.,**
Scholarly and Reference Division,
175 Fifth Avenue, New York, N.Y. 10010

ISBN 0–312–17266–4

Library of Congress Cataloging-in-Publication Data
Green, Andy, 1954–
Education, globalization and the nation state / Andy Green.
p.   cm.
Includes bibliographical references (p.    ) and index.
ISBN 0–312–17266–4 (cloth)
1. Education and state—History—Case studies.   2. Education–
–History—Case studies.   3. Comparative education.   I. Title.
LC71.G76   1997
370'.9—dc21                                    96–46320
                                                      CIP

This book is printed on paper suitable for recycling and made from fully managed and sustained forest sources.

10   9   8   7   6   5   4   3   2   1
06   05   04   03   02   01   00   99   98   97

Printed in Great Britain by
The Ipswich Book Company Ltd
Ipswich, Suffolk

For Caroline

# Contents

# Acknowledgements

Many of the chapters in this book are based on essays of mine which originally appeared in journals and edited books over the past three years: Chapter 1 from 'Postmodernism and State Education' in *Journal of Education Policy*; Chapter 2 from 'Education and State Formation in Europe and Asia' in A. Heikkinen (ed.), *Vocational Education and Culture – European Prospects from Theory and Practice*, Tampere; Chapter 3 from 'Technical Education and State Formation in Nineteenth-Century England and France' in *History of Education Journal*; Chapter 4 from 'The Roles of the State and the Social Partners in Vocational Education and Training Systems' in L. Bash and A. Green (eds), *Youth, Education and Work: World Yearbook of Education 1995*, Kogan Page. Chapter 5 is from an article written jointly with Richard Aldrich which appeared as 'Education and Cultural Identity in the United Kingdom' in B. Hildebrand and S. Sting (eds), *Erziehung und Kulturelle Identität*, Waxman. My thanks to the editors and publishers of those volumes and particularly to Richard Aldrich for allowing me to publish a revised version of our essay here.

A number of people have been generous enough to read and comment on various versions of these essays. I would like to thank in particular Pat Ainley for his sound advice on Chapters 1 and 7, and Hugh Lauder, Brian Simon and Michael Young for their very helpful comments on the final chapter. My thanks also to Hilary Steedman with whom I have collaborated on a number of research projects, the results of which I have drawn on in Chapter 6. Needless to say in the course of writing these essays I have been helped and influenced by many others, not least my students at the Institute of Education. I am grateful to them all but take full responsibility for the outcome here.

# Introduction

Historically, education has been both parent and child to the developing nation state. The national education system as a universal and public institution first emerged in post-revolutionary Europe as an instrument of state formation. It provided a powerful vehicle for the construction and integration of the new nation state and became one of its chief institutional supports. Since then few nations have embarked on independent statehood without recourse to its ideological potential; even the older states, at least in periods of war and crisis, have continued to view education as a valuable source of national cohesion and a key tool for economic development. However, the role of the nation state is now changing, and with it the place of education.

The world system of nation states is being transformed by new global forces. For many social scientists globalization has revolutionary consequences, not only in terms of the world economy but also in the realms of politics and culture. National economies are eroded by the growing interdependence of world markets in capital, goods, services and information. Multinational corporations become transnational entities, relocating their operations as profit dictates, and beyond the power of national controls. Financial capital becomes equally mobile and ubiquitous – like power to Foucault (or God to deists), it is immanent everywhere and at the same time. Faced with these uncontrollable world market forces, so it is argued, governments no longer have sovereign control of monetary, fiscal and labour market policies; national economies can no longer be managed.

Information technologies and modern communications are likewise transforming cultures and politics. Time and space are compressed and a new global culture emerges, at once both more uniform and more particular than the national cultures it replaces. The autonomy of the nation state is curtailed by new levels of political agency, from outside by the growth of supra-national, regional and world associations, and from inside by subnational regionalisms.

The nation state, it is argued, is also fast losing its military sovereignty; it no longer has that monopoly of legitimate violence which was, to Max Weber at least, its defining condition. The year 1989 marked the end of the Cold War and of a world divided into superpower military blocs. The old 'balance of power' system, which kept the world at war and at peace for the last two hundred years, is now finished. We are entering an era of fluid international relations, where areas of relative order and safety coexist uneasily with zones of disorder and uncertainty (Cooper, 1996). The advanced states of the West and East have lost their imperial urge and their territorial ambitions. They no longer want to fight each other and, even if they did, so the argument goes, would be constrained by nuclear weapons and the regionalization of defence. In the developing world there are still areas of danger and tension, exacerbated by the ever widening gap between rich and poor nations which is made daily more visible through global communications. But, as the Gulf War demonstrated, the advanced world still retains the overwhelming military power to contain challenges to the status quo. For the moment, at least, there is a new, if precarious, order in world relations, based on new prin-ciples.

This so-called 'cooling out' of international relations, and the weakened military rationale for nationhood, it is argued, has left the advanced nation states with a crisis of identity. Since the development of a world system of states from the seventeenth century, the military imperative provided the principal *raison d'être* for the nation state. In fact it was primarily through warfare that it came into existence (Tilly, 1990). Since the Reformation, it was a commonplace of statecraft, as Elizabeth I famously noted, that national unity could be won through facing a common enemy abroad. The Cold War embodied this principal to an extreme (Chomksy, 1969) but by then it was already becoming a politics of 'virtual war', hastened by the US débâcle in Vietnam and the 'media war' in the Gulf. Now the advanced states no longer have this 'easy' option. They have to find new bases for national identity and social cohesion.

In the twenty-first century the dangers to the nation state will come as much from within as from without. Massacres in Lockerbie, Hungerford, Dunblane, Oklahoma, the Tokyo Metro and Port Arthur have all tragically emphasized just how far the means of violence have been privatized and internalized. But the problems of social violence go deeper than these extreme examples – bearing on the very basis of social solidarity in modern pluralistic societies. In the coming century the main challenge to nation states will be to find renewed forms of social solidarity commensurate with their new roles in the global order.

What is the role of education in this 'post-national' era? How far can national states control their education systems in a world of global markets and supra-national political organization? How distinctive will national education systems remain against pressures for international convergence? How far can states promote 'national cultures' through education and what forms should these take in pluralistic societies? Does the national education system have a future at all?

Postmodernism would suggest that it does not (Usher and Edwards, 1994). Indeed the whole logic of both postmodern and globalization theory is that the national education system *per se* is now defunct, at once irrelevant, anachronistic and impossible. Governments no longer have the power to determine their national systems. They increasingly cede control to regional and international organizations on the one hand (Sultana, 1995), and to consumers on the other (Chubb and Moe, 1990). In the face of common global imperatives and influenced by supra-national bodies, education systems converge on a common, instrumental norm, no longer able to maintain their distinctive national characters (Avis *et al.*, 1996). With growing social diversity and cultural fragmentation they become increasingly privatized and individualistic, shorn of their public and collective associations. Governments can no longer use education to promote social cohesion and to transmit national cultures and should not attempt to do so (Donald, 1992). As the national state becomes a marginal force in the new world order so education becomes an individualized consumer good delivered in a global market and accessed through satellite and cable links. National education ceases to exist.

There are clearly some grounds for these arguments. The devastating consequences of two world wars have made the advanced nations rightly cautious about promoting national identities through education, just as the absorption of immigrant populations has forced reconsideration of what in any case this national identity might comprise. In the so-called postmodern world of the 1990s, states find it harder to decide what a 'national' education might be and how to control it. Social pluralism forces fundamental questions about national cultures and the potential sources of social integration. Governments find it more difficult to manage the costs and complexities of a public education system. New global trends reduce some aspects of state sovereignty and authority, and the breakdown of post-war Keynesianism raises questions about the degree to which governments can manage and deliver essential services to the standards demanded by ever more discriminating and demanding publics. Faced with all this, some governments have retreated into a kind of Know-Nothing politics, emphasizing the limitations of state action, and adopting less costly and less politically risky strategies of decentralization or privatization in education. While national education thrives among the emerging nations of East Asia, in the older advanced states the very notion of the national, public education system is increasingly placed in question.

The role of the national education system has changed, particularly in the older advanced nation states, and governments cannot manage education in the old ways. The original function of education systems was to cultivate social integration and cohesion, forging new notions of national citizenship and identity. This continued to be the case with the development of new nations since 1917 and among the old nations in periods of national crisis and war. However, as this book argues, the dynamics of education within the older nation states have changed. As nationhood has been consolidated and sustained, and with growing international economic competition in the postwar period, education has partially lost sight of this formative mission and purpose. In the advanced states now, with the possible exception of Japan, education is seen primarily as a means of individual and collective economic advancement. Citizen formation has given way to skills formation, nation-building to national economic competitiveness. The public and collective nature of the educational project has been partially eclipsed, at least for the moment, by individualist as-pirations and norms. This process has not occurred evenly, even among the advanced older nation states. Indeed it is much less evident in the continental European states than in the English-speaking world of Britain, North America and Australasia. Nevertheless the tendency is widespread.

However, the overall argument here is against the extreme scenarios of the postmodernists and globalization theorists. Nation states, it is argued, will survive as the only viable sites of political representation and accountability, and as the building blocks of international governance. There will still be national economies, albeit increasingly dependent on the world market. National governments will continue to see education as an important vehicle of national development, both economic and social, and seek to direct it towards these ends, however difficult this may prove to be. In fact, they may come to rely on it more. As capital, goods and ideas become increasingly global, and as people and skills remain one of the few national resources which remain relatively rooted, governments may come to regard education as one of the most effective remaining instruments of national policy. It becomes increasingly essential for national economic competitiveness in a global market. It may also come to be seen again as the key instrument of social cohesion and civic identity. In secular societies, characterized by cultural diversity and less cohesive and binding patterns of family life, there are few institutions left which can perform this function.

Education systems, though increasingly open to international markets in students and ideas, will remain national institutions, primarily under national control. They will continue to pursue national goals in economic and social development, forming citizens and skills. But hopefully they will discard the ideological trappings of an inward-looking cultural nationalism, which emphasizes ethnicity and language as the basis of national identity.

A modern citizen education, conscious of the interdependence of nations, the diversity of societies, and the necessarily global nature of solutions to the world's problems, would eschew the narrow cultural chauvinism which has characterized much of what has passed for national education. But equally, recognizing the importance of cohesion and solidarity in modern societies, it would seek to promote new and more inclusive forms of national identity. This would be a civic national identity based on common political commitments and understandings not divisive cultural myths. It would be oriented to the future not the past. The modern education project is to form new, more democratic societies and the citizens which sustain them – not to transmit and reproduce historic cultures and identities.

To understand this, and to understand the changing role of education in the global era, it is important to see how the relation between education and the process of state formation has evolved.

This book comprises a collection of essays which seek to address these questions, both historically and comparatively. Some have been published before or have been reworked from previously published pieces, and some are entirely new. Although all were written within the past three years, the essays reflect the time and purposes of their original composition. Inevitably their collection here involves some repetition in places and, in order to maintain the coherence of each piece, I have not sought to edit all of this out. It is hoped that despite their heteroclite origins, the chapters in this book form a coherent whole and a sustained argument, although the latter must remain, given the nature of global change, both provisional and evolving.

Chapter 1 reviews the literature on postmodernism and assesses the claims of postmodern education theorists as regards the current and future trends in education. Chapter 2 builds on my earlier work in *Education and State Formation* by comparing the role of education in nation-building in European and East Asian 'developmental' states. Chapters 3 and 4 examine the historical and contemporary role of the state in technical education and training in Britain, Germany and France. Chapter 5, from an original article written with Professor Richard Aldrich, looks at the relations between education and national consciousness in one multinational state: the United Kingdom. Chapter 6 draws on the author's recent research with Hilary Steedman on qualification rates in Britain, France, Germany, Singapore and the USA, and analyses the causes of differential outcomes in centralized and decentralized education systems. Chapter 7 is an extended essay on globalization theory and its implications for the future of national education systems.

# 1 Postmodernism and State Education

Like other Parisian theoretical exports before it (structuralism and post-structuralism), postmodernism has been relatively slow to penetrate the intellectual discourse of Anglo-American sociology, and even slower to make its mark on the sociology of education. However, in the last five years the ideas of Jean-François Lyotard and Jean Baudrillard have increasingly preoccupied intellectuals in Britain, America and other, predominantly English-speaking, countries. While few writers outside the cultural studies heartlands of deconstructionism will unequivocally associate themselves with postmodernism – which indeed is hard to do since no one seems able to define it precisely – there are many who draw on its conceptual repertoire to add 'cultural capital' to a diversity of new theoretical commodities, and even more who vaguely allude to it as a signifier of cultural and social change. Indeed postmodernism has become so central to theoretical debates in the UK that it serves as the structuring paradigm of several new Open University Sociology Readers (Hall, Held and McGrew, 1992; Hall and Gieben, 1992). The discourse generally has now attained such currency that it can no longer be ignored. It has become a kind of theoretical benchmark against which all intellectual products have to be assessed.

It comes as no surprise then that debates in the sociology of education have assumed an increasingly postmodern tone. As in other disciplines there are few unqualified postmodernists among educational sociologists but there are many who assert the relevance of its ideas. Most notable in the USA are Henry Giroux and Stanley Aronowitz who proclaim a left libertarian rhetoric of choice and diversity in education which is bolstered by frequent reference to postmodernism (Aronowitz and Giroux, 1991). Notable in the UK is James Donald whose book, *Sentimental Education* (1992), draws heavily on postmodern ideas, celebrating the contemporary cultural fragmentation which allegedly renders futile the search for a 'common curriculum', and calling for greater diversity and pluralism in education. Writers on race and gender relations in education in the USA and the UK have also made plentiful use of postmodern ideas (Boyne and Rattansi, 1990; Rattansi, 1992).

The impact of postmodernism is not, however, confined to the mainstream of sociological theory, nor, indeed, to Anglo-American commenta-

7

tors. Val Rust argues in *Comparative Education Review* that comparativists must take postmodernism seriously because it puts into question the continuing relevance in the 'postmodern' age of education systems which were designed to fit 'modern' purposes, i.e. when 'schools served as universalizing institutions, promoting unifying ideals and fostering notions of nationalism and civic pride' (1991, p. 619). In Australia, Jane Kenway (1992) argues that cultural commodification, economic globalization and the compression of time and space which has attended the 'information revolution', all imply radical transformations in education; and that these are already prefigured in the 'commercialization' of education and the shift away from institution-based learning, for which a paradigm case would be the development of full-fee, offshore distance education.

There is clearly no such thing yet as a postmodern theory of education. However, there has been an increasing tendency for writers on education, both from the Left and the Right, to question many of those core values and organizing concepts which have underpinned social democratic systems of state education in the postwar era and which postmodernists have identified as typical products of modernity. Writers on the Right have often denied the desirability and feasibility of universal education and have been generally hostile to the notion that a 'common education' can or should be used for progressive social ends such as increasing social equality (Scruton, 1980). They have also criticized state schooling for being an inefficient bureaucratic monopoly, subject to 'producer-capture', and have proclaimed the advantages of greater diversity and choice in systems regulated by the mechanisms of the market (Sexton, 1987; Chubb and Moe, 1990). Writers on the Left have often also been critical of the bureaucracy of state systems, if for different reasons; they have often denied the possibility of education achieving progressive social transformation, and have rejected the use of state education to impose a uniform (and variously ethnocentric, sexist, capitalist) culture on diverse populations (CCCS, 1981; Aronowitz and Giroux, 1991; Donald, 1992). Postmodernism, with its scepticism towards the 'Enlightenment metanarratives' of universalism, unity, reason and progress, has had something to say to both groups but particularly for Left sociologists who have sought to abandon their former allegiance to Marxist and socialist theory but without seeking refuge in the Right's neoliberal philosophy of Hayeck and Friedman.

Broadly speaking, the body of ideas loosely represented by the term postmodernism has emerged from the confluence of three currents of thought, each with a long and complex history (Callinicos, 1989). Their recent forms can be roughly distinguished as follows: (a) cultural critiques of 'modernist' art forms and, in particular, of the so-called 'international' style of architecture, which seek to theorize a new postmodern aesthetic, claimed to be radically removed from traditions of modernism; (b) the 'post-structuralist' writings of French theorists like Foucault, Derrida and Deleuze, whose philosophy, echoing Nietzsche, stresses the fragmentary, heterogeneous and plural nature of reality and the inherently unstable and shifting nature of the subject and individual consciousness; and (c) general theories of contemporary society, dating from the 1960s, which see new developments in technology, work organization and social forms as so distinctive as to force a complete reconceptualization of social organization in advanced capitalist societies which are now variously designated as 'post-industrial', 'post-capitalist' or 'post-Fordist' (Kumar, 1992). Within each of these strands there has been a range of intellectual output which varies from the profound and challenging to the ephemeral and jejune. Those, like Lyotard and Baudrillard, who have written most sweepingly about the 'postmodern condition', tend to draw eclectically on all three currents, often incorporating the most extreme positions from each.

The most obvious manifestation of a cultural break lies in the debate around architecture that has been raging since the 1960s. Here one can clearly identify a stylistic and aesthetic shift from an earlier form that can be accurately described as modernist. Ever since cityscapes have become dominated by the concrete and wall-of-glass brutalism of the high-rise flats and office blocks, people living in cities have demonstrated a palpable yearning for an environment built on a more human scale which would better reflect the diverse needs and local patterns of urban lives. Architects and urban planners who have attempted to respond to these desires, designing less imposing and more decorative buildings and recreating more habitable, village-like spaces in the midst of the urban jungle, have often defined their work as a rejection of the 'international' style of architecture that has dominated postwar building. Inasmuch as the latter dates back to the prewar modernism of Walter Gropius, Mies van der Rohe and the Weimar Bauhaus school, with its celebration of the monumental, the technocratic and the linear, the new architecture can be seen as genuinely postmodernist. Similarly, the rejection among some painters and sculptors of the 'heroic', technology-celebrating work of earlier generations of Russian Constructivists and European Futurists, all of whom saw themselves as quintessentially modernist, can also be seen as a genuine manifestation of postmodernism. However, whether this sense of a definitive aesthetic transition can be extended to other arts and cultural formations in general is far more problematic.

The philosophical, historical and aesthetic writings of Gilles Deleuze, Jacques Derrida and Michael Foucault form an extensive and complex theoretical corpus with considerable internal variations and disagreements. Derrida's 'textualism' involves treating all phenomena as literary genre to be deconstructed; there is, in his famous dictum, 'no outside-text', but merely an endless proliferation of signifiers. Foucault, by contrast, is concerned with the whole social apparatus (*dispositif*) of institutions, discourses, administrative procedures and architectural forms and the relations of power-knowledge that are dispersed within them. For Foucault it is power that is omnipresent and radically decentred: for Deleuze it is 'desire'. However, what all the post-structuralists share is a common debt to the writings of Frederick Nietzsche. It is from Nietzsche that they derive their stress on the multiple and heterogeneous character of reality and the unstable and contingent nature of the individual subject beneath whose apparent unity lies only a welter of conflicting desires and drives. What Nietzsche concluded from this was that all knowledge is relative, valid only within its own conceptual framework: the grounds for accepting this or that claim to truth lie not in its verifiability with reference to reality but rather in the purposes it serves. Truth and identity are merely intentional, the product of the Will to Power (Nietzsche, 1968). Post-structuralists stop short of Nietzsche's celebration of Might and Mastery but they fully embrace his relativism.

The third intellectual current drawn on by postmodernist writers is represented by the theories of contemporary economic and social change which posit a radical break with earlier forms of industrial capitalism and variously label modern social formations as post-industrial, post-capitalist and post-Fordist (Kumar, 1992). Dating from the 1960s, the first of this wave of theories noted a secular tendency in advanced capitalist societies towards the substitution of manufacturing industry by new service industries and the replacement of knowledge and expertize for capital as the central variables of modern society. Some writers, following Burnham (1945), stressed the changing relations of production, arguing that a 'managerial revolution' was occurring which separated ownership and control of productive capacity making the new managers and experts more critical for capitalist organization than the owners of capital in the traditional Marxist model. More frequently the theorists of the first wave emphasized the dramatic changes occurring in the forces of production, claiming that new technology was promoting an 'information revolution' which would transform the shape of the modern world. Most notably, Daniel Bell (1974) argued the emergence of an 'information society' in which knowledge production, rather than the production of material commodities, was becoming the principal activity of capitalist societies. The global spread of the information society would break down older divisions between social and political systems, marking the arrival of McLuhan's 'global village' and the 'end of ideology' – a theme recently recycled in the wake of the collapse of the communist regimes of Eastern Europe in the shape of Francis Fukuyama's vapid 'end of history' thesis (Fukuyama, 1992).[1]

Post-Fordism has a somewhat different ancestry and focus. Writers like Piore and Sabel in the USA, Robin Murray in England and John Mathews in Australia echo some of the arguments of the Information Society school, but they owe more to the work of the French Regulation school and writers like Lipietz and Aglietta whose thought is more concerned with changing regimes of control and work organization in capitalist societies (Piore and Sabel, 1984; Murray, 1988; Mathews, 1989). In other words their stress is more on the changing relations of production than the new forces of production: new technologies are seen as an important but not a determining element.

Post-Fordists argue that advanced industrial societies reached a watershed sometime in the late 1960s and early 1970s. This represented the limits of the postwar socio–economic system based on cheap energy supplies; the compromise between capital and labour constituted by the welfare state and Keynesian macroeconomic policies of full employment and demand management; and production regimes based on the work organization theories of Frederick Taylor and the methods epitomized by Henry Ford's automobile manufacture.

Fordism was based on the mass production of cheap and relatively uniform commodities for the mass commodity market which was gradually consolidated in the 40 years after the end of the First World War – a period during which world recession was followed by upturn and world war and then the longest period of uninterrupted capitalist growth in history. Fordist mass production, as originally characterized by Gramsci (1971), was facilitated by the new flow-line assembly methods pioneered by Ford at his famous Detroit plants. Based on dedicated production technology, massed semiskilled labour, and 'Taylorist' work organization involving maximum task differentiation and centralized bureaucratic control, the Fordist factory proved capable of producing standardized and cheap commodities on a scale hitherto unknown. Securing a mass market for these commodities was initially achieved through new forms of mass marketing, advertising and hire purchase, helped by the enhanced pay rates afforded initially by manufacturing giants like Ford and General Motors. In the longer term, as the overproduction-induced 1930s slump was dramatically to illustrate, further conditions would have to be met:

sustained continuous production could only be achieved at the expense of new deals reached with labour, giving trade unions more power and control, and by other social 'contracts' like full employment and welfare provision, which required the mushrooming apparatus of the interventionist, welfare state.

The system was reaching its limits, according to the post-Fordists, by the end of the 1960s. The costs of the welfare state were becoming prohibitive, the power of labour unions imposed rigidities on the economy which threatened profits, and the 1973 oil crisis finally ended the era of cheap energy, the supply of which had underpinned mass production technologies of the 'smokestack' era. Less perceptible, but equally important, were the gradual changes in social patterns and lifestyles which produced new demands for diversity and quality in commodities and services which Fordist systems were ill-equipped to meet (Piore and Sabel, 1984). What has emerged from this crisis, so the argument goes, are the new forms of production, enabled but not determined by new technologies, which have characterized the leading edge of the high-tech, high value-added sectors in Japan, and areas of Italy and western Germany.

The advanced guard of post-Fordist organization is said to be represented by new regimes of production characterized by flexible specialization (Piore and Sabel, 1984). Microtechnology has made it possible to move from the production of mass standardized products by dedicated machinery to the flexible, small-batch production of differentiated commodities through the use of computer-aided design and computer-numerically-controlled machines. Advanced information systems also make possible the 'Kanban' and 'just-in-time' systems which achieve the day-to-day coordination of production and orders through the minute control of supplies, stocks and deliveries. These flexible production systems are also said to be able to cater to the ever more specialized and design-conscious demands of the so-called 'niche markets'; they are responsive to rapid changes in fashion and have the potential to deliver the high quality goods increasingly demanded by affluent consumers.

It is not the new technology alone, however, which constitutes the most important aspect of the break with Fordism. Post-Fordists invariably place greater stress on the necessary social determinants of the shift. The new technology can be set to work in thoroughly Fordist ways, using the old forms of work organization, as has often been the case in England and the USA. What characterizes the post-Fordist regime is the use of new technology in a transformed labour process. This typically involves the replacement of centralized bureaucratic control by 'flat hierarchies' where responsibility and decision-making are increasingly devolved to the lower levels, as in the use in Japan of quality-control circles and incentive systems for encouraging process and product innovation on the shop floor. The other major departure from the Taylorist system is said to lie in the replacement of rigid and specialized work roles by fluid and multi-functional roles and by the widespread use of teamworking: hence the need for the multiskilled or polyvalent worker who is sufficiently flexible to move between design, production, maintenance and quality control tasks as occurs in some German car plants.

Much of the literature on post-Fordism is insightful and generally illu-minating of certain economic trends. It is often based on close observation of the labour process in advanced production facilities in Japan, Germany and Sweden or of the commercial networks in industrial districts like Emilia-Romagna in Italy, and, at its best, it is careful to stress the uneven nature of the trends it is describing and the politically contingent nature of future developments. In the hands of writers like Piore and Sabel concepts like flexible specialization are used to explore a range of possibilities not as a means to proclaim the inevitability of a future determined by tech-nological innovation. However, others have been less circumspect, and have fallen into the trap of over-generalizing from certain local develop-ments and slipping from social analysis to futurology.

Daniel Bell and the theorists of 'post-industrial society' have somewhat exaggerated the shift from manufacture to services in advanced economies. The share of employment in the service sector in countries like the USA has indeed increased, but largely at the expense of agriculture initially and then as a result of greater increases in productivity in manu-facture as against the service industries. The share of manufacture in GDP has declined less markedly in the USA, whereas in Japan and in many newly industrialized countries it has increased. Likewise, many of the post-Fordists have exaggerated the tendency for new technologies and labour processes to generate high-skills workforces. Depending on how they are introduced, systems derived from new information technologies and robotics have as much potential to deskill workers as to upgrade their skills. The most commonly observed pattern in fact is for an increasing polarization of the workforce into a core of highly skilled, flexible and well paid workers and a periphery of casualized, low-skill, low-pay workers whose flexibility consists of horizontal movement between semi-skilled jobs and in and out of work, i.e. contractual rather than functional flexibility (Ainley, 1993). This labour force segmentation generally re-inforces existing gender divisions (Jensen, 1989; Pollert, 1988). Arguments about the tendency for increased democratization of work in post-Fordist enterprises have also been greatly exaggerated (Mathews,

1989). Flattened hierarchies can often simply mean the curtailing of middle management leading to increasingly centralized decision-making and the intensification of work among lower grade staff who lack any real autonomy and see their career paths cut off. The economic miracle in Japan, Taiwan and South Korea has been achieved in part by the excessive working hours of employees at all levels (Amsden, 1992; Wade, 1990).

Postmodernism is a derivation from these three currents of thought, but a very eclectic and often unfaithfully sensationalist one. The post-modernists – Lyotard, Baudrillard and their epigones – revel in hyperbole, ignoring the more qualified and nuanced arguments of their precursors, and elevating their most casual and throw-away generalizations into the new dicta of their post-discourse. For them everything is different even when it is the same, because different is new and new is good. Postmodernism is defined by what it is against – the modern – and if that proves awkwardly postmodern, then modernity must be reinvented. To the postmodernists history has no meaning in any case.

Lyotard defines the postmodern as 'incredulity towards metanarratives' (1984). Modernity, therefore, must be 'any science that legitimizes itself with reference to a metadiscourse'. Modernism is constructed as a set of 'grand narratives' which are said to derive historically from the Enlightenment (see 1984, pp. xxxiii–iv, 5). They include belief in scientific rationality, historical progress, the autonomy of the individual subject, the possibility of objective reason, and indeed any integrated or coherent thought-system which attempts to find an overall pattern in social structures or historical development. Postmodernism is against all these, holding that any 'totalizing' system of thought, like Marxism or Liberalism or science, is inherently totalitarian. For postmodernists experience is transitory and ephemeral, reality is fragmentary and unknowable, and history is arbitrary and directionless. The individual subject has no stable identity and consciousness is merely a temporary conjuncture of shifting discourses and perspectives which allow no fixed point of reference. Postmodern art, therefore, must be a refusal of all metanarratives. It is typically ambiguous, paradoxical and 'self-ironizing', celebrating the uncertain and heterogeneous nature of reality through pastiche, montage and intertextuality. As David Harvey puts it: 'postmodernism swims, even wallows, in the fragmentary and chaotic currents of change as if that is all there is' (1989, p. 44). At its limit it becomes deliberately 'depthless', even reified, wilfully embracing commodification. For Baudrillard (1986) postmodernity tends inevitably towards 'hyper-reality', the simulated state where the real and the image are indistinguishable. In the postmodern condition, says Lyotard, rational thought is impossible; all that is left is surrender to the indeterminate multiplicity of phenomena celebrated in the games of language.

The first problem with all this is that it is deeply ahistorical. Most of the concepts which postmodernists seek to claim as their own, and which they associate with the characteristics of contemporary society, can be found also in the aesthetics and philosophies of modernity (Berman, 1982). Since the onset of the Enlightenment, there has been a powerful current of thought and artistic production which was consciously anti-rationalist. That tradition in England runs from Blake, Fuseli and the Swedenborgians at the end of the eighteenth century, through the 'romantic conservative' line of Coleridge and Wordsworth, down to Carlyle and Ruskin. While this tradition is in many ways anti-modern, it partially fuses in the last decades of the century with another French tradition which evolved from the self-proclaimed 'modernism' of Rimbaud, Baudelaire and the Impressionists to produce that unique blend of pro-modern and anti-modern sensibility which is the *fin-de-siècle* culture of Pater, Wilde, Huysmans and Beardsley. The artistic movements which flourished between then and the 1930s – Symbolism, Cubism, Futurism, Constructivism, etc. – self-consciously identified themselves with modernity, in the early period typically in sympathy with revolutionary movements (i.e. Mayakovski and Picasso), and between the wars often veering to the Right (i.e. Eliot, Pound, Lawrence and Celine) (Hobsbawm, 1990), and they are generally taken to represent the modernist period proper as far as one can define such a thing (Anderson, 1984).

There is little in the writings of Lyotard and Baudrillard which is not already evident in the art of the modernist period and sometimes even in the anti-rationalist works of earlier periods. William Blake, though supporting the revolutionary movements of his day, was virulently anti-rationalist, celebrating the power of the imagination against the 'mind-forged manacles' of contemporary reason (which he satirized as the tyrannical deity, Urizen); so too Coleridge and the later critics of utilitarian thought like Carlyle, with his polemics against the 'dismal science' of Political Economy and the sterile cash-nexus mentality. The fragmentary and transient nature of experience was a favourite theme of later poets like Baudelaire, who defined modernity as 'that which is ephemeral, fugitive, contingent upon the occasion', and even of Marx himself – the arch system-builder – who was, as Marshall Berman reminds us, ever mindful of the ceaselessly changing nature of capitalist society where 'all that is solid melts into air' (Marx in *Communist Manifesto*, 1844; Baudelaire quoted in Berman, 1982, p. 133).

In the modernist period proper, artists and writers explicitly adopted many of the notions claimed by postmodernists. From the mid-nineteenth century onwards many writers were preoccupied by the absence of moral absolutes and the relativity of knowledge. Dostoevski's Raskolnikov proclaims in *Crime and Punishment* that 'everything is possible' and writers of the *fin de siècle* are constantly exploring the limits and relativities of perceptions (Huysmans), time (Proust and Bergson) and individual identity (Wilde). Lawrence's attempt to redefine the novel by dissolving 'the stable ego of character' in *The Rainbow* and *Women in Love* prefigures later literary developments, just as his statement that 'everything is true in its own relationship, and no further' might be taken as a desideratum of postmodernism (quoted in Kermode, 1973). If the postmoderns are obsessed with surface appearances, ambiguities and shifting identities so were precursors like Yeats, with his poetic 'masks', and Wilde, who made a career out of paradox and the conflation of art and life and illusion and reality. When he says 'we live, I regret to say, in an age of surfaces' it is only his regret that separates him from Baudrillard (quoted in Callinicos, 1987, p. 9).

Postmodernism has borrowed its sentiments from the past and also its typical stylistic forms. The self-parodying, ironical style celebrated by postmodern writers can be traced back at least to Lawrence Sterne in the eighteenth century and its pre-eminent exponents in this century, like Flann O'Brien and Vladimir Nabokov, developed the form without recourse to postmodern theory; pastiche and intertextuality were the stock in trade of James Joyce, Ezra Pound and T.S. Eliot, writers *par excellence* of the modernist movement; the graphic montage of John Heartfield, the communist cartoonist, predates and surpasses anything produced by Andy Warhol and Roy Lichtenstein. One of the few aspects of postmodern aesthetics which is genuinely new is the cultivation of 'contrived depthlessness' or meaninglessness (Harvey, 1987). This is the true hallmark of the postmodern and, as Frederick Jameson argues, this should be seen as part of the extreme commodification of art in the late twentieth century which marks out postmodernism as the aesthetic of late capitalism (Jameson, 1984).

The second, and most profound, problem with postmodern thought is its relativism and extreme anti-rationalism which should, if applied consistently, lead postmodernists to abstain from making general statements about society altogether. The fact that it has not is best explained perhaps by Ernest Gellner in his book, *Postmodernism, Reason and Religion* (Gellner, 1992). That postmodern thought has thrived, and thrived most in America, Gellner puts down to three causes. Firstly, and paradoxically, the growth of the new anti-rationalist relativism can be attributed to the overwhelming dominance of rationalist and non-relativist scientific thought across the world, and particularly in the USA, the traditional heartland of positivism. In the face of this international scientific hegemony social theorists have experienced intellectual marginalization: rather than pursue the more rigorous path of a critical rationalism many have lapsed into an easy oppositionalism which they justify through a confused moral and cultural relativism. Secondly, the commercialization of academia in many western countries has put unprecedented pressure on academics to be intellectually productive and this, particularly in the American context, means producing novel ideas. Postmodernism is, as Stuart Hall notes, 'another version of that historical amnesia characteristic of American culture – the tyranny of the new' (Aronowitz and Giroux, 1991, p. 63). Thirdly, the growth of postmodernism can be related to another common trait in American culture: provincialism. American academia has so long taken for granted the primacy of American culture that the waning of US political and economic hegemony has come as something of a shock to some. The recent discovery that other cultures actually exist and that they have their own systems of values seems to have induced a state of moral shock in some intellectuals, a trauma which they rationalize by asserting that all cultures are incommensurable and all moral values relative – until, of course, they impinge on some unspoken moral bottom-line when value judgements furtively reappear.

Postmodernism should be seen, therefore, not as a development beyond modernism but rather as a continuation of a certain idealist current within it. This current it conveniently represses in its own analysis of modernity, the more to accentuate its own novelty. Postmodernism is really, as Habermas has contended, an extension of the ever-present anti-rationalism of the modern period (Habermas, 1985). Its insights are the same and so are its dangers. Taken to extremes it can only lead to moral nihilism, political apathy and the abandonment of the intellect to the chaos of the contingent. Logically it should end in silence, but like one of Samuel Beckett's characters, the postmodernists continue to speak even when there is nothing left to say.

## SO WHAT CAN POSTMODERNISM CONTRIBUTE TO EDUCATIONAL THEORY?

Many educational theorists in Britain, America and Australia have clearly found the encounter with certain theoretical strands within and around postmodernism fruitful. Foucauldian discourse analysis has sometimes provided a flexible and useful tool for decoding ideologies, policies and power relations at the macro and micro levels (Ball, 1990a); it has also allowed analysts of gender and ethnic relations conceptual space for thinking about the subject and relations between subjects in education (Rattansi, 1992). Post-Fordist analysis has provided a new language for thinking about social and economic change and has led to some innovative and cogent theorizations of the relations between education and economic relations (Brown and Lauder, 1992). These developments should be welcomed. However, postmodernism proper (i.e. as propounded by Lyotard, Baudrillard et al.) has so far contributed little that is distinctive or theoretically fruitful and it seems unlikely that it will.

The main advocates to date of a postmodern approach to educational theory are Stanley Aronowitz and Henry Giroux in their volume: *Post-Modern Education: Politics, Culture and Social Criticism* (1991) (and more recently Giroux in *Border Crossings* (1992) and James Donald in his book: *Sentimental Education* (1992)). (The recent work of Usher and Edwards (1994) is discussed in the final chapter of this book.)

Giroux and Aronowitz do little more than fashion-model the latest theoretical costumes for the educational audience. They make grand claims for the theoretical value of postmodern ideas: postmodernism 'offers new theoretical tools to rethink both broad and specific contexts in which authority is defined ... by combining the best insights of modernism and postmodernism, educators can deepen and extend what is generally referred to as critical pedagogy...' and so on (1991, p. 117). Not wishing to abandon their former neo-Marxism they seek to annex some of the ideas of postmodernism to the unashamedly modernist project of radical democracy and social justice (Hill and Cole, 1993). But how, one might ask, can postmodernism extend 'critical discourse' when it rejects the very rationalist foundation on which critique is built? The authors here show little interest in answering the difficult questions; their intention, rather, is to resuscitate a now somewhat moribund libertarian progressivism with the latest theoretical tonic. Never mind that this involves an incoherent admixture of two philosophically antithetical discourses: Marxism and postmodernism. It seems not to trouble them that the origins of Lyotard's thought lies in an explicit rejection of his former '68 Marxism.

In his later book, *Border Crossings*, Giroux has apparently acknowledged these contradictions and now claims to have made a political and theoretical shift into 'post-Marxism'. *Border Crossings* is about traversing intellectual domains: the borders referred to in the title are the 'boundaries of knowledge that claim the status of master narratives ... within feminist and postmodern discourses this has expressed itself in recognizing the situated nature of knowledge, the partiality of knowledge claims, the indeterminacy of history, and the shifting, multiple and often contradictory nature of identity' (Giroux, 1992, p. 26). The discourse is unequivocally postmodernist and the authors' position is now at least overt. However, the new theoretical paradigm has little commensurate pay-off in terms of educational theory. Giroux's 'border pedagogy' involves the study of popular culture, 'texts which must be decentred and understood as historical and social constructions', students creating their own texts, and systematic analyses of the ways in which the dominant culture creates borders saturated in terror, inequality and forced exclusions (Cole and Hill 1993; Giroux, 1992, pp. 31–3). His postmodern high school would involve students and teachers negotiating courses, a variety of pedagogic styles, including open learning, and democratic forms of organization. The language has changed, but there is little here that was not common currency in the liberal progressivism of the 1970s. While it is undoubtedly necessary to continue to reassert the importance of democracy in schools and the value of critical and contextualized study there is a striking naivety about a study written in the 1990s which fails to address the pervasive and sometimes trenchant criticisms of progressivism which have dominated educational debates for the past 20 years. It would seem clear now that a student-centred and critical pedagogy is a necessary but not sufficient condition of effective learning in schools and no guarantor in itself of increased educational equality.

James Donald (1992) is altogether more urbane: his style is light and witty and his theoretical footwork good enough to avoid the obvious conceptual pitfalls. However, after 180 pages of circuitous peregrination on the heterogeneity of modern cultures and the impossibility of common curricula, he has still not managed to say anything about what should constitute the curriculum in a modern society or who should construct it. This may amuse some people but it will not help much with the questions of what to do on a Monday morning in the classroom, and nor, one imagines, will it give much guidance to the policy-makers. Instead he calls for a sustained critique of 'regimes of truth' and the 'patient and practical reform of existing institutions' to achieve 'greater diversity and pluralism, more democratic accountability and control and improved quality' (pp. 179, 133). Somehow one had hoped that a new theoretical approach would deliver more, for this is now familiar stuff. Aside from the word 'democratic', the rhetoric could come straight out of *Choice and Diversity* (DFE, 1992); the policy: Education Reform Act (ERA) minus the national curriculum.

Postmodernism has little of value to offer educational theory but it has many dangers. The greatest of these is that the logic of the postmodern argument points towards an individualistic educational consumerism in many respects similar to that advocated by the free-marketeers of the new Right. While some postmoderns, like Giroux, would resist this association, there are others, like Rorty in the USA, who clearly align themselves with the free-market Right. Most common in the educational field is probably the open ambivalence displayed, for instance, by Jane Kenway, who acknowledges that the 'rapid rise of the market form in education is best understood as a post-modern phenomenon', and calls for the development of the 'educational possibilities and oppositional politics within and against post-modern markets in education' (Kenway, 1992, p. 12).

The inherent dangers of free-market education policies have been too often rehearsed to need extensive elaboration here. The main point is that regulation by the market is likely to create education systems which are less democratic than those which are regulated by public authorities, where overall standards are no better, and where inequalities of provision and outcomes are more accentuated. Since the marketization of education in the UK and USA is still in its infancy there are no hard data as yet to prove the point. However, it seems very clear from changes in patterns of recruitment to schools in Scotland (Adler, Petch and Tweedie, 1986) and in areas like Chicago in the US (Moore, 1990) that open enrolment or 'school choice' policies lead to a greater concentration of children from less advantaged backgrounds in certain schools and the colonization of the more popular schools by the better-off and better-informed. This is for two reasons. Firstly, the more affluent parents tend to be more mobile, more 'system-wise' and more aspiring for their children and use their advantages and contacts to get them into the higher performing schools. Secondly, the more parents exercise choice in the selection of schools, the less choices are available, because popular schools, which cannot grow infinitely and remain effective and popular, have to start selecting the pupils. Since their success in the market and hence resources depend largely on their academic results, they will inevitably select on the basis of academic attainments thus leading to greater differentiation in the ability intakes of different schools (Edwards and Whitty, 1992). It would defy all the results of educational sociology over the last 40 years if this did not lead to greater differentiation in average levels of achievement between schools and hence between social groups.

Whether aggregate levels of achievement are improved by school choice and autonomy remains to be seen but the arguments put forward by its advocates are less than convincing. The logical case offered by free-marketeers is crude in the extreme. School choice they say will make institutions more efficient because they have more power over decisions and because they have to compete with each other to attract students and money. School diversity will encourage a variety of school types which will enrich provision and cater for the varying needs of pupils and parents. The results may be very different. School autonomy can have beneficial effects in motivating staff and giving them an enhanced sense of commitment but, equally, it may overburden teachers and heads with administration, marketing and fund-raising responsibilities which they are often ill-equipped to carry out and which will detract from the main business of education (Ball, 1990b). School competition will no doubt raise the game of some institutions which are well placed to improve their position in the market. However, it will likely lead to extreme demoralization in other schools less well placed and hence to a decline in performance. It is unlikely that a national curriculum and national testing will be sufficient to prevent certain schools failing. The UK government now tacitly acknowledges this in its provisions for powers to 'rescue' failing schools to be vested in new Education Associations – the much ridiculed 'hit squads' of retired teachers and others who are supposed to achieve what current heads and LEAs cannot (DFE, 1992).

Equally, the promotion of school autonomy may well lead less to an enriching diversity of schools with high standards but differing specialisms than to a new uniformity where all schools try to maximize their market position by concentrating exclusively on the academic results most prized by the parents, thus reducing the current diversity of schools whose excellence lies in their provision for those with special educational needs or particular aptitudes and talents. Research into the effects of school diversification programmes in Chicago suggests that, despite the proliferation of exotic new names for schools, there is, in fact, little specialization and most schools allowed to select do so generally on the basis of traditional academic criteria (Moore, 1990). Furthermore, the new market orientation of schools in the UK is bringing with it a whole new commercial culture – the culture of public relations, promotions, unit costing and quality control, where students are clients, parents are consumers, teachers are managers and learning is 'value-added'. This new culture promises to be as uniform as anything that went before it and rather less inspiring as an environment for young people.

So far the statistical evidence to support the claims of the 'school choice' lobby are feeble in the extreme. Chubb and Moe (1990), the current doyens of the movement, argue that their research shows that effective schools tend to be those least subject to external control and bureaucracy thus supporting the argument for the deregulation or market-ization of schooling. However, their statistical methods are self-evidently flawed. Their data shows only a weak correlation between state schools with high effectiveness traits and low levels of external control. Such a level of correlation can easily be explained as a methodological artefact since data on levels of external control are based upon the self-perceptions of school heads who are clearly likely to report that they experience low levels of external control if they are effective – if they are doing well it is less likely that they will feel that the state educational bureaucracies are on their backs. Chubb and Moe's data show that private organization is a much more powerful indicator of school effectiveness than low levels of bureaucratic control in the state sector. They claim that this shows that private schools are less bureaucratic than state schools and hence more effective. In fact, church school systems in the USA are often as bureau-cratic as the public schools. The correlations in Chubb and Moe's data between private organization and school effectiveness can more simply be explained in terms of other factors associated with private schools, such as selective recruitment, which may make it easier for schools to exhibit characteristics of effectiveness. Interestingly, Chubb and Moe present no data to demonstrate that private schools achieve greater value-added in educational terms than the public schools in their sample. They also ignore the evidence which demonstrates the relatively high standards achieved in schools in countries like Germany, France and Japan which maintain strong external controls (see Chapter 6).

While postmodern advocates of school choice and diversity share certain policy orientations with the free-marketeers they do not generally rest their case on the same grounds. Their argument is not so much that choice and diversity will raise standards and efficiency but rather that they are an inevitable concomitant of the changing cultural configurations of modern societies. In the postmodern world, they argue, societies are so heterogeneous and fragmented that increasing differentiation, diversification and fragmentation within education systems is inevitable: we should welcome it rather than practise futile resistance in the face of self-evident global trends. If this is true then clearly the argument must be taken seriously.

It is certainly the case that diversification policies of the kind favoured by the free-market Right in the UK have been adopted in a number of countries, not all of which are governed by neoliberal regimes. Market policies in education made the biggest impact in the USA under Reagan and Bush and in the UK under Thatcher and Major. Generally, they have had most influence in the English-speaking countries which have been particularly prone to neoliberal ideas, even when under nominally Labour regimes as in New Zealand. However, there are signs that these policies are making an impression beyond the English-speaking heartlands of neoliberalism both in eastern Europe and in western continental states. Deregulation and choice are at the centre of debates about educational reform in Hungary, Poland and the former Czechoslovakia (Mitter, 1992a; Mitter 1992b; Szebenyi, 1992); Spain is experimenting with school-based management policies (Hanson, 1990); France has allowed parents some choice over secondary schools (Derouet, 1991); and legislation has occurred in Sweden which will reduce central regulation of the curriculum and teaching methods and encourage more private schools (Swedish Ministry of Education and Science, 1993). The international evidence has certainly been sufficient to convince some of the most intelligent critics of educational markets that important changes are indeed occurring. Geoff Whitty, in a circumspect and perceptive evaluation of the claims of post-modernism, concludes that 'policies which seem to emphasize heterogeneity, fragmentation and difference certainly seem to represent more than a passing fashion amongst New Right politicians' (1992).

However, we should remain sceptical of claims that a global policy-shift is occurring for a number of reasons. Firstly, most, if not all, cases of market policies in education *have* been associated with regimes of the Right and it is far from clear that there is a secular global trend towards neoliberal political economy. Only three years after announcing the 'End of History' in the global ascendancy of the free-market ideal, the American sage, Francis Fukuyama, has now discovered another, more successful, model of Asian capitalism which is based, he says, on 'trust' not American-style *laissez-faire* (Fukuyama, 1995). Secondly, the spread of market education policies in Europe is clearly very uneven. The reforms in countries like Sweden and France are essentially about the decentralization of powers to the regional and local state and to the social partners. Privatization in Sweden is still limited and increased school autonomy relates mainly to pedagogic decisions rather than financial decisions. While France has introduced a degree of school choice there is little sign as yet of local management of schools. In Germany and Japan there have been no serious moves to break up the state education bureaucracies or to introduce school choice. Outcome-related funding and performance-related pay for teachers are unknown in most of continental Europe. Thirdly, even in eastern European states like Poland, Hungary and the former Czechoslovakia, where there has been an understandable reaction against centralized statism in education, there is still considerable resistance to the break-up of educational bureaucracies and to full-blown policies of deregulation and school autonomy. Fears that this might lead towards reduced democratic accountability, inefficiency and increased inequalities may well stem the initial enthusiasm for liberalization policies (Szebenyi, 1992).

Lastly, in the fast developing countries of the Asian Pacific Rim, there is little evidence of educational marketization. In fact, in countries like Taiwan and South Korea centralized planning and bureaucratic corporatist forms of control dominate in education as well as, arguably, in economic production. As these countries increasingly come to dominate the world economy, it would seem likely that the free-market dogmas of the Anglophone countries will come under growing ideological challenge from the policies associated with the 'governed markets' and 'developmental states' in East Asia (Wade, 1990; Castells, 1992). The latter can hardly be described as 'postmodern'.

Neoliberal education policies have found favour with policy-makers in some countries in part because their promises of increased efficiency can be seen as 'solutions' to the problem of runaway costs in ever-expanding national education systems. However, they may well run up against bedrock opposition in countries which have strong traditions of state regulation, social partnership and corporatist planning. In many countries these are still seen as essential for democratic accountability, consistency of standards and the maintenance of equality of opportunity. In Japan, Nakasone repeatedly tried to steer the education system towards liberalization but failed due to lukewarm public support, the opposition of the powerful teachers' union, Nikkyoso, and the lack of consensus within Monbusho, the central educational bureaucracy (Schoppa, 1991). Despite public unease about the pressures in Japanese schools, there is an awareness that standards are high by international comparisons and that the system is relatively egalitarian: the liberalization proposed by Nakasone was seen as a threat to this. Likewise in France and Germany, great stress is placed on the responsibility of the state for maintaining consistency of standards throughout the system. As Detlef Glowka put it in 1989:

> To German observers the phenomenon of Thatcherite education policy appears very strange. The tendencies towards privatization and commercialization of the education system would encounter massive resistance in the FRG and would not be supported by a political majority ... Most people believe that the school system has to be regulated by the state authorities in order to ensure effectiveness and social balance. For this we have the special term 'Ordnungspolitik'.

There is little evidence that this has changed in the intervening period in Germany and one doubts whether even in France, with the Right now in control, deregulation will make much headway in the face of powerful traditions of state control in education. The problem for neoliberal reformers is not just entrenched traditions but also the current logic of international comparisons which show that the high achieving educational systems, like those in Germany, France and Japan, are generally those which place considerable emphasis on public regulation and consistency of practice, whether this be in relation to the curriculum, assessment, teaching methods or learning materials (Green and Steedman, 1993). It is only governments in the grip of blind dogma who will ignore this and opt for the undiluted free-market policies of countries like the USA, whose school standards are among the lowest in the OECD (see Chapter 6).

The last ten years have certainly seen important changes in the way public services are delivered in modern societies. There has been widespread questioning of the crude Morrisonian model of public ownership and a desire to move beyond the paternalism inherent in the Fabian conception of welfare services dominated by the 'experts'. New relationships have evolved between states and markets, between central, regional and local authorities and between the public and private sectors. In the undemocratic 'government by quango' model described by Ainley and Corney (1990), the state sector is privatized and the private sector state-subsidized; public services are delivered privately on contract to the state, where the state defines the terms (Ainley, 1993). However, in other, more democratic models services are delivered and controlled through collaboration between social partners. Contrary to the view of the free-marketeers, this involves not an overall reduction in the scope of state regulation, but rather a change in form (Blackstone et al., 1992).

In education, likewise, one can see various changes in regimes of finance and control, but these by no means suggest a global shift towards deregulation and free-market principles. In Britain and the USA, market forms have indeed been taken furthest. Some services have been privatized, while others have remained in the public realm but in institutions which have been 'opened up' to market forces through local management and competition policies. However, even in these countries government controls over the curriculum and assessment have grown and output-related funding regimes have provided increasing central steerage over the priorities of institutions. In continental Europe thus far there has been only limited privatization, and devolution has most often meant giving more control to regional and local authorities rather than to institutions. Where private sector and state combine in delivering services, as in the celebrated

German Dual System of training, it is on the cooperative rather than the contract model: the social partners collaborate in all aspects of service provision from policy-formulation to administration, finance and delivery (CEDEFOP, 1987).

The promotion of diversification and differentiation within public services need not, of course, only be associated with free-market mechanisms. It is quite possible to promote greater differentiation in provision within a traditional public service model and to some extent this may be desirable providing that it does not increase inequalities and undermine the essential functions of education (Ranson, 1993). The dangers of the first have already been suggested. It remains to consider the second which is at the heart of the postmodern argument.

The postmoderns argue that greater pluralism and 'choice' in education is good because it empowers individuals and subordinated cultures. They also suggest that it is somehow inevitable in the modern world because society and culture itself has become so fragmented. Both of these claims are highly questionable.

Historically, England has had one of the most pluralistic and 'liberal' education system in the world. LEAs and school heads have had considerable powers in the organization of schools, there has been little central regulation of curricula or assessment and no central control over teaching methods. The result has been an immense plurality in types of school, curricula and examinations (Green, 1990). Whatever the benefits of this arrangement, it is not at all clear that this has empowered the majority of individuals or legitimated subordinate cultures to a greater degree than in other western European states where education has been more regulated and less pluralistic. What is clear is that pluralism and diversity in England has been synonymous with the most hierarchical, elitist and class-differentiated system in the world. There is no reason to believe that the diversity and pluralism advocated by the postmoderns would be any different.

It is also questionable whether greater diversification in education is inevitable in the modern world. The postmoderns argue that society and culture have become increasingly fragmented and disaggregated. But how true is this? It is certainly the case that there has been a gradual dissolution of many of the old solidarities and cultural affinities based on class, region and religion and that this can be seen as a breaking down of older unities and commonalities within groups. But it also represents a weakening of some of the sharper social divisions between groups and thus the potential for new collective identities. Surely the most remarkable feature of the modern cultural landscape is the overwhelming dominance of the mass media with their massive potential for homogenizing national – and global

– cultures. The problems facing a common school system are no greater now than they ever were; in fact they are probably less and this may explain why the drift in continental Europe at least is still away from selection in education and increasingly towards comprehensive models of organization and common curricula (OECD, 1990).

Clearly, as Donald says, there is no such thing as a 'common culture', undifferentiated by class, race, gender and region; but there never was. The arguments of the postmoderns against national common curricula are superficially attractive but fundamentally damaging. A radically relativist postmodern approach to cultural politics (which refuses the national imposition of common curricula) may appear to encourage more critical approaches to the dominant culture and thus to valorize the marginal and excluded. However, the gains are strictly limited since, as Ken Jones points out (1992), the very nature of the project prevents it going beyond pure deconstruction and disaggregation towards the development of a more coherent and positive 'multicultural' discourse, which fosters solidarity as well as acknowledging difference. What we are left with in the end is a 'free market' in classroom cultural politics where the powerful dominant discourses will continue to subordinate other voices and where equality in education will become an ever-more chimerical prospect. The best alternative to a monocultural, exclusionary, national curriculum is not the abandonment of common curricula altogether but the development of more *inclusive* and more genuinely pluralist forms within a common curriculum framework which is applied consistently to all schools. The latter does not imply complete uniformity since teachers must always be empowered to adapt their teaching to the cultures of the students they teach, but there must be a level of consistency in the learning experiences available to all children if we are to avoid the extreme variation in standards between schools which is the peculiar blight of the English system. This may be a difficult task but there can be no progress towards more egalitarian and more effective schooling without it.

The national education systems which developed in nineteenth-century Europe did so in societies which were massively differentiated and fragmented. When La Chalotais first advocated national education in France the country was still a disaggregated collection of communities speaking countless different languages (Green, 1990; Weber, 1976). The main reason for creating national education systems, as Durkheim later noted (1977), was to foster social solidarity and national cohesion – or, to put it in a more Gramscian way, to promote a 'national-popular' cultural hegemony defined predominantly by the dominant classes. Since that time the state-forming role of education has increasingly involved meeting national economic needs as well as social and political imperatives. However, there is no reason to think that modern states will cease to expect education systems to perform that Durkheimian function; and so long as this is the case it is hard to agree with the postmoderns that diversification and fragmentation are the order of the day.

# 2 Education and State Formation in Europe and Asia

The historical role of education in the process of state formation or 'nation-building' is now widely accepted. The development of national education systems in nineteenth-century Europe, Japan and North America, though occurring at different times, invariably overlapped with the process of nation-building, both contributing to it and as a function of it. The leading role which the state apparatus, or political state, played in this process in many countries is also widely, if not universally, accepted as a historical fact (Bendix, 1964; Boli, 1989; Curtis, 1988; Green, 1990; Melton, 1988).

However, if the links between education and state formation are fairly common currency for historians, the same cannot be said for analysts of contemporary education, particularly in the English-speaking world. In many countries, both Anglophone and otherwise, there is now considerable scepticism regarding the role of the state in education and the role of education in the process of state formation. There are a number of reasons for this.

The first, and most obvious, is that the resurgence of neoliberal politics and *laissez-faire* economics have decisively undermined the leading role which Keynesian welfarism formerly assigned to the state in the direction and regulation of economies and societies (Harvey, 1990). The second is that a combination of economic globalization and growth of supra-national and regional political organization has problematized the role of nation state and possibly reduced the powers of the state apparatus within it, at least in certain areas (Held, 1989; Hobsbawm, 1994). Thirdly, and not least, the increasingly plural and heterogeneous character of modern advanced societies has provided a challenge to the concept of national identity and, even, to the concept of society itself. It is not only to Margaret Thatcher that 'there is no such thing as society'. To postmoderns such as Baudrillard societies have been replaced by the hyper-reality of virtual cities and imagined communities (Green, 1994), and this perception has spread way beyond the Anglo-Saxon heartlands of deconstructionism.

In almost all countries politicians and others accord education and training an important role in economic development, and this has become
increasingly evident as globalization has heightened international economic competition. However, there is now much less confidence in the
ability of education systems to perform other developmental functions
such as the cultivation of social solidarity, democratic citizenship and
national identity. These classic functions were the essence of national education to nineteenth-century thinkers such as Durkheim but they are seen
as increasingly problematic today (Durkheim, 1956). To some educational
analysts such aims have become positively anachronistic in the postmodern world with its increasing social fragmentation and cultural
diversity. According to Rust (1991) and Usher and Edwards (1994), postmodernism fundamentally questions the relevance today of the whole
'modernist' education project where schools were universalizing institutions which aimed to assimilate and integrate diverse populations and
promote unifying national cultures. In the extreme postmodern vision education becomes a matter of individualized consumption in a market of differentiated educational products. Information technology replaces the
school and college with the virtual classroom individually customized for
each office and living room (Usher and Edwards, 1994). Education as a
public, collective and social process disappears.

The argument here, however, is that this view is not universally shared in
these countries and is certainly not yet the dominant belief outside of the
Anglophone world. There are other paradigms which continue to assert the
primacy of education in the processes of social integration and citizen-
building, and other conceptions of the 'learning society' which go beyond the
purely economic and instrumental (Ranson, 1994). There are also models of
development which continue to stress the importance of the leading role of
the state. One such model is the concept of the 'developmental state'.

This chapter seeks to explore the relationship between education and
state formation in a number of countries, and particularly those which may
be defined as 'developmental states'. Various countries might qualify for
this description and those considered here are not a methodologically rigorous sample; rather they consist of a number of countries from the Asian
Pacific and western Europe which have been defined as 'developmental
states' at different periods and which have coincidentally gone through
rapid periods of educational growth. The chapter thus deliberately crosses
centuries and continents in order to ask whether there is anything common
about the role of education in state formation in certain types of 'developmental state', even where these are manifested in diverse geopolitical and
historical contexts.

The hypothesis here is that education has played a particularly important role in the so-called 'developmental states' and that its rapid growth in
certain periods has been closely linked with the intensive process of state
formation engendered by the developmental ambitions of the state. Rapid
educational advance was both a product of the developmental state and an
important vehicle for its work. The argument so stated might seem unex-
ceptional, as merely a restatement of a human capital theory of development given a *dirigiste* twist. However, what is suggested here is somewhat
more controversial since it specifically relates economic development with
the broader aspects of state formation which concern the cultivation of
social cohesion and national identity.

## STATE FORMATION AND THE DEVELOPMENTAL STATE

It is useful to start by defining some concepts. The term 'nation state' is
used in the classical nineteenth-century sense of sovereign or citizen
states, even where these include a diversity of 'nations' or 'peoples'
(Gellner, 1993; Hobsbawm, 1990). It is not a very helpful term conceptually since it is sometimes taken to imply the existence within the
territorial political state of a culturally homogeneous 'nation', which is
rarely the case. Nevertheless, it is employed here as a concession to
common usage and because it usefully serves to distinguish the idea of
nation state as citizen population plus political state, from the idea of the
'state' as simply the state apparatus, which is how the latter is sometimes
used.[1]

State formation is taken here to refer to the historical process by which
'states' or 'nation states' are formed or reformed. In its broad sense 'state
formation' encompasses the achievement and maintenance of national/
state sovereignty; the construction of national public institutions and economic infrastructures; and also the popularization of the notions of citizenship, statehood and national identity which bind it together. The term is
deliberately bi-vocal: it connotes both the process by which 'states' are
formed and the active role played by the state apparatus in this process,
particularly in states which may be termed 'developmental'.

The term 'developmental state' was first used by Chalmers Johnson in
his classic study of Japan's postwar economic transformation (Johnson,
1982) and has since been adopted by Manuel Castells and others to define
the mode of development of the four 'Asian tigers': Taiwan, South Korea,
Singapore and Hong Kong. David Marquand has also used the same term
to describe certain postwar European states such as France, Sweden,

Germany and Austria, as well as nineteenth-century Prussia and Meiji Japan (Marquand, 1988, p. 106).

The defining characteristic of the developmental state is the dynamic, shaping role played by the state leadership and bureaucracy in relation to civil society. According to Castells a 'state is developmental when it establishes as its principle of legitimacy its ability to promote and sustain (economic) development' (1992, p. 56). Marquand understands the role of the developmental state more broadly to encompass both political and economic modernization (Marquand, 1988). He describes this process in postwar France in the period of state planning and the *économie con-certée*: 'the state', he writes, 'acting in close collaboration with large, private sector firms, prodded, bullied, bribed, cajoled and argued a pre-dominantly private-owned economy into a more advanced and more com-petitive shape' (1988, p. 106). Both authors note that rapid educational advance was an inherent part of the developmental process in these states. This can be traced historically in a number of instances.

## THE DEVELOPMENTAL STATE AND THE FORMATION OF NATIONAL EDUCATION SYSTEMS IN THE NINETEENTH CENTURY

National or public education systems developed in most major European states during the course of the nineteenth century as well as in the northern states of the USA and in Japan. They were distinctly new forms of public education involving state-funded networks of elementary schools and later secondary schools, teacher training and accreditation provided by the state, the inspection and licensing of schools and state control over curric-ula and examinations (Green, 1990). These new systems represented a decisive break with the family-, church- and apprentice-based forms of education which prevailed in Early Modern Europe, replacing the particu-laristic and essentially clerical educational forms of the earlier period with a new universalistic mission of schooling to serve the interests of the indi-vidual and, above all, the state. The national education systems were the precursors of modern state schooling.

While the national systems developed in most major states at some point between 1770 and 1900, they did not develop at the same rate or in quite the same forms in different countries. The first systems were pion-eered by eighteenth-century absolutist monarchs like Frederick the Great in Prussia and Maria Theresa in Austria. They were consolidated during the first three decades of the nineteenth century along with the systems in some other German states and in France. Holland, Sweden and the northern states in the USA were not far behind, consolidating their public systems in the 1830s and 1840s. In other areas, however, national systems were much slower to develop. The Catholic Mediterranean states developed public education considerably later, led by Italy's pioneering regional initiatives after unification in 1870. Japan laid the foundations of its system in the 1880s as part of the reforming efforts of the Meiji Restoration, and the southern states of the USA delayed implementing public education until the decades after the Civil War. England was the most tardy of the major states, delaying the development of a public system of elementary schools until after 1870 and not instituting a national system of secondary schools until 1902, almost a hundred years after Napoleon had created the state *lycées* in France. On the whole the pioneer education systems in France and the German states tended to be more comprehensive and coherent in their forms than those in states like Britain, which had long clung to the earlier voluntarist forms and only reluctantly brought the state into education (Archer, 1979).

Exactly why these new systems developed, and why they developed faster and more completely in some states than others, has long been a subject of historical debate (Archer, 1979; Boli, 1989; Green, 1990; Melton, 1988). Many of the traditional theories of educational change cannot explain the uneven development of these systems (Archer, 1979). Theories linking educational development with industrialization and urbanization cannot explain why national systems developed first in countries like Prussia and France when they were predominantly pre-industrial and rural societies, while Britain, the most industrialized and urbanized nation, was relatively slow to develop its national system. Equally, Whiggish historical accounts, which link educational advance with Protestantism and the steady progress of reason and democracy, cannot explain why educational development occurred more rapidly in the more authoritarian states like Prussia and Austria than in liberal Britain, and why there were major exceptions to the general rule of Protestant ascendancy in education, as provided by the relative advance of Catholic areas of France and Austria (Green, 1990).

A more satisfactory explanation of the uneven rise of national education systems would seem to lie in the theory of state formation. In essence what the argument suggests is that educational advance was an integral part of the general process of state formation and was most apparent in states and at times when this process was most intensive and most accelerated, as was the case in France and Prussia after the French Revolution and in the northern USA during the Early Republic.

In states like Britain and Italy, where, for various reasons, the process of state formation was relatively gradual, protracted or delayed, the pressure for educational development seems to have been less insistent, despite other attendant factors, like British economic and urban development, which might otherwise have seemed conducive towards educational reform.

What gave rise to these accelerated periods of state formation? In each case it would appear to have been a concerted drive towards national development led by the state and prompted by crises in state viability. These crises usually resulted from protracted territorial conflicts and foreign invasion as in Prussia, revolution as in France, or struggles for independence as in the USA. Powerful popular nationalisms which, as Tom Nairn has noted, are often products of historical conditions such as these, were also evident in each case, although necessarily in different forms (Nairn, 1981). In each case economic and technological backwardness, relative at least to some other rival powers, appears to have been an attendant feature although not necessarily at this stage the overriding motivation. Each of these conditions left the countries concerned with major tasks of national reconstruction, usually involving widespread political and constitutional reforms, accelerated economic development, and extensive cultural and ideological transformations to establish and popularize new notions of national identity.

Countries involved in domestic and international wars and conflicts generally experience a centralization of power and the efforts of reconstruction after such conflicts also, typically, necessitate enhanced activity on the part of the state. Likewise, countries determined to catch up economically with other more advanced states generally find that this requires exceptional state activity since the efforts of individual entrepreneurs are unlikely to be sufficient for this task. As Eric Hobsbawm and Paul Bairoch have both noted, *laissez-faire* economics and free trade generally favour the already strong, as Britain well knew in the mid-nineteenth century (Bairoch, 1993; Hobsbawm, 1969). It is not surprising, therefore, that reconstruction and modernization in France and Prussia in the early nineteenth century was largely driven and directed by the central state. Barrington Moore describes the Prussian experience, like that of Meiji Japan at the end of the century, as 'revolution from above' (Moore, 1967). In the Early Republic of the USA, constituted in reaction against the overweening centralism of the old Europe, this was less obviously the case since, as both Marx and de Tocqueville noted, here the central state tended to underplay and mask its presence (de Tocqueville, 1956). However, even in the land of democratic localism, nationalism was a most powerful force and the local state was intensely active in building the foundations of the new republic (Kaestle, 1983).

The importance of education in this process of state formation is evident. The major impetus for the creation of national education systems lay in the need to provide the state with trained administrators, engineers and military personnel, to spread the dominant cultures and inculcate popular ideologies of nationhood, to forge the political and cultural unity of the burgeoning nation states, and to cement the ideological hegemony of their dominant classes. In all counties there was a need to promulgate popular literacy and to generalize the use of the dominant language or dialect as part of the process of fostering national identity. In new nations, such as the USA, education also had to play a major part in assimilating immigrant cultures (Kaestle, 1983).

Schooling, as Hobsbawm has written, was 'the most powerful weapon for forming ... nations' (Hobsbawm, 1977, p. 120). National education helped to construct the very subjectivities of citizenship, justifying the ways of the state to the people and the duties of the people to the state. Furthermore, if state formation involved using schooling to create new subjects or citizens, it was also about creating new gendered social roles for these subjects. As Miller and Davey have shown (1990), notions of rights, citizenship and social contract rarely included women as equals. Rousseau's plans for the education of Sophie were very different from his plans for Emile, and even Jacobins like Lepelletier, who wanted girls educated alongside boys, thought girls needed less education than boys (Archer and Vaughan, 1971). Typically, schools were entrusted with making boys into useful citizens and girls into wives and mothers who would rear the next generation of male citizens.

The role of the developmental state in this process of accelerated state formation and educational development can be seen most clearly in Prussia, France and Japan. Each of these countries experienced intensive periods of state formation, following either revolution, foreign invasion or, in Japan's case, the threat of foreign invasion. Each was a pioneer educational state in their region; Japan somewhat after France and Prussia, but certainly precocious for its geopolitical context and for a scarcely post-feudal state. In each case social transformation was essentially state-led, with the political powers and the state bureaucracies playing crucial roles. Other countries, like England and Canada, followed different paths and could not be considered as examples of the developmentalist state in action. However, in these countries, no less than in the developmentalist states, education was still integral to the process of state formation.

## PRUSSIA

The consolidation of a full national education system in Prussia dates from the first three decades of the nineteenth century. It occurred during the 'era of reforms' which followed the Napoleonic occupation of Prussia and represented part of the process by which the Prussian state was regenerated in the wake of military defeat and national humiliation. The immediate causes of those subsequent educational developments, which were to so impress foreign observers, lay in that historic moment of state formation when the Prussian Junker class, pumped up by fierce nationalistic reaction to French occupation, re-established its power after the abolition of serfdom through a reformed state apparatus and the imposition of new social relations among its subjects (Anderson, 1974).

The characteristic forms of Prussian education were clearly rooted in its historical origins in the absolutism of the eighteenth century. The right of the state to impose compulsory schooling on the masses and the patriotic duty of the latter to conform to this had been well established in the earlier period and required no major cultural revolution to be made effective in the following century. The drive for military power and bureaucratic efficiency which had prompted educational development earlier was still a motive force and continued to provide the shaping spirit behind educational innovation. What was added to this in the subsequent period was a virulent nationalistic impulse, epitomized in the writings of Johann Fichte, and a desire to use education to promote the reform of the Prussian state and later to galvanize industrial development through technical expertise. Educational development was to become one of the most active ingredients in a process of compacted and forced state formation that transformed a society based on serfdom and royal absolutism to the reformed Junker state that was capable of hauling Germany into the capitalist world (Green, 1990; Landes, 1969).

## FRANCE

Educational development in France, unlike in Prussia, owed less to absolutism and more to the process of post-revolutionary bourgeois reconstruction. National education in France was first conceived by the *philosophes* of the eighteenth-century Enlightenment. However, it was not actually constructed until the period of Empire and as part of Napoleon's project of using the exceptional form of the Bonapartist state to restore order to post-revolutionary France and to finalize the revolutionary task of

unifying and fortifying the state according to the principles of the bourgeois revolution of 1789 (Artz, 1966; Prost, 1968).

The educational innovations of the Empire reflected the purposes and
structures of the Napoleonic state. The development of centralized educational bureaucracy and the subordination of education to state control was
designed to promote bourgois interests and the collective goals of the
nation state. The development of the public lycée embodied the secular
rationalist philosophy of the revolutionary period and offered a limited
form of meritocratic promotion for the middle orders (Anderson, 1975).
The continuation and development of the vocational and special schools
reflected the desire for efficient and well-trained recruits for the military
and public authorities, providing a technical education that complemented
the broad humanistic education of the *lycée* (Artz, 1966). Finally, the re-
admission of the Church into education under state control was calculated
to ensure that elementary education for the masses was still steeped in
patriotic and moral values. Throughout the accent was on the use of education to promote a unified and cohesive national culture which would celebrate the glory of France and underwrite the hegemony of the Bonapartist
state. 'To instruct is secondary,' said Napoleon, 'the main thing is to train
and to do so according to the pattern which suits the state' (Archer and
Vaughan, 1971; Green, 1990).

## JAPAN

The development of a national education system in Japan after the Meiji
Restoration of 1688 can also be understood as part of a process of intensive state formation. As Herbert Passin (1965) has written, 'educational
reform ranks as one of the key measures in the transformation of Japan
from a feudal to a modern nation state .... Through the use of uniform
teaching materials and the diffusion of a national language..., the schools
helped promote a common sense of nationhood and the displacement of
regional by national loyalties' (p. 62).

During the pre-Meiji Tokugawa period, Japan had a thriving educational culture among the Samurai elite whose children were educated in
the domain schools run by the feudal authorities, but less than 50 per cent
of the population as a whole (by 1860) went to school and most of these in
the privately-run Terakoya basic schools (Passin, 1965; Dore, 1984).
Towards the end of the Shogunate, and after the arrival of Commodore
Perry in 1853, Japanese culture began to be more open to western science,
but the schools remained dominated by traditional Confucian values. It

was the Samurai reformers after the Meiji Restoration who sought to modernize Japan and saw education as a means of mobilizing the entire population in this process of state formation.

As in Prussia half a century earlier, the impetus towards state formation in Japan was driven primarily by the fear of foreign domination. In this case, unlike in Prussia, the invasion was cultural and only putatively military, but it evoked no less a reaction for that, not least because it came after centuries of isolation such as no European state had experienced. The Meiji Restoration of 1868 was the result of a social movement triggered in part by the opening up of Japan to western influences during the 1840s and 1850s. It was the realization of the superiority and threat of western technology which prompted the formation of new social alliances dedicated to resisting foreign domination. This was to be achieved through the adoption of western technology and the reassertion of Japanese identity symbolized by the restoration of the Emperor.

Under the new Meiji regime it was the Samurai reformers and the enlightened bureaucracy who spearheaded an intensive programme of modernization which drew on and adapted western principles to the Japanese context. With the abolition of the feudal class system in 1871, the adoption of a new constitution, and the introduction of representative political institutions a new order was established. Under the slogan of *slogen shokusan koguo* ('develop industry and private enterprise'), the reformers promoted a national banking system; built railways, harbours and telegraph networks; established and later sold-off plants in the cement, silk, copper and glass industries; and provided start-up loans and subsidies to the private sector (Marquand, 1988, pp. 102–3).

Education had a major part to play in all this. It was required to furnish the new bureaucratic elite so vital to the modernizing process; to inculcate new modernizing principles among the masses, while reinforcing traditional Japanese traditions and identity; and it was critical for the administrative and linguistic integration of a nation formerly divided into over 300 separate feudal units (Cummings, 1980, p. 8). The Japanese authorities proved themselves to be particularly adept at all this, simultaneously emphasizing the importance of adapting western science and technology whilst stressing the uniqueness and historical continuity of Japanese culture and traditions. As Burkes has noted: 'In Japan certainly, experience has demonstrated that an education system can be a powerful instrument in the forging of national unity' (Burkes, 1985, p. 257).

With the establishment of a Ministry of Education in 1871, a new education system was developed which drew heavily on western influences, incorporating French principles of centralized administration and American modern curricula. A later conservative backlash against westernization led to a return to traditional Japanese values in education, epitomized in the revised Education Ordinance of 1880 and later in the ultra conservative Imperial Rescript, which stressed the role of education in promoting loyalty to the state and to the Emperor. After 1885, Japan's celebrated education minister, Mori Arinori, sought to reconcile modernity and tradition by promoting a westernized secondary education for the elite while preserving traditional values in popular education. Though later assassinated by nationalists, Arinori expressed his mission for education in classic nation-building terms: 'In the administration of all schools ... what is to be done is not for the sake of the pupils, but for the sake of the country'; 'Our country must move from its third class position to second class, and from second class to first, and ultimately to the leading position amongst countries in the world' (quoted in Passin, 1965, pp. 88 and 68).

Japan, though modernizing later than France and Germany, provides one of the clearest examples of a developmental state using education as a vehicle for state formation. Cummings' statement that: 'Japan, as a late developer, was one of the first societies to treat education as a tool of national development' (1980, p. 7) may not be strictly true in global terms, but it certainly captures several important ancillary truths. Japan under the Meiji regime was exceptionally clear sighted in its understanding of the role of education in modernization, and it provided the first example of this process in Asia, which several other countries were subsequently to follow. Cummings' statement also recognizes that late development required an especial attention to education – a point which is developed by Amsden in her work on South Korea (Amsden, 1992).

## CANADA

The construction of the 'educational state' in Ontario in the mid-nineteenth century provides another illustration of education as state formation but in rather a difference sense from the other examples cited here since the formative period of educational development occurred during a period of as yet unresolved struggle over colonial rule. As Bruce Curtis (1988) clearly demonstrates, educational reform in the period 1830–70 was inextricably tied up with struggles over the nature of the colonial state and different parties had different ideas about what kind of state they wished to promote through their educational reforms. What they had in common was a belief that education was essential for the creation of a new type of political subject whose own internalization of discipline and moral responsibility was seen as a precondition for political order in an emerging polity, which, whatever form it eventually took, would involve greater independence and more representative government. As elsewhere, the reforms were essentially constructed from above, and reflected the class aims of the dominant groups, but they cannot be construed as a crude process of imposition and unmediated social control. What Curtis demonstrates so well in his book is the process by which the reformers sought through education to 'anchor ... the conditions of political governance in the selves of the governed' (p. 15). As described by Curtis, this amounted to a classic exercise in the construction of a cultural hegemony by dominant groups through education, whereby 'official knowledge presented the patriarchal, linguistic, ethical, political, economic and religious interests of the ruling class as the general interests of society' (Curtis, 1988, p. 371).

## ENGLAND

In England the development of education was no less a process of state formation than it was in these other countries. However, due to the particular nature of the state and its relationship to civil society, a national education system did not occur until relatively late compared at least with France and Prussia. Although the terminology can be deceptive, this can be seen as a question of early 'strengths' and later 'weaknesses'. Throughout the sixteenth, seventeenth and eighteenth centuries, the British state was characterized by the relative unity of its kingdom and the relative stability and durability of its institutions and ruling groups. One of the first consolidated nation states in Europe (despite the protracted and bloody process of colonization in Ireland), the British state benefited from the early centralization of state power under the Tudors, and the advantages afforded by its geographical insularity and maritime strength, from which grew its colonial power. The early termination of absolutism through Cromwell's revolution, added to its other advantages, made possible the early development of capitalist relations in agriculture, commerce and, later, industry. During the eighteenth century, the relative absence of military conflict, combined with the economic advantages of natural resources and colonial trade, allowed capitalist development to take advantage of the home markets provided by a relatively fluid society undergoing a demographic explosion. Early industrialization could thus occur organically, from the bottom up, without excessive intervention from the state (Perkin, 1985).

State formation, or 'nation-building' to use Walter Bagehot's nineteenth-century phrase, was thus a comparatively precocious affair in Britain, and though bloody and violent at times, to be sure, occurred more gradually than in many other countries considered here. It also occurred without the enlarged, 'forcing' apparatus of the absolutist state which was so central to modernization in other countries. With a history of long-standing and relatively stable institutions and ruling groups to draw on, national identity did not have to be invented as in other countries where nation-building required the elaboration of various nationalist ideologies which literally had to manufacture traditions. If nationalism in other countries meant creating what Benedict Anderson calls 'imagined communities' (1983), Britain had no need of it, since the nation was the past. Such a state also had less need for national education during the eighteenth century, since there was not the great demand for bureaucrats and military recruits which existed in absolutist states and since the population scarcely had to be schooled in 'nationhood'.

The absence of a national education system in eighteenth-century England was thus certainly not the product of a 'weak state', as some have construed the argument (Davey and Miller, 1991). What can be argued, however, following Hobsbawm (1969), Gamble (1981) and Marquand (1988), is that the early 'strengths' of the British state and economy later became fetters on the development of a modern state and economy.

During the period 1815–60 it would be quite inaccurate to talk of a 'weak state' in Britain for, as Polanyi (1957) famously argued, the creation of a *laissez-faire* system precisely required a strong – albeit stream-lined – state to remove all the old barriers and restrictions to 'free enterprise'. The state properly described as 'liberal' or *laissez-faire* emerged after the end of the Napoleonic Wars (although its principles derived, of course, from Adam Smith in the previous century), and then only developed gradually through deliberate state action. The liberal state was deliberately minimalist, or tried to be, but was not so much weak as limited in the extent of its apparatus and functions. This became a problem after 1860 and has remained so since, in the sense that after the so-called second Industrial Revolution, and in what later became known as the era of monopoly capitalism, successful economies came to require more effective state intervention in all spheres of life to ensure their conditions of existence. Corrigan and Sayer's account of British state formation, which consciously plays down its uniquely *laissez-faire* features, is unable to explain these later obstacles to modernization, and it is to explain this later course of development that emphasis has been placed on the so-called 'peculiarities' of the English (Gamble, 1981; Green, 1990).

However, while that *laissez-faire* was certainly a defining characteristic of the British liberal state in the nineteenth century, 'weakness' was not. During the 'golden age' of Victorian capitalism, the British state certainly did not appear as 'weak', even though it may be said to have been storing up problems for the next generations.

Education was, however, in a sense, 'weak' or 'underdeveloped' in that provision was in various respects both less extensive and less appropriate than it might have been to the needs of the time and compared with other comparable countries. Admittedly these 'needs' were often not generally recognized, except by the long-sighted, until later (say in the 1860s) and one may thus be accused of hindsight and anachronism in applying them to earlier periods like the 1840s and 1850s. However, there were clear social and political 'needs' for more education even at that time, as many did in fact recognize, and arguably also long-term economic needs, for even if the British economy developed rapidly in these years without improved education, the absence of that education would have consequences for the economy of the next generation.

This underdevelopment of education was the result of the failure to develop a national system until late in the day; this in turn was the result of the specific nature of state formation in Britain where *laissez-faire* liberalism continued to provide powerful arguments against the use of the state in education.

## STATE FORMATION FROM THE AGE OF EMPIRE

Since the period when national systems of education were first consolidated, the process of state formation has gone through many changes and the role of education in it likewise. The function of education in economic development has become more important, whereas in the earlier period it was probably the political and social aspects of nation formation which most exercised educational reformers. The nature and role of the nation state – and the ideologies of nationalism which underscored it – have changed.

National education systems were first formed at a point when the modern, capitalist state was emerging through the twin revolution in industry and society: nationalism meant support for the liberal Mazzinian ideal of the viable nation state as formed through the agglomeration of smaller territorial and ethnic units; education was important to the formation of a cohesive citizenry out of these heterogeneous populations, particularly in immigrant nations such as the USA.

Since that time concepts of nationalism and nation state have been through successive changes. The late nineteenth century saw the emergence of expansionist imperial states and the recrudescence of new forms of nationalism which, unlike the earlier nationalisms, stressed the ethnic and linguistic bases of national identity (Gellner, 1983; Hobsbawm, 1990). The First World War led to the break-up of the old empires and the emergence of a multitude of smaller nation states under the Wilsonian doctrine of national sovereignty. The unstable political settlement reached at Versailles, combined with the economic catastrophes of the late 1920s, led to the ultra nationalist and fascist regimes of the prewar era. In the post-Second World War period we have seen the rise and fall of new superpowers, successful national independence movements and, with the demise of the former communist regimes, a resurgence of small state formation.

This and the other nationalisms associated with it has occurred simultaneously, and possibly in reaction to, other apparently long-term tendencies which suggest the partial supersession of the nation state. Economic and cultural globalization facilitated by the information revolution, and the proliferation of super-national entities like the EC, have fundamentally placed in question the role of the nation state and its sovereign powers. While Hobsbawm (1990) has suggested that nationalism and the nation state can no longer be considered the 'primary vector' of historical development, current movements across the world suggest a major resurgence of nationalism.

Education has clearly played different roles at different times and in different national contexts in this changing process of state formation. While the economic function of education may have become increasingly important, and while in the older nation states increasing cultural pluralism and internationalism would seem to be weakening the roles of education in fostering national cohesion (as the postmoderns would have us believe), there are clearly still notable instances in this century where education has been closely associated with nationalist objectives, and this continues to be the case. This includes both the negative examples of the roles played by education in the fascist regimes of the 1930s and the more positive roles played by education in forging national identity in the emerging nations of East Asia. Arguably, education's role in fostering social cohesion and national solidarity in these countries is part and parcel of the process of accelerated economic development (Wielemans and Chan, 1994).

There are certainly examples in the postwar western world of countries going through intensive periods of state formation where education was also a major factor in development. Reconstruction in postwar France and West Germany was rapid and led to long periods of sustained economic growth, with both countries achieving average annual rates of growth of over 4.5 per cent in the postwar decades (Porter, 1990). In both cases the state played a major role in planning and directing development. Sweden provides another case of a relatively corporatist centralized state engineering simultaneous economic growth and substantial educational expansion during the three postwar decades. The first country to institute comprehensive secondary schooling in Europe (in the 1950s), and the first also to create a comprehensive upper secondary system (in the 1970s), Sweden has long been seen as a pacesetter in educational reform. One could also, of course, find examples of expansionary periods in education in states not committed to the state-developmental model, like Britain and the USA after the Sputnik shock and with the Keynesian welfare surges of the 1960s, although these were short lived. In what follows, however, the focus is on the East Asian states since they would seem to provide the clearest example of the developmental state using education in the pursuit of rapid state formation.

## EDUCATION AND STATE FORMATION IN EAST ASIA

In the last three decades East Asia has experienced a period of economic development which has been described as 'unprecedented' and 'miraculous' (World Bank, 1994). During the quarter century from 1960, the four 'little tigers' of East Asia – Hong Kong, Singapore, South Korea and the Taiwan (ROC) – grew by over 8 per cent a year (Wade, 1990, p. 34). This was faster than any other region in the world at the time and represents a level of sustained regional growth over three decades that has few, if any, historical precedents. It took Britain 58 years to double its real per capita income from 1780. The USA did it in 47 years from 1839 and Japan in 34 years from 1900. South Korea took 11 years from 1966 (Morris, 1995). At current rates of development Taiwan will probably have the same average rates of income as Italy and Britain by the end of the century, if not before (Wade, 1990, p. 38).

The same period has seen enormous expansion in education in the region. Each of the four countries had quite high levels of basic education prior to industrial take-off; primary schooling expanded fast during the early period of growth so that enrolment was more or less universal in each country by 1965. Secondary school expansion followed. In 1965 the enrolment rates in secondary schools were generally below 50 per cent in each country. By 1986 they had reached 92 per cent in Taiwan, 95 per cent in South Korea and 69 per cent in Hong Kong (Morris, 1994). Expansion in tertiary education in the recent period has been equally dramatic. Taiwan and South Korea now have among the highest rates of upper secondary completion in the world, and a large proportion of those who complete go on to higher education. South Korea has over 100 universities for a population of some 42 million and well over 30 per cent of its 18–22 year olds in higher education, significantly more than in the UK (Adams and Gottlieb, 1993; Porter, 1990, p. 465).

The coincidence in these countries of rapid economic advance with educational expansion clearly suggests a close relationship between the two; indeed, there have been few accounts of the 'economic miracle' in East Asia which have not stressed the contribution of education and human capital development to economic growth (Amsden, 1992; Porter, 1990; Wade, 1990; World Bank, 1984). It is not always an easy matter to separate cause and effect in this relationship, but few would doubt that the two are connected. My purpose here, however, is not so much to enter this debate but to consider more broadly the relationship between educational development, state formation and the developmental state in these countries and how it compares with the relationships described earlier for certain nineteenth-century states.

One parallel is immediately obvious. The intensive process of state formation with which educational expansion has been associated in each of the four tigers has been about much more than economic development. As in the nineteenth-century states experiencing this process, state formation in at least three of the East Asian states has involved an effort of nation-building prompted by nothing less than the need for national survival. Not only has each state experienced protracted and unresolved conflicts with other states in the region but the whole area, in the period before economic take-off, found itself at the front-line of Cold War tensions involving substantial financial and military investments by the then superpowers.

At the time of independence in 1965 Singapore was experiencing multiple political, social and economic crises. Manuel Castells has described it as 'a devastated economy ... forcibly cut off from its natural Malaysian hinterland, and abandoned as an entrepôt and military base by a retreating British Empire' (1992, p. 37). In addition to its ambivalent and contested regional status it was a multicultural society torn by violent internal ethnic and religious strife between the Chinese majority, and the Muslim Malay and Hindu Tamil minorities. South Korea in the late 1950s was economically depressed and still recovering from one of the bloodiest wars of the postwar era. Four decades of Japanese colonialism shortly followed by a civil war which became a primary global focus of the Cold War had left South Korea, like Singapore, with an enormous task of reconstruction to repair its social fabric and re-establish its national identity. Taiwan in the 1950s, like South Korea, found itself at the centre of Cold War tensions and thus also the recipient of considerable US aid. Like South Korea, it was the product of a national territorial division which remained unresolved and which, arguably, provided an enormous impetus for national reconstruction.

Each of these countries had a lot to do and a great deal to prove. As Castells has written: 'If there is a fundamental common thread to the policies of [these] ... countries it is that, at the origin of their development we find policies dictated by the politics of survival' (1992, pp. 522–3). In this they also had much in common with those nineteenth-century states, like Prussia, France and Japan, whose accelerated state formation was also a form of reconstruction for national survival made necessary by the dislocations of revolution, military conquest or foreign cultural invasion.

The other obvious feature common to these diverse instances of state formation is the degree to which they were state-driven. There has been much debate about the common factors underlying the rapid simultaneous development of these East Asian states. Sociologists and political scientists have debated the effects of cultural and religious traditions and the common geopolitical context. Economists have stressed the fortuitous conjuncture of global growth and free trade with the existence of industrializing nations with the right characteristics and policies to take advantage of the situation, i.e. low labour costs, high rates of savings and the ability to respond swiftly to changing export markets (Castells, 1992; Wade, 1990). However, the one common factor which seems to overarch all others – indeed which seems to set the others in motion – is the existence of a certain type of developmental state. As Castells has put it: 'Behind the economic performance of the Asian tigers breathes the dragon of the developmental state' (1992, p. 56).

In economic terms the developmental state is a state which consistently intervenes to direct and regulate economic activity towards certain national goals. While not directly owning or controlling the majority of production, the state exercises strategic influence through its policy levers. In the cases of Taiwan, South Korea and Singapore this has variously involved government subsidies for exports and new product developments, controls over banking and capital movements, the use of differential interest rates, measures to encourage domestic saving and foreign investment, imports and licensing controls to protect infant industries, and substantial support for education and research and development. In Wade's model such methods are seen not as a contravention of market realities but as ways of 'governing markets' (Wade, 1990). They are successful to the degree that state planners and policy-makers understand global market trends and are able to encourage others in the economy to respond to them in ways which promote the best long-term interest of the national economy.

The role of the developmental state, however, goes beyond economic planning and regulation. It also involves the construction of national identity and the legitimation of state power. As Castells argues: 'Ultimately for the developmental state, economic development is not a goal but a means. To become competitive in the world economy, for all Asian NICs, [is] first their way of surviving both as a state and as a society' (1992, p. 57). From these beginnings it becomes 'a nationalist project of self-affirmation of cultural/political identity in the world system' (p. 58).

The state has therefore intervened not only to promote economic development but also to improve social conditions. The emphases have, of course, varied between states. Governments in Singapore and Hong Kong have invested heavily in health care and housing but relatively less (as a proportion of their public spending) on social security and welfare. Taiwan has invested proportionally more on social security and welfare than health and housing. All, however, have invested heavily in education. Public spending on education as a proportion of total public spending in 1987 was 62.5 per cent in South Korea, 47.2 per cent in Taiwan, 49 per cent in Singapore and 34.4 per cent in Hong Kong (Deyo, 1992).

Another common feature of the developmental states has been their ability to plan strategically, and their authority, in most cases, to win consent or compliance to the policies chosen to promote the planning goals. Given the problems faced by many western democracies in implementing policies in the face of volatile electorates and strong interest groups (Olson, 1982) this often seems remarkable. A number of factors have been associated with this facility. The developmental states in South Korea, Taiwan and Singapore have certainly faced crises and unrest at different periods. However, they appear to have achieved a certain degree of autonomy relative to the different social classes and interest groups in society and this has given them an added authority. As Ashton and Sung have commented in relation to Singapore: 'in order to achieve these political goals, the government has had to act independently of the immediate interests of capital and labour' (1994, p. 9).

The governments of the 1960s and 1970s had some advantages in this. Rural landowning classes, which have sometimes provided resistance to modernization in other states, were practically non-existent in Hong Kong and Singapore and partially destroyed by US-inspired land-reform in the 1950s in South Korea and Taiwan. Trade unions were also severely weakened in several of these countries in the more labour-repressive periods of early industrialization (Castells, 1992). Taiwan and South Korea also grant exceptional powers to the President and have been through substantial periods of presidential rule when elections have been largely suspended and the state has achieved a transcendence of the political process reminiscent of Bonapartism in France. The legitimacy of the state during these periods has depended very largely on its ability to deliver rapid economic growth and to make sure the benefits accrued to all sections of society.

Now, with the electoral process restored in all the countries, and democratic politics undergoing rapid revival, these developmental states face new challenges. However, they will continue to benefit from their expert bureaucracies which, working closely with the business and financial leaders, have an impressive record in economic and social planning. The commitment and relative success of these technocratic bureaucracies in long-term strategic planning would seem to be another common feature of the 'developmental state' (Wade, 1980).

Clearly education is of fundamental importance to this project. It not only provides the high-level technical skills and knowledge which future industry will need and on which the state bureaucracies rely for effective strategic planning; it also develops the attitudes and motivations in individuals which will ensure continuing collective commitment to and active participation in the goals of national development. This means not only a commitment to work discipline and individual achievement but also an understanding of the collective social meaning of the development goals. It involves cultivating productive employees and active citizens. Where, as in Singapore, the society is multicultural and multifaith, it also means developing social solidarity and cultural cohesion through the integration of different traditions.

Two characteristics, above all, distinguish educational developments in these states, and they both relate to the function of education in this process of state formation. The first is the degree to which educational development is planned and the role the central state and bureaucracy plays in this. The second is the emphasis placed on the moral and social dimensions of education . These would seem to be defining characteristics of the educational systems of not only Singapore, Taiwan and South Korea, but also of Japan.

Educational planning, at least in its more explicit and directive forms, is not currently so fashionable in many western countries. There has been growing scepticism among governments about the efficacy of central planning in general and particularly that which links educational development with future manpower needs. Many governments have preferred to limit their role to indicative planning and leave the rest to the workings of the market. However, in many East Asian states, government planning has remained absolutely central to development, and this has generally entailed an integrated approach to the planning of economic development and human capital formation. Medium-term (four and five year) plans have been a common feature of government strategy in South Korea, Taiwan and Singapore since the 1960s. Numerous planning authorities in each of these countries have been active in translating economic plans into education and training plans and in devising policies to meet the targets set in these plans. Actual developments do not, of course, always follow exactly the intentions of the planners. However, the existence of clear goals and targets has had clear effects in stimulating and focusing activity in a concerted national effort of educational development (Ashton and Sung, 1994).

The second defining feature – the emphasis on moral and social education – is particularly evident to observers from Britain, whose national curriculum, uniquely, omits social or civic education from its compulsory core. National curricula in most of the East Asian states reserve a central place for learning which encourages moral understanding and which promotes social cohesion through appreciation of national traditions and goals and the meaning of citizenship. This can take various forms but it is always in evidence. The reintroduction of moral education was one of the first reforms undertaken in Japan in the 1950s as the country began to reassess the educational changes instituted under American influence during the postwar occupation, and it has remained important since (Schoppa, 1991). In Taiwan, the national curriculum prescribes courses on Life and Ethics designed, in the official language, to develop 'traditional values', inspire 'patriotism' and 'cultivate good citizens' (Young, 1994). In South Korea, Ministry of Education guidelines on middle school education (1988) explicitly refer to the importance of developing 'skills and attitudes essential for citizenship in a democratic society' and of instilling in students 'an awareness of the mission of the nation' (Adams and Gottlieb, 1993, p. 50).

These social goals often seem to be more fundamental to education in many Asian societies than are the more strictly economic goals of human capital development, despite the importance accorded to economic growth. It is notable for instance that the majority of education at the high school level in Japan and South Korea is general rather than vocational and that even the vocational education remains fairly general in character. This does not, however, seem to have undermined economic development and may, indeed, have been beneficial to it since employers seem to value recruits with broad, general skills and good work discipline, rather than those with specific job skills (Dore and Sako, 1989; Stephens, 1991). Indeed, as McGinn et al. have noted, 'what distinguishes the curriculum of Korean schools from that of countries whose attempts at development have failed is not the emphasis on science and technology ... [but rather] the heavy stress on moral education and discipline' (Amsden, 1992, p. 219).

In each of these countries it would seem that the primary motivation behind educational development lies in the drive towards achieving national identity and cohesion. In South Korea in the 1960s the slogan was 'nation-building through education' and that sentiment still remains central to the educational mission of elementary schools which, according to Adams and Gottlieb, is to provide 'basic skills and general education in support of Korean culture and national integration' (1993, p. 50). National integration and social cohesion is likewise a primary objective of education in Taiwan, according to Young (1994). In both cases this motive has been intensified by the territorial divisions which continue to put national identity in question. As the authors of *Korean Education 2000* have put it: 'The repeated pounding of hammers steeled the will of the people to develop education as the driving force of national development' (KEDI, 1985, p. 33).

It is the importance of education to this wider project of state formation which has been the driving force behind educational development in all the countries mentioned. It is also the reason why the 'developmental states' have intervened and forced this educational development more deliberately and purposefully than in other states. Other reasons can be found for the rapid educational advances of East Asian states. Cultural traditions have no doubt played their part. Confucian values, like Protestant values in nineteenth-century Europe, have provided certain dispositions towards valuing education in certain countries where they are predominant. However, they provide no explanation for the educational advances of Asian states like Malaysia, where they are not part of the majority culture, and nor do they explain the sudden surge of educational development in a particular historical conjuncture. Like Protestantism in Europe, they can be considered only a predisposing factor, but not a necessary or sufficient condition. The main spur for educational development, rather, has been the drive towards accelerated state development and the historical causes which have engendered that drive.

# 3 Technical Education and State Formation in Nineteenth-Century England and France

Modern economists generally see human skills as *the* key factor in economic competitiveness (Porter, 1990). Vocational education has consequently been a high priority for policy-makers, particularly in Britain where provision is seen to lag behind that of other competitor nations (Green and Steedman, 1993). This situation has given rise to intense public debate about the causes of underachievement among young people in post-compulsory education and training. Current discussions focus on the narrow and over-specialized nature of academic study, the relative unpopularity and low status of alternative vocational tracks, and on the fragmented and incoherent nature of the post-compulsory system as a whole (National Commission on Education, 1993). In addition to multiple institutional distinctions in the sector, and the fragmented and dispersed nature of control over these institutions and over the qualifications system, there is a deep and damaging divide between 'academic' and 'vocational' learning. This is often believed to impede access and achievement among students and to perpetuate the low status of the vocational routes which the government wishes to enhance (Ball, 1991; IPPR, 1991).

Although the current intensity of the debate over these issues is unparalleled in this century, there were similar debates in the nineteenth century. This was particularly the case during the period from 1870 when, as now, the country was undergoing an economic recession and also experiencing the first bitter taste of the relative economic decline which has dominated subsequent British history (Gamble, 1981). Contemporary policy-making has much to learn from revisiting these historic debates to understand better the nature of this problem and the specific national causes which underlie it. A comparative analysis of the development of technical education in France and England can assist this process.

THE UNDERDEVELOPMENT OF SCIENTIFIC AND TECHNICAL
EDUCATION IN NINETEENTH-CENTURY ENGLAND

With the exception of pure science, which developed largely independently of formal educational institutions, England was, throughout the
nineteenth century, notably backward in most areas of scientific and technical education by comparison with other major states in northern Europe.
This judgement, shared by many late nineteenth-century commentators
and the vast majority of subsequent economic and educational historians,
applied not only to the state of science teaching, or the lack of it, in
schools and universities, but also to post-school vocational education,
whether in institutes, colleges or universities.[1]

For working-class boys and girls, elementary education was too sparse
and narrow to provide a proper foundation for technical and scientific
study, and facilities for full-time post-elementary education were largely
absent. State-organized trade schools for artisans and skilled workers,
which were common in continental Europe, had not developed in England
where received opinion regarded the workshop as the only fit place for
learning a trade (Huxley, 1971). There was also a virtual absence of those
intermediate vocational schools, like the *écoles des arts et métiers* and the
*écoles primaires supérieures* in France, which trained students from the
upper ranks of the working class and from the lower rungs of the middle
class for supervisory and lower managerial positions in commerce and
industry. While in France and Prussia there was a plethora of such institutions by the 1840s, England had to wait until the 1880s for the development of the higher grade schools and the first technical colleges which
would perform a similar function (Roderick and Stephens, 1978).

Provision for the middle class was equally deficient in this area. Public
and grammar schools remained frozen in the classical mould, and, until
the last quarter of the century at least, universities contributed virtually
nothing towards scientific and technical needs (Ashby, 1961). Engineering
did not become an examination subject in Cambridge until 1894 and
Oxford had no Chair in Engineering until 1908 (Roderick and Stephens,
1978). This again was in striking contrast to major continental states
where not only was secondary and university education somewhat more
scientific (Ringer, 1985), but where also a layer of higher technological
institutions had emerged in the form of the *polytechnique*, the French
*grandes écoles* and the German *Technische Hochschule* (technical high
school). Equivalent polytechnics and civic universities did not begin to

emerge in England until the 1880s and then remained chronically under-funded until the beginning of the next century (Roderick and Stephens, 1978; Weiss, 1982). By 1910 Germany had 25 000 university students of science and technology compared to some 3000 in England (Roderick and Stephens, 1978, p. 107).

Until the last quarter of the nineteenth century England had thus not even begun to develop a system of full-time state technical schools, at either elementary, intermediate or higher levels, such as existed in many continental states and this was the true measure of its backwardness in vocational education. What it had instead was an apprenticeship system, which was the sole means of training for most trades and for many of the new professions, and a profusion of adult evening classes, first in the form of the popular Mechanics Institutes and later supplemented by the classes funded by the Department of Science and Art. However, the apprentice-ship was often of dubious efficacy and rarely sought to train beyond the level of basic practical skills, and the evening class provision was geo-graphically uneven and often ineffective as training, hampered as it was by the lack of prior learning among students and the often desultory and unsystematic nature of the teaching (Thompson, 1879; Sadler, 1979).

During the first half of the century, while Britain was still basking in the sunshine of its first successful industrial revolution and its still unchal-lenged economic supremacy, this state of affairs caused relatively little alarm. However, from the mid-century onwards it was increasingly appar-ent that continental countries were fast developing economically and this raised considerable concern about the state of Britain's education and training. This was fuelled by the reports of German and French technical achievements displayed at the various international exhibitions and by the writings of educational lobbyists, like Playfair, Huxley, Samuelson, Arnold, Thompson and Russell, who came back from their investigative travels on the continent with dire warnings about the superiority of con-tinental education and training and the dangers this posed for Britain's economic position.

These writers offered substantially different accounts of the problems inherent in English education and training. Some, like Huxley (1971) and Playfair (1821), were strong supporters of workshop training and some-what suspicious of the theoretical nature of continental trade schools. Others, like Sylvanus Thompson (1879), the first Principal of Finsbury Technical College, and John Scott Russell (1869), civil engineer and fellow of the Royal Society of London, were keen to adopt the school-based training model.[2] However, they were unanimously agreed on two points: that English technical training was deficient and that this was endangering the economic health of the country. As Thompson put it in his book, *Apprentice Schools in France*:

> The lack of technical education is costing us dearly – has cost us terribly dear – in spite of the oft repeated warnings of those who saw the efforts which continental nations were making to surpass us, as they could only surpass a nation possessing vast natural advantages, by organizing the technical education of their artisans, and by giving to the sons of the wealthier commercial classes and employers of labour that sound scientific training which alone would qualify them to use to the highest advantage the technical training given to the artisans. (1879, p. 4)

These warnings about the deficiencies in English technical education began with individual lobbyists and their beliefs were certainly not shared by all commentators or indeed, as far as we can tell, the majority of manufacturers at the time. However, in time they gained increasing credibility, reinforced by the verdict of successive Royal Commissions which noted the backwardness not only of technical training but of English education in general. The Schools Inquiry Commission reported in graphic terms to this effect in 1868:

> ...our evidence appears to show that our industrial classes have not even the basis of sound general education on which alone technical education can rest ... In fact our deficiency is not merely in technical education, but ... in general intelligence, and unless we remedy this want we shall gradually but surely find that our undeniable superiority in wealth and perhaps in energy will not save us from decline. (Roderick and Stephens, 1978, p. 205)

The Royal Commission on Technical Instruction (1884), chaired by Berhardt Samuelson, later reinforced the judgement about England's comparative disadvantage with a wealth of data on continental schooling. It found that the 'dense ignorance so common among English workmen' was unknown in Germany[3] and that the advance of continental manufactures could not have been achieved had it not been:

> ...for the system of high technical instruction in their schools, for the facilities for carrying on original scientific investigation, and for the general appreciation of the value of that instruction and of original research, which is felt in these countries.[4]

## EXPLANATIONS OF ENGLISH UNDERDEVELOPMENT

The most popular explanation of English backwardness in scientific and technical education is the so-called 'cultural critique' which focuses on the supposedly anti-industrial and anti-utilitarian culture of the Victorian political elite and the landed class from which they mostly came. Versions of this thesis have emerged both from the Right and the Left and can be found in the works of a series of eminent historians and social commentators – most notably: G.C. Allen, Perry Anderson, Correlli Barnett, Anthony Sampson, Martin Wiener and, most recently, Michael Sanderson.[5] The argument, broadly summarized, is that Britain, the first successful industrialized nation, never experienced a full bourgeois revolution and thus never fully displaced the landowner class from its dominant political and ideological position. The culture of the landed class, and of the old professions and sections of the bourgeoisie which became assimilated to it, was predominantly rural and conservative, suspicious and sometimes contemptuous of industry and commerce, and disinterested in science and technology and anything that smacked of base utilitarianism. Since this class continued to dominate the British establishment it fostered a style of political leadership which was more amateur than expert and policies which were hostile to modernization and economic development. The dominance of this 'anti-industrial' culture is said to have determined the resistance of the Anglican-controlled universities and secondary schools towards science and technology and the failure of governments to modernize the educational system.

The problem with the argument is that while these traits were predominant among the landed classes, and some of the older professional groups allied to them, they by no means constituted the dominant or hegemonic ideology of Victorian England (Green, 1990; Perkin, 1985). Certainly there were aspects of the traditional landed ideology that remained distinctly influential in some areas, particularly in the Anglican Church, in the rural areas and in certain branches of the state, like the Army, the Home Office and the Foreign Office. There was also a powerful current of thought among sections of the intelligentsia which was overtly antagonistic to the dominant bourgeois ethos of the time. The romantic conservative tradition, which extended down from Coleridge to Carlyle, Ruskin and even Dickens in his later years, was deeply opposed to the narrow materialism and harsh self-interest of the liberal creed and at times appeared both unsympathetic to the urban world and hostile to industrialism itself. As both Wiener and Anderson rightly insist, these influences, combined with the lure of the gentlemanly, pastoral lifestyle,

proved uniquely attractive to sections of the bourgeoisie and the old professional class.

However, the wide resonance and compelling attraction of this view of
the world owed precisely to the very dominance of liberal and materialist
values in this the most urbanized and industrial country in the world. It
was an inevitable reaction and had important consequences, particularly in
the later period, but it hardly dislodged the mainstream bourgeois values
from their hegemonic position. The overwhelmingly dominant values of
the Victorian era were those of individualism, enterprise and *laissez-faire*
liberalism, at once both tempered and sharpened by religion. Whatever
their antecedents, these were nothing now if not the values of a confident
and predominantly bourgeois capitalism, and the heart of the metropolitan
culture which held sway in the politics of the industrial cities. The Liberal
governments of the middle decades of the century may have been dominated by landowners, but many of these had been won over to the values
of the middle classes and where it mattered most succumbed to their
wishes. For the most part, as Marx (1993) well observed, the 'aristocratic
state' served as representative of the bourgeois interest. This bourgeois
interest, though perhaps dominated more by finance and commerce than
manufacture, was nevertheless, as Rubinstein has recently argued (1993),
triumphantly pro-business.

Thus while it is certainly true that the anti-modern attitudes of the old
elites still fashioned the character of the Anglican public schools and the
grammar schools, and contributed towards their characteristic elevation of
character over intellect and classics over science, it can hardly be said that
the wholesale failure of the state to create other, more modern, institutions
derived from this cause. After all, the old landed classes still maintained
immense influence in most continental states during the nineteenth
century, as Arno Mayer has demonstrated (1981), but this did not prevent
the development of technical education. The remnants of the *ancien
régime* in France and the Junkers and old bureaucracy in Germany all
retained residual cultural traces of the old conservative values and were
sometimes overtly hostile to modernization. All over Europe, the traditional humanist education, dominated by the study of classics, continued
to retain the high status it had enjoyed since Aristotle first designated it as
the only civilized education proper for the leisured classes, and it continued to be defined in opposition to utilitarian learning (Silver and
Brennan, 1988). The German concept of *Bildung*, as defined by Von
Humboldt, and the French concept of *culture générale,* as lauded by the
likes of Victor Cousin, no less than Cardinal Newman's notion of learning
for its own sake, were all anti-utilitarian and were used by the educational

establishment in secondary schools and universities in all countries to resist the encroachments of professional or vocational education (Albisetti, 1983; Anderson, 1985). Where England differed from France and Germany was in the failure of the rising middle classes to secure reforms to these recalcitrant institutions or to ensure the development of alternative institutions. On the continent, and in Meiji Restoration Japan, these reforms were generally achieved through the action of a modernizing state. In England decisive state action was slower to occur, thus prolonging the retarding influence on education of the old cultural conservatism.

The underlying causes of the peculiarly delayed development of scientific and technical education in England should be sought, therefore, not so much in the culture of the old establishment but rather in the responses of the new industrial and bourgeois classes to it. The most striking aspect of this whole story is the failure of the bourgeoisie to secure adequate reforms in technical education despite the fact that they were clearly in favour of industrial development and in other respects quite capable of fighting for and winning those conditions which would secure it. The paradoxical fact is that the majority of this pioneer class was neither generally aware of the singular importance of scientific and technical education to economic advance nor willing, when they became aware of it, to argue for the state to take the necessary remedies. Underlying this were two historical causes which more than anything else constituted the peculiarities of the English situation. The first of these was the fact and consequences of having the first Industrial Revolution and the second was the nature of the liberal state and the individualist creed that underpinned it (Green, 1990).

In continental Europe industrialization occurred under the tutelage of the state and began its accelerated development later when techniques were already becoming more scientific; technical and scientific education had been vigorously promoted from the centre as an essential adjunct of economic growth and one that was recognized to be indispensable for countries which wished to close on Britain's industrial lead. By contrast, Britain's early industrialization had occurred without direct state intervention and developed successfully, at least in its early stages, within a *laissez-faire* framework. This meretricious industrial start had two consequences for technical education. Firstly, state intervention was thought unnecessary for developing technical skills, where the initial requirements were slight and adequately met by traditional means. The customary empirical approach of the apprenticeship seemed adequate and eminently practical. In fact, Political Economy suggested that state intervention might be positively injurious. Not only would it offend against liberal principles and create an unwanted additional tax burden, but it would interfere in the market, undermine the manufacturer's own training provision and endanger trade secrets. Secondly, the very success of Britain's early industrial expansion encouraged a complacency about the importance of scientific skills and theoretical knowledge which became a liability in a later period when empirical knowledge, inventiveness and rule-of-thumb methods were no longer adequate.

The first cause of England's failure to develop scientific and technical education was thus a deeply entrenched complacency which derived from its uniquely fortunate position. As John Scott Russell put it in 1869:

> We have been enjoying the fruits of the inventions of a few men of genius who had created the whole system of modern manufacturing industry, and providence had also endowed [us] with the accumulated wealth of countless centuries shored up in the bowels of the earth in the shape of iron and coal. (p. 80)

Such complacent confidence lasted well into the mid-century and goes some way to explaining the lack of urgency felt in matters of technical education until this time. However, there was also another cause for inaction which outlasted the first for a further 20 years and this was the resistance to state involvement in education of any sort, whether elementary, secondary or technical.

The doctrine of *laissez-faire* and the minimal state, as first advocated by Adam Smith in the eighteenth century, became the fundamental tenet of nineteenth-century liberalism, permeating the culture and values not only of dissent and the middle class but of all sections of society. When applied to education it provided powerful arguments against state involvement and led to the failure of countless reform initiatives during the first half of the century (Simon, 1969). Although various liberal ideologists, like Jeremy Bentham and John Stuart Mill, recognized that there must be exceptions to the rule of non-intervention, and particularly in the case of public goods like education, the predominant view of Political Economy during the first 60 years of the nineteenth century was that the state should let alone wherever possible, including in the field of education. State education was frequently condemned as a 'Prussian' heresy – as alien to the English national character and tradition.[6] As well as costing the taxpayers money, it was often claimed to be prejudicial to voluntary effort, detrimental to the family and enfeebling for the individual. Above all it was considered to be fundamentally illiberal and conducive towards state tyranny over the minds of individuals. Despite the small encroachments made by the state into education since the 1830s, this view was still widely held in the 1850s, as evidenced by the considerable popularity of Herbert Spencer's *State Education Self Defeating* (1851) and Samuel Smiles' *Self Help* (1859), both of which eulogized the individualist creed and berated state involvement in education.

When, in the decades following the Franco-Prussian war, *laissez-faire* ideas came to be increasingly questioned and state intervention seen more favourably, there emerged a body of opinion which was frankly sceptical of voluntarism in education. By the 1870s both John Stuart Mill and Matthew Arnold had acknowledged that opposition to state intervention was a major cause of English educational backwardness. Although he saw good cause for not allowing the state a monopoly of education, Mill (1971) recognized in his later years that 'jealousy of government interference' and opposition to 'centralization' could be a mere prejudice and one to which the middle class were particularly prone. Matthew Arnold, like his father a long-time advocate of state intervention, roundly condemned the English middle class for their opposition to state secondary education which he believed the only way to achieve schools for the middle class comparable in excellence to the *lycées* of France and the German *Gymnasien*. Writing on *Higher Schools and Universities in Germany* (1882), he quite accurately linked this opposition to state action to the characteristic British hostility to expertise and science:

> Our dislike of authority and our disbelief in science have combined to make us leave our school system ... to take care of itself as best it could. Under such auspices, our school system has very naturally fallen into confusion; it has done nothing to counteract the indisposition to science which is our great intellectual fault. (Roderick and Stephens, 1978, p. 6)

From a later vantage point Michael Sadler, who was certainly no supporter of unfettered state control, summed up the particular problem of English educational development by a series of contrasts with Germany:

> The crucial difference between the history of German education and that of English during the nineteenth century lay in the different use which the two countries made of the power of the state. In Germany that power was exercised unflinchingly, with great foresight and clearness of purpose and without any serious resistance from public opinion. In England it was used reluctantly, with deliberate rejection of any comprehensive plan of national reorganization and in the teeth of opposition

which had to be conciliated at every turn. As a result, Germany has constructed an educational system which works with fairly simple machinery; England has a complicated machinery, but no well-defined system of national education. (1979, p. 93)

By the 1900s even the Board of Education could acknowledge, in retrospect, that voluntarism had failed, arguing, in its 1905/6 Report, that reforms had been held up by 'the formidable inertia of the nation reinforced by intense jealousy of state interference and dislike of public control' (Roderick and Stephens, 1978, p. 30).

English technical education, like elementary and secondary schooling, was a major casualty of voluntarism and *laissez-faire*, and by the 1870s there was an increasing number who were prepared to acknowledge this. Few of its advocates were as sanguine about state intervention as Arnold in respect of secondary schools, and indeed it would not have been politic to be so given the importance of the industrial lobby in the cause. However, there were some, like J. Scott Russell, whose analysis of the problems in technical education closely mirrored those of Arnold and Sadler. Russell identified the same popular impediment to reform as Arnold:

[W]e dislike System, organization, and methodical control ... We despise the paternal governments of foreign nations, and spurn interference, control or direction from the executive of our own government. (1869, p. 3)

The result of this aversion to systematic organization in English education, Russell argued, was all-pervasive, affecting every branch of the system, including technical education. Most specifically, it had prevented the development of an organized system of full-time technical institutions, such as had developed in many continental states since early in the century.

## THE DEVELOPMENT OF FRENCH TECHNICAL EDUCATION

We can see more clearly the particularities of English technical educational development by comparing it with France. In France the development of vocational schools predated both the Revolution and industrialization by over a century. Technical education developed under the tutelage of the absolutist state from the time of Louis XIV onwards. It was an important part of the process of early state formation underscored by the mercantilist doctrines which argued for the enhancement of national wealth and prestige through the exercise of state power. The *ancien régime* established schools of art and design and also a number of higher vocational schools such as the *École des Ponts et Chaussées* (1747), the *École du Corps Royale du Génie* (1749), the *École Royale Militaire* (1753), the *École de Marine* (1773) and the *École des Mines* (1783). The Revolution which, as de Tocqueville argued (1955), perpetuated many of the centralizing tendencies of the *ancien régime*, destroyed many of the religious schools, but had positive results for vocational schooling. The Thermidorean regime set up the *Écoles Centrales*, which were arguably the pioneers of a modern model of secondary schooling; the Directory (1795–99) created the *École Polytechnique*, soon to become the foremost science faculty in Europe, and numerous *écoles d'application*. The latter provided training for a diverse range of occupations including sailors, agriculturalists, pharmacists, veterinarians and midwives (Artz, 1966).

After the Revolution, the centralized, etatist policies first promulgated by the absolutist monarchs, and later consolidated by the revolutionary regimes, continued to support the development of technical education. Napoleon, although the architect of the *Université*, the heart of the burgeoning French national education system, was notably conservative in his beliefs on education, abandoning the revolutionary principles of the *Écoles Centrales* for a quasi-meritocratic but still traditionalist classicism in the new state *lycées* which he founded (Anderson, 1985). More concerned with the creation of loyal and disciplined officers and expert public administrators than with the needs of industry and commerce, he gave little attention to technical education for civil occupations. However, he did give his support to the *école des arts et métiers*, which had originally been founded by the Duc de la Rochefoucauld on his estate at Liancourt for training war orphans in skilled trades. He also had two similar institutions set up at Chalons (1806) and Angers (1811) and, according to Frederick Artz, the Chalons school quickly gained the reputation for being the best elementary trade school in Europe (Anderson, 1985). Later in the century these schools, which combined practical training with theoretical instruction in applied science, became a key source of engineering skills. Their graduates, known as *Gadzarts*, often came to occupy key positions as managers and production engineers in small and medium-sized companies concerned with the design, construction, installation and maintenance of heavy machinery and power plants (Day, 1987).

After the ravages of the Napoleonic Wars France was far behind England in the development of industry and manufacturing. However, the Restoration brought a revival of economic activity which increased the demand for skills which would no longer be available from Britain which had banned the emigration of artisans to France. Initially, the Bourbon regime did little to promote technical education and the *Université* remained wedded to the ideas of classical education. However, there was increasing pressure from industrial and business leaders to provide more technical education and this received growing support from liberals, like the economist J.B. Say, and from technologically minded Saint-Simonians; the desire to see France catch up with English industrial development gave impetus to this movement. During the 1820s the main initiatives came from private individuals with encouragement from the state. In 1820 a group of Parisian capitalists, including Jacques Laffitte and Casimir Périer, set up the *École Supérieure de Commerce de Paris*. Initially encouraged by government officials like Chaptal, this finally received government funding in 1839. Likewise the *École Centrale des Arts et Manufactures* was originally founded in 1829 by a group of private individuals including the Saint-Simonian Eugéne Péclet and scientists Olivier, Binet and Lavallée. The school was designed to train civil engineers for the private sector, originally recruiting from among unsuccessful but able candidates for the *École Polytechnique*. With a supremely talented scientific faculty the school was dedicated to promoting the new field of applied science (*la science industrielle*) as a holistic discipline. Its motto – 'industrial science is one, and every *industrielle* must know it in its totality or suffer the penalty of remaining inferior to his task' – well symbolized its novel and demanding aspiration to unite the theory of pure science and the practice of engineering and in so doing helped reinforce the high status already acquired by the engineering profession through its association with the state and public works (Weiss, 1982). In time it became one of the chief sources for highly trained civil engineers in France, becoming a state institution in 1857.

During the July Monarchy the state played a more active role in promoting vocational and technical education. The 1833 *Loi Guizot* did much to improve primary education and also required the creation in every commune of over 6000 people of an *école primaire supérieure*. These taught a modern curriculum with some commercial subjects. While seen as inferior to the *collèges* by many, they grew in strength to 352 by 1841 (Artz, 1966). Although out of favour during the Second Empire they were revived during the Third Republic. By 1887 there were 700 of these institutions (about two hundred of which were for girls) providing children from petit-bourgeois families with a vocationally oriented education to fit them for work as small manufacturers, artisans and white-collar employees (Grew and Harrigan, 1991). During the July Monarchy the state, both local and central, also created a wide range of elementary vocational schools. By the mid-century there were some 50 trade schools, 35 agricultural schools as well as numerous naval, mining and design schools (Artz, 1966). Although some of these were private establishments the majority existed by virtue of state support.

The Second Empire took relatively few initiatives in vocational education but substantial progress did occur in the development of a more modern secondary education. Louis Napoleon instructed his minister Fortoul to create a modern scientific stream in the *collèges* but his bifurcation policy was fiercely resisted by the *Université* and the scheme was finally scrapped by Duruy. However, there was clearly a strong demand for a more modern secondary curriculum and local initiative saw to it that this was at least partly met. A survey by Gustav Rouland found that a sixth of all *lycéens* and 50 per cent of those in municipal *collèges* were already involved in vocational courses during the 1850s (Day, 1987). In 1865 Victor Duruy's law on *l'enseignement secondaire spéciale* was finally successful in creating a viable modern programme in the *collèges*. This scheme flourished and in 1880 its status as a full secondary course was acknowledged by the creation of a *baccalauréat* for special education. By this time some 33 per cent of children were following the special modern programmes which involved systematic science education (Day, 1987).

The Third Republic was most noted for its achievement in primary and secondary education, but there were also important new initiatives in vocational and technical education. Jules Ferry battled successfully against the traditionalists in the *Université* to create a new range of applied science faculties which could recruit students from the technical schools. Although their degrees did not at first have parity with the state diplomas, the faculties were popular and developed good links with industry. There were also important developments at the lower levels of technical education. During this period a strong lobby for technical education grew up around the Ministry of Industry and Commerce's *Conseil Supérieur de l'Enseignement Technique* and a tussle ensued between this ministry and the Ministry of Public Instruction for control over vocational education. The two ministries between them created a new network of vocational schools. From the 1880s onwards they instigated numerous *écoles manuelles d'apprentissage* which later became known as *écoles pratiques de commerce et l'industrie*. These recruited the sons and daughters of workers and petit-bourgeois families from primary schools and trained them to be skilled workers and office employees. By 1913 there were some 14 766 students in such schools, one quarter of whom were girls (Day, 1987, p. 43). The government also set up four regional boarding schools, known as *Écoles nationales professionnelles* for the training of foremen and supervisors as well as reviving the higher primary schools. Day estimates that these together with the intermediate technical schools were by 1914 enrolling at least 150 000 students.

Despite opposition from the *Université* and some of the old elites, the French state, in collaboration with progressive private individuals, had created a system of technical education probably only rivalled in Europe by that in Germany (Day, 1987).

## THE DEVELOPMENT OF TECHNICAL EDUCATION IN ENGLAND

In contrast to the state-led development of technical education in France, England relied for the greater part of the century on individual private initiative for the development of its skills training. Apart from the Government School of Mines, the School of Naval Architecture, Owen's College, and a handful of agricultural and military schools, there were few full-time state-funded vocational schools during the first half of the century, and this reflected the deep hostility within liberal opinion for state intervention in education.

For the greater part of the nineteenth century English training was based on apprenticeship and this remained the paradigmatic form of all future technical education. Privately organized by employers and independent craftsmen, the apprenticeship system received no public funds and embodied a characteristically practical approach based upon on-the-job experience rather than theoretical study. The same principle was adopted in training for professional engineering. While vocational education for doctors and lawyers was widespread, particularly with the numerous medical schools, a scientific and technical education for engineers and manufacturers was hard to find, reflecting the bias against science and the new professions in much middle-class education. This contrasted strongly with the typical practice in continental states. The 1968 Report of the Institute of civil engineers noted:

> The education of foreign engineers is strongly contrasted with that in England in every particular. Practical training by apprenticeship is unknown; the education begins at the other end, namely, by the acquirement of a high degree of theoretical knowledge, under the direction, and

generally at the expense of government. (Roderick and Stephens, 1978, p. 132)

Where government intervention later supplemented this system it was in an ancillary role that left its fundamental features intact. State-assisted technical education was predominantly part-time, practically oriented and in administration largely marginalized from mainstream educational provision. When anxieties about the superiority of French design in silk manufactures prompted the government to create a school of design and later to fund other such schools in industrial areas (of which there were 17 by 1852), the council which administered them was characteristically located within the Board of Trade, insulated from contact with educational administration. The schools were bedevilled by bureaucratic and factional conflicts and represented a very inauspicious beginning for state intervention in technical education. They were intended as a stimulus to technical education, but never as an alternative form to the apprenticeship (Bishop, 1971).

By the 1850s the limitations of this approach were becoming increasingly evident. Industrial development was entering into a new phase which made different demands on education. As Eric Hobsbawm has written:

The major technical advances of the second half of the nineteenth century were essentially scientific, that is to say they required at the very least some knowledge of recent development in pure science for original invention, a far more consistent process of scientific experiment and testing for their development and an increasingly close and continuous link between industrialists, technologists, professional scientists and scientific institutions. (1968, p. 173)

What was absent in England was precisely this link between pure science and its application, such as had been pioneered in the *École Centrale* and the *écoles des arts et métiers* – in short, technical education. The limitations of this were becoming increasingly obvious with the development of new technologies – the electric telegraph, the synthesis of aniline dyes, artificial fertilizers and so on – which were highly dependent on scientific knowledge, particularly on chemistry, and in which Britain was at some disadvantage.

The pragmatic approach of on-the-job training appeared to be inadequate and a more rigorous and systematic form of training was required. However, private and voluntary initiatives were not responding sufficiently. This was not surprising, since there was an inherent limitation in the *laissez-faire* approach to training which lay in the very nature of the market itself. Capitalist enterprise was, by definition, competitive and individualistic and recourse to any collective strategies to improve technical skills, for instance setting up technical schools, went against the grain of entrepreneurial values. Competitive entrepreneurs would not sponsor schools for technical training because they feared for their trade secrets, suspected that others would poach their trainees, and reckoned the investment was not warranted by its potential return in immediate profit. Their judgement was not untypical of their class. In no country did individual capitalist enterprise produce a collective strategy for training without state intervention. In this, the area of education with most economic importance, the market principles of Political Economy were found wanting.

Thus by the mid-century there was increasing anxiety about the state of technical education. The Great Exhibition of 1851 had alerted more far-sighted observers to the potential industrial challenge from the Continent. Lyon Playfair, a leading chemist and champion of scientific education, returned from a tour of the Continent to warn of the superiority of their technical schools. In a much publicized lecture entitled *Industrial Instruction on the Continent*, he argued that as improved transport lessened the competitive advantage to be gained from an abundance of raw materials, so science and technical skills would become increasingly important. However, it was in this area of technology that 'we English are weak. Philosophy we have in abundance. Manual skills we possess abundantly. But we have failed to bridge the interval between the two. On the contrary, there is a dead wall separating our men of theory from our men of practice' (Playfair, 1852, p. 31).

Changing economic circumstances and the agitation of men like Playfair and Henry Cole, the recently appointed Secretary of the School of Design, prompted government intervention and in 1853 the Department of Science and Art was created under the Board of Trade. The aim was to create a more effective central body to stimulate and coordinate efforts in technical education, including existing schools and sundry public institutions like the Government School of Mines and the Division of Practical Geology. However, the system it supported would remain 'local and voluntary ... (and) in the main self-supporting' (Bishop, 1971, p. 161). The department had mixed fortunes. Under Cole's energetic supervision the existing design schools were revived and by 1858 there were 56 flourishing schools of art with 35 000 students (Bishop, 1971, p. 159). The science division was less successful, initially: most of the new science schools failed and by 1859 only 450 students attended courses. Aid to science classes from the department between 1853 and 1859 amounted to a mere

£898. However, in the following decade, with Henry Cole as sole secretary of the department and Captain Donelly as Inspector of Science, a more energetic regime evolved and pupils in science schools and evening classes increased to 10 230 (Bishop, 1971, p. 167). Payment by results was instituted throughout the schools and classes receiving funds and outside examiners were brought in to assess the school results.

However, this limited government action still left scientific and technical education in an inadequate state. The Department-funded schools, like those in the Mechanics Institutes, were predominantly part-time, and their effectiveness was undermined by the paucity of elementary education among their students and the desultory nature of the classes. Michael Sadler's later reflection on this tradition of evening schools was characteristically perceptive:

> Thus alike in their excellence and their effects, the evening classes have borne the characteristic features of the English educational organization. Free in their development, vigorous in some of their achievements, and often well-adapted to the requirements of the persevering and strong, they were unsystematic in arrangement, weakened by deficits in the early training of their pupils, and from a national point of view, insufficiently adjusted to the needs of the rank and file. (Roderick and Stephens, 1978, p. 21)

Criticism of existing provision continued and intensified, as burgeoning economic realities kept this issue alive in public debate. The Paris Exhibition of 1867 had a chastening effect since the failings of Britain's industrial performance were now evident. In all of the 90 classes of manufacturers, Britain was pre-eminent in only ten. Lyon Playfair, who was one of the jurors, reported back on the exhibition with some foreboding and, in a much quoted open letter to Lord Taunton, warned that Britain was losing its industrial lead due to the fact that continental countries 'possess good systems of industrial education and that England possesses none' (Bishop, p. 174).

Growing anxiety about the scientific ignorance of foremen, industrial managers and proprietors and the deleterious effects of this on the economy prompted a series of public enquiries into the state of technical education. In the year following the Exhibition, the Select Committee on Scientific Instruction reported; this was followed by eight reports from the Devonshire Royal Commission on Scientific Instruction and the Advancement of Science (1872–75) and then in 1884 with reports from the Samuelson Royal Commission on Technical Instruction. Each report praised the achievement of continental education and noted the industrial advances that could not have occurred without it. While all reports defended the notion of workshop training, they each found many defects in English provision.

The primary concerns of the reports lay in the results of inadequate training for supervisors, managers and proprietors. Most managers and 'capitalists of the great industrial enterprises' were only educated up to higher elementary level, although in 'rare' cases they followed courses at institutions like the Royal College of Mines or Owen's College, Manchester. There was a great insufficiency of modern grammar schools. In public and endowed grammar schools 'science is as yet very far from receiving the attention to which it is entitled'.[7] Although some improvements had been made since the Clarendon Committee reported, still only 18 out of 128 schools investigated had more than four hours of science teaching per week. Various witnesses noted the effects of this inadequate scientific background in managers and proprietors: many of them did not understand the manufacturing process and thus failed to promote efficiency, avoid waste and instigate innovative techniques. Furthermore, having little interest in science themselves, they did not value it in their workmen.

The second area of deficiency lay in the ignorance of foremen and supervisors. Ordinary workmen were not thought to require much scientific education but since the foremen and sometimes the managers also were drawn from this class, it was desirable that there should be a pool of expertise there. The absence of this was put down to a number of causes. The Revised Code had narrowed the focus of elementary schools to such an extent that they imparted little scientific or technical knowledge. Their standards were inadequate as a foundation for further study. Continuation schools and evening classes were 'unsystematic' and 'desultory' in their provision and they were hampered by the lack of preparation and fatigue of their students whose efforts to acquire further education after work were not recognized by employers. Furthermore, there was a shortage of qualified science teachers, and the administrative separation of Department of Science and Art classes and the remainder of elementary and secondary education was a handicap.

As to the apprenticeship system, opinions expressed in the reports varied. The Samuelson Report acknowledged the benefits of continental trade schools, concluding that 'secondary instruction of a superior kind is placed within the reach of children of parents of limited means to an extent [of] which we have no conception in this country.'[8] However, a number of witnesses criticized the overly theoretical nature of these schools and maintained the superiority of the workshop as a means of imparting practical skills. Some of the most perceptive comments were offered in evidence given by Flemming Jenkins, a Professor of Civil Engineering at University College. Explaining that in his experience apprentice supervision was often very lax, he maintained that while the best apprentices learnt a good deal, the idle ones learnt nothing at all. Comparing the apprenticeship system with the continental trade schools Jenkins argued that, in terms of practical ability and common sense, the English apprentice was a match for anyone, and even for the products of the Polytechnic. However, he continued:

> When in after life, the two men came to fill the higher stations, the English engineer would begin to feel the want of elementary training very severely, and he is at a disadvantage compared with the man abroad, in the judging of new problems which come under his eye.[9]

Other contemporary commentators, like John Scott Russell and Silvanus Thompson, were less generous to the apprenticeship system, claiming that in all respects it was inferior to the continental trade school. Thompson, in his book, *The Apprentice Schools in France* (1879), argued that the English apprentice spent six years in repetitive drudgery that failed 'to make anything but a bad, unintelligent machine'. By contrast the French trade school, with its combination of theoretical and practical training, had demonstrably better results with its students:

> They are more methodical and intelligent in their work, steadier in general conduct, have a far better grasp of the whole subject, and are pronounced to be more competent than the average workman at executing repairs, since they have learned the principles and have not been kept doing the same thing ... all through the years of their apprenticeship. (pp. 8 and 44)

The reports made various recommendations for the improvement of science teaching in elementary and secondary schools and the better training of science teachers. Most significant was probably the recommendation of both the Devonshire and Samuelson Commissions that means should be found to integrate the work of the Department of Science and Art and the Education Department. Samuelson found much to criticize in the confusion and overlapping between the two departments and suggested that scientific and technical education was best advanced in the context of a broad and integrated secondary provision. Unable to go beyond the technical brief the report recommended the creation of a central authority for all matters relating to scientific and technical education.

Despite widespread acceptance of the findings of the Commissions, their more wide-ranging proposals were not immediately adopted. During the next ten years technical education expanded within its existing structures. The Department of Science and Art, which had become linked to the Education Department in 1856 but still remained essentially separate, expanded its support and supervision of science and art schools and classes. However, these remained unintegrated with elementary and secondary education and the dual administration of these sectors became increasingly fractious, wasteful and inefficient (Bishop, 1971). With the instigation in 1880 of the independent City and Guilds London Institute for the Advancement of Technical Education and with the creation of the new polytechnics in the 1880s, this *ad hoc* proliferation of technical provision was becoming increasingly muddled and chaotic.

The last decade of the century did finally bring some important advances in technical education. The 1889 Technical Instruction Act allowed the new local councils to set up technical instruction committees which could be financed by a one penny rate. As often happened with such permissive legislation the take-up of this was very uneven at local level with only 12 among 108 councils using this provision by 1894 (Roderick and Stephens, 1978). However, the 1990 Local Taxation (Whisky Money) Act also provided public funds which could be spent on technical education and this was more widely used. Together the measures contributed to considerable growth in technical education and encouraged many towns to build their first technical colleges.

This was the 'golden age' of the English technical education movement. The changes it brought were made possible through reform in the structures of the state. There were two aspects to this. Firstly, there was the reform of local government. Prior to 1888 England, unlike France and Germany, had no local state apparatus as such and this had been an enormous handicap in setting up a nationwide education system. After the 1888 Local Government Act, this situation was rectified creating the basis for systematic development through local state initiative. Secondly there was a general change in attitude towards the role of the state which occurred during the last quarter of the century.

The nature of this change has been much debated. Some contemporaries like Dicey regarded the Liberal reforms of the late nineteenth century as a manifestation of the wholesale abandonment of *laissez-faire* for a new anti-individualist collectivism (Dicey, 1914). Later historians, like Polanyi (1957), have tended to see these changes merely as pragmatic responses by the state to the recognition of overwhelming social needs which could not be met by the market. The truth is probably somewhere in between. There were strong immediate problems, both economic and social, whose solution seemed to require new responses. The economic challenge of Germany and the USA after 1870, along with the price depression of that period, suggested the need for more vigorous state action to maintain Britain's economic supremacy, not least in the field of education. Likewise, the social problems brought graphically to light by the investigations of Booth, Mearns and Rowntree imposed themselves on the social conscience of the middle class which, given the political implications of the extended franchise and the rise of mass democracy, increasingly felt the need for decisive action. All these factors suggested the necessity of more government intervention.

At the same time new ideologies were emerging in the closing decades of the century which embodied new conceptions of the role of the state. Chamberlain's radical followers broke with orthodox liberalism to develop a new philosophy of 'Social Imperialism'. This yoked together ideas of imperial strength abroad with national efficiency and social reform at home in a new reactionary collectivism under the sign of the strong state. The new Fabian Society, created in 1884, combined the Benthamite tradition of expert administration with notions of national efficiency in a top-down programme of gradualist social reform and municipal socialism. In the same year the Social Democratic Federation was formed which marked the rise of a more revolutionary socialist tradition. These political movements all, in different ways, echoed the emergence of new and more interventionist conceptions of the role of the state in academic disciplines from philosophy (T.H. Green) to economics (Jevons and Marshall). Together they marked the beginning of what Harold Perkin (1989) has termed the 'rise of professional society'.

The beginning of concerted government action, now made possible in a climate less hostile to state intervention, drove the reforms in technical education in this period, and their relative success only highlighted the limitations of the former voluntarist creed. However, despite this late outbreak of good sense, the long record of neglect left an enduring legacy. Technical education had been cast in a mould that subsequent legislation would find hard to break. Growing up as an extension of the apprenticeship system and reliant on employer initiatives, it developed in a fragmented and improvised manner: perennially low in status, conservatively rooted in workshop practice and hostile to theoretical knowledge, publicly funded technical education became normatively part-time and institutionally marooned between the workplace and mainstream education. A century later we have still not overcome the deep divisions between theory and practice and between academic and vocational learning which were first entrenched in these nineteenth-century institutional structures. Nor, it would seem, have we quite outgrown the voluntarist reflex which gave rise to them.

# 4 The Roles of the State and the Social Partners in Vocational Education and Training Systems

The historic demise of the centralized command economies of the communist world has prompted ideologists in the West to proclaim the 'end of history' and the secular evolutionary ascendancy of the liberal, market system as a means of organizing societies and economies (Fukuyama, 1992). However, more sustained examination of the different trajectories of the western capitalist states suggests more discriminating judgements, for while the recent Anglo-American experiments in free-market economics have proved unsustainable, and have merely consolidated the relative decline of Britain and the USA as world powers (Kennedy, 1989), the neo-corporatist, social-market policies of the continental European Union states have, in many cases, proved to be comparatively successful, providing the basis for continued economic innovation and growth through a combination of market dynamism and state regulation. Moreover, whereas advocates of the free market have often explicitly abandoned equity and fair distribution as political goals and have been prepared to see the decline of public services as a necessary cost of rejuvenating private enterprise, elsewhere social justice has remained at least on the political agenda and the effective provision of public services has been seen as a precondition of economic prosperity. The fundamental political debate in industrialized countries still appears now to revolve around the relative merits of free-market economies versus socialized mixed economies and, while this is by no means yet resolved, the case for variations on the 'third way' remains powerful.

Education and training policy, in all advanced economies, occupies a central position in this debate. Not only does it bear critically on questions both of social justice and economic efficiency but it is also subject to very contrary 'solutions' which well illustrate the still marked ideological cleavages within western politics. While all governments appear to recognize the importance of a wide distribution of education and training throughout their populations, especially in the current context of rapid technological advance and intensified global economic competition, the policies they have adopted to achieve this have varied widely.

74

Typically, Britain and the USA, and some other English-speaking countries like New Zealand, have attempted to raise participation and achievement in education and training systems through institutional reforms that attempt to install market mechanisms, fostering greater competition and efficiency. In Britain this has been accompanied by measures that greatly increase central state control in education as regards curricula and qualifications, while reducing the powers of local education authorities and minimizing the decision-making roles of educationalists and trades unions.

In continental EU states the trends have been somewhat different. Centralized control has generally been reduced by attempts to devolve decision-making to the lowest effective level (the subsidiarity principle). This has generally meant giving more powers to the regions and encouraging the social partners to play increasingly prominent roles at national, regional, local and enterprise levels. The Social Chapter of the Maastricht Treaty, endorsed by all member states except Britain, makes social partnership and subsidiarity the cornerstones of its vocational training policy (CEDEFOP, 1992). However, this devolution, which diffuses control in both vertical and horizontal directions, occurs within the overall context of regulation by the central state, which determines both the roles and responsibilities of the different actors. Neoliberal policies, involving unfettered control by the markets, have found little favour in systems where the principle remains that public authorities bear ultimate responsibility for collective services.

The different roles played by the state and other social partners in the determination and implementation of policies constitutes one of the most significant variables between different national systems of education and training. This chapter focuses on one particular area of the policy debate – vocational education and training (VET). Its main objective is to offer a preliminary analysis of the roles played by the state and other social partners in different areas of VET within a number of different national systems and to point to some of the effects of such differences. Reference will be made mainly to the systems of VET in England and Germany.

## VOCATIONAL EDUCATION AND TRAINING IN ENGLAND AND WALES

VET in England and Wales is frequently seen as one of the weakest areas of the education system, traditionally suffering from a lack of prestige and of coherent planning and organization (Ball, 1991; Green, 1990; Royal

Society, 1991; Sanderson, 1994). Currently, despite widespread recent reforms, rates of participation in post-compulsory education and training are still much lower in Britain than most other EU countries with levels of qualification, particularly in vocational areas, likewise (Green and Steedman, 1993, 1996; OECD, 1995). The reasons for this are various and complex but much of the explanation arguably hinges on historical traditions of *laissez faire* which go back deep into history.


THE LIBERAL LEGACY

Britain was one of the last major European countries in the nineteenth century to create a national education system and, contrary to the pattern in continental Europe, the state was particularly slow to intervene in promoting technical education. This was partly due to a general complacency about the importance of technical education that was one of the legacies of an early, successful industrial revolution that appeared to owe little to formal education. It was also partly due to the fact that manufacturers were reluctant to lose child labour to the education system, particularly if they had to pay for it through their taxes, and particularly if it involved training in trade schools that might endanger their trade secrets. Most importantly, however, it was the inevitable consequence of a dominant liberal, *laissez-faire* philosophy that discouraged state intervention in anything except where it was absolutely unavoidable.

The result of this voluntarist policy was that, with the exception of the evening classes provided by the Mechanics Institutes and the Department of Science and Art, there was no technical education to speak of before 1880 except that provided on the job. France by the mid-century had a wide range of vocational schools at different levels. These included 85 elementary trade and agricultural schools; various intermediate vocational schools like the *écoles des arts et métiers* and the *École Centrale* and a number of higher vocational schools (*grandes écoles*) including the celebrated *École Polytechnique*. England had few comparable full-time vocational schools which could impart both the theory and practice of different vocations. Nor, until the higher grade schools were developed, did it have much to compare with the vocationally oriented post-elementary schools on the continent like the German *Realschulen* and the French *écoles primaires supérieures* which numbered 700 by 1887 (Grew and Harrigan, 1991; Day, 1987; Weiss, 1982). In the absence of these institutions England relied largely on the apprenticeship. This was stoutly defended as the most effective way of imparting practical skills but few apprentices received the grounding in scientific principles or indeed basic education which was necessary for the skilled worker promoted to higher supervisory levels at the time when new technology and more complex processes began to make more demands on the scientific and technical knowledge of engineers and managers.

During the last two decades of the nineteenth century the situation did begin to change as the political climate became more conducive to state intervention and as the threat of foreign competition pressed home the importance of improving education and training. However, despite the achievements of the technical education movement in promoting the development of technical colleges and the civic universities, English technical education and training by the end of the century were still significantly underdeveloped by comparison with what had been achieved in many continental states (Barnett, 1986). It was still not widespread and what there was of it was generally still anti-theoretical, low in status and marginalized from mainstream education.

Throughout the first half of the twentieth century vocational education and training continued to lag behind and until the late 1950s remained largely on a voluntary footing. Part-time enrolments at technical colleges grew steadily if unspectacularly, but post-compulsory technical schooling remained a minority experience. Though twice enacted, in 1918 and 1944, compulsory continuation schooling was never implemented and most young people left school without receiving any further education or training. Sporadic attempts were made to develop technical secondary schooling with the pre-Second World War junior technical schools and the post-1944 secondary technical schools, but neither initiative gained much momentum or broke the status monopoly of academic secondary schooling, as recent studies by Gary McCulloch (1987) and Michael Sanderson (1994) have shown. By 1937 only around 30 000 pupils attended junior technical schools and attendance at secondary technical schools never grew beyond 4 per cent of the age cohort (Bailey, 1990).

The apprenticeship remained the main vehicle of vocational training throughout the period and was usually completed without any parallel off-the-job general or technical education. For all its strengths as a means for imparting job-specific vocational skills the apprenticeship system was never an adequate vehicle for meeting the skills needs of the economy. The craft unions tended to see the apprentice system as a means by which they could protect their skill status and differentials through restricting entry into tightly demarcated trades, while employers often valued the system as a way of gaining cheap labour without statutory obligations to provide expensive investment in training to given standards (Rainbird,

1990). Both sides of industry agreed on limiting the numbers of apprentices so that there were repeated skills shortage crises not only before and during the world wars but also increasingly during the expansionary post-1945 period. Not only did the apprentice system provide an inadequate supply of skilled workers but it was deficient in many other ways as the 1958 Carr Report made plain (Perry, 1976). It involved unduly lengthy periods of time-serving, failed to train to any specified standards, and was overly narrow in the skills it imparted and impoverished in terms of general education and theory; most damagingly, it ignored the training needs of semi-skilled workers and severely limited access to many groups, most notably women (Sheldrake and Vickerstaff, 1987).

Numerous reports (including the government's own 1956 White Paper on Technical Instruction) pointed to the relative deficiencies of British training and the 1945 Ince Report called for the creation of a national training scheme (see Ainley and Corney, 1990). However, no government action was forthcoming. In 1952 the Ministry of Labour and National Service was still upholding the traditional government line that 'employers bear the major responsibility for the training of their own employees' (Sheldrake and Vickerstaff, 1987, p. 27). The *'laissez-faire'* era in British training policy thus continued until the beginning of the 1960s when renewed skills shortages, the challenge of Soviet technology and the bulging youth cohort finally convinced government that policies on vocational training had to change.

Since 1964 and the Industrial Training Act, which marked the first major departure from the traditional *laissez-faire* approach, government policy on training has undergone repeated shifts but only to arrive in the 1990s very much where it started. The period can be divided into three main parts characterized by different forms of state control and social partnership.

The 1964–73 period, defined by the terms of the Industrial Training Act, saw training organized through a devolved form of social partnership between employers and industry with relatively light central state intervention. The period from 1974 to 1979 was the era of the Manpower Services Commission (MSC) under a Labour government, characterized by a more centralized form of social partnership under a highly interventionist government agency. The period from 1979 to 1988 was a transitional period during which central government intervened ever more directly through the MSC to shape training policy while simultaneously dismantling the apparatuses of social partnership in both the education and training fields. Since 1988 there has been a return to the voluntarist model and this time with one of the social partners, the trade unions, largely removed from influence and control. Although numerous initiatives have been tried and despite the fact that vocational education and training has been higher on the political agenda than ever before, the policies of these periods have had limited success in reversing the historic backwardness of British vocational education and training. It is important to see why.

## THE ERA OF THE INDUSTRIAL TRAINING BOARDS, 1964–73

The 1964 Act inaugurated the tripartite Industrial Training Boards (ITBs) to promote and coordinate training in the different sectors and empowered them to redistribute the costs of training between employers by means of the levy-grant system. Being organized by industrial sectors but without achieving full coverage, this was never quite a national apprenticeship system, still less a national training system for all grades of employees. However, it was as near as the country had come to such a thing in its history. During the brief ten years while the system was in operation the volume of training did marginally increase (up by 15 per cent in those areas of manufacturing covered by the ITBs between 1964 and 1969) and notable advances were made in improving the quality of training (Sheldrake and Vickerstaff, 1987). Day-release became common in many apprentice schemes; group training schemes proliferated, helping smaller firms to participate in formal training programmes; and the engineering ITB's modular training systems paved the way for greater flexibility and breadth in apprentice training (Perry, 1976). However, the system was far from achieving its objectives.

The quantitative gains in training provision were limited to skilled areas and were, in any case, soon wiped out by the secular decline in apprentice places which followed the onset of the recession in 1973. The ITBs failed to open up access to apprenticeships for previously excluded groups and did little to change the old practices of time-serving and age entry restrictions. Most seriously, little headway was made in the setting and monitoring of standards in training.

These shortcomings were not attributable to the principle of social partnership in training and nor do they undermine the argument for government intervention. What they did show was that a national training system could not be created on the basis of devolved sectoral organization and that the social partners in the different sectors could not be induced to act in a coordinated way to create a national system of training to standards without a strong central body to coordinate them. Unlike in Germany, Britain's national federations and 'peak bodies' for employers and unions (including the Confederation of British Industry and the Trades Union Congress) lacked binding powers over their members and the local chambers of commerce never attained great influence. The Central Training Council, as the TUC frequently complained, never had adequate powers to compensate for this and to ensure that the system fulfilled its objectives in meeting those long-term skills needs of the national economy which individual employers were always prone to ignore (Perry, 1976; Ainley and Corney, 1990).

## THE ERA OF MSC TRIPARTISM, 1973–79

The next phase of training policy was inaugurated by the 1973 Employment and Training Act which created the Manpower Services Commission, and can be said to have lasted until the Conservative government was elected in 1979 with a new economic agenda. The tripartite composition of the MSC suggested that the principle of social partnership was still to govern training but this time it was to be coordinated through a much more powerful central government agency with considerable public funds at its disposal. The TUC had, it appeared, finally got the Swedish-style central manpower planning body which it had long sought and in its early years the MSC indeed seemed determined to provide the strategic manpower planning and to facilitate the comprehensive national training system which had so long been lacking. In some areas it was remarkably successful. The Training Opportunities Programmes provided a new and viable form of publicly funded accelerated skills training for adults on 6–12 month courses. Numerous other initiatives, although not markedly successful in themselves, did also raise the profile of vocational training to a level not seen before.

However, two factors decisively undermined the MSC's efforts to revolutionize Britain's VET. The first concerned the limited nature of the social partnership which it represented. The MSC, which never gave equal representation to educational interests, soon managed to antagonize the powers in the education sector who viewed it, not without reason as it turned out, as a body that would be used by governments hostile to the education system as a Trojan horse to force changes on that system from without. The MSC, in its relations with education, thus soon came to exacerbate that long-standing historical division between education and training which it was part of its proclaimed mission to eradicate. The split deepened and the possibility of creating an integrated system of post-compulsory education and training receded. The second factor, which lay outside of the MSC's control, was the state of the economy. With the deep recession which followed the oil price rises, and the massive increases in youth and adult unemployment which resulted, government training priorities swiftly changed. The MSC was pressed into service to provide emergency unemployment schemes and soon lost sight of its original goal of creating comprehensive and high-quality skills training for the long-term needs of the national economy. The MSC was, in effect, blown off course by economic events. As Ainley and Corney have argued, by 1976 it had all but abandoned its original mission of comprehensive manpower planning and now played a kind of firefighting role, dealing with the social consequences of youth unemployment (Ainley and Corney, 1990).

## TRAINING IN TRANSITION, 1979–87

The third phase in recent training policy covered the years of the first two Thatcher governments and represented something of a transitional phase. Despite early signs that the new government would wind up the Commission in line with its general policy of 'rolling back the frontiers of the state', the MSC remained and even expanded, partly no doubt because the new recession of 1980–81 caused rocketing unemployment and a summer of urban riots which made the MSC's firefighting role ever more important. However, the MSC was to become a different kind of body with a different mission, a shift that was decisively signalled by the government's decision to dispense with its Director, Geoffrey Holland, and replace him by their own man, David Young (Ainley and Vickerstaff, 1993). Government took increasingly direct control of the MSC, using it now in a more interventionist and authoritarian fashion to impose new forms of vocationalism on the education system and to transform the apprenticeship system, ridding it of time-serving and restrictive trade union controls. The notion of partnership was quickly abandoned. The 1981 Employment Training Act abolished 17 out of the 24 ITBs and replaced them with non-statutory Industry Training Organizations. These rarely included union representatives and the unions were thus deprived of an important forum for representing their views on training. Educational bodies also saw their influence diminished as government initiatives in education increasingly bypassed the DES (as with TVEI, the technical and vocational education initiative) and the local authorities. Relations between the latter and the MSC reached an all-time low in 1985 when government announced its intention to hand over control of a large slice of LEA funding for non-advanced further education to the MSC.

Central government intervention in VET during this phase was probably more intensive than in any other period this century and yet at the end of it British training seems to have been lagging as far behind other countries as ever. What went wrong? The simple answer is that government directed its interventions to the wrong ends. The policies were misconceived. The Youth Training Scheme was set up in a blaze of publicity which proclaimed that this was the first ever comprehensive national training scheme aimed at high-quality training for both the employed and the unemployed. In fact it was cobbled together at breakneck speed without many of the preconditions for high-quality training. The schemes were designed in such a way that they inevitably involved much routine work experience but little supervised training or education. The pressure to provide places to meet government targets was such that schemes were accepted even where there was little likelihood that training would be of a high standard and this was rarely monitored with any rigour. The removal of the statutory grant levy system meant that employers were actually investing less in training than before. Between 1979 and 1987 apprenticeships in manufacturing declined from 155 000 to 58 000 only to be replaced by often lower quality Youth Training Schemes largely paid for by the state (Vickerstaff, 1992). The qualification system was not reformed to provide suitable certification for trainees and consequently less than a third came out with any recognized qualification (Green and Steedman, 1993). Without the prospect of a useful qualification or any guaranteed employment afterwards trainees inevitably tended to have little motivation on the schemes. In short the Youth Training Scheme never managed to throw off the reputation for low-quality training which had dogged all previous MSC training schemes (Ainley and Corney, 1990).

THE RETURN TO VOLUNTARISM, 1987–

Since 1988 training policy has undergone another radical shift which has involved the final abandonment of social partnership and a return to the voluntarist principles of the pre-1964 period. A third election victory in 1987, followed by the short-lived 'Lawson' economic boom, encouraged the government to apply in the training field the market-led policies it had been pursuing so vigorously in education. The long dispute with the unions over the Employment Training initiative proved the decisive catalyst for the decision to return to a demand-led, employer-controlled training system. The Youth Training Scheme was substantially deregulated and relaunched as Youth Training, the MSC was abolished and the control of training was handed over to the new, employer-dominated, local Training and Enterprise Councils (TECs). This, according to the Employment Department 1988 White Paper, *Employment for the 1990s*, would 'give leadership of the training system to employers, where it belongs'. Since then further measures have been adopted to place increased responsibility for training on individuals and employers and to replace the corporatist control over training with a new training market.

TECs have been promoted by government as 'one of the most radical and important initiatives ever undertaken in this country' (Shephard, 1992). Originally modelled on the US Private Industry Councils (PICs), the TECs were designed as an entrepreneurial and strategic local mechanism for reversing Britain's skills deficit. They would make training responsive to local economic needs, inject a bottom-line, business-like approach to programme management and use their influence in commerce and industry to persuade employers to take the initiative in solving their own training problems. Unlike the PICs in the USA, they would be responsible not just for training programmes for the disadvantaged but for a range of measures to stimulate all kinds of training and to promote local economic development. Their ability to provide strategic local leadership was seen as a key catalyst for solving Britain's skills problems and for restoring economic competitiveness.

Since 1990 TECs have been formed in 82 areas in England and Wales and there are a further 22 Local Enterprise Councils in Scotland. Their boards, of whom two-thirds must be local business leaders, and the civil servants who service them manage budgets which average around £18 m each and which accounted for a total national budget of £2.3 billion in 1993/4. Originally responsible for training programmes for unemployed youths and adults (the Youth Training Programme and the Employment Training Programme) and for a range of schemes to help local business (Business Growth Training, the Enterprise Allowance Scheme and the Small Firm Service), their responsibilities have been systematically increased during the past five years. They now have a significant role in the finance and governance of further education colleges, play the major part in a range of Education–Business Partnerships and Compacts, and are increasingly involved in the running of local careers services (Bennett et al., 1994). As the role of the local education authorities has declined in relation to secondary schools, colleges and training, so the TECs' importance has increased. They are now *de facto* among the most important agencies of planning in local education and training.

TECs are also centrally involved in several further initiatives which are designed to shift responsibility for training to employers and individuals.

Firstly, employers have been exhorted to take more responsibility for training through the promotion of targets for National Vocational Qualifications in firms and through the award of Investors in People kitemarks to companies with demonstrated standards of human resource development. Secondly, individuals have been encouraged to take more responsibility through schemes like Gateway to Learning and Skills Choice, which have sought to improve the range of careers guidance opportunities available to young people and adults, and also through the introduction of Training Credits (Felstead, 1993).

Training Credits are vouchers which can be used to purchase education and training from a range of accredited providers including colleges, training agencies and employers. Young people are counselled on how to 'spend' the vouchers through a process of Individual Action Planning which identifies suitable career/training progression paths and providers of suitable education or training. When the providers have received the Training Credits from the individual, payments are made through the TECs to providers by instalments and on the attainment of the target outcome (Outcome-Related Funding). The idea of the initiative is to encourage young people to see themselves as consumers making discriminating choices in the training market. According to the Employment Department 'this will put buying power into the hands of young people so that they can chose the training and training provider which best meets their needs' (1992). The recent White Paper, *Competitiveness: Helping Business to Win* (HM Government, 1994) proposed extending the system to the funding of all post-compulsory education and training.

## THE LIMITS OF VOLUNTARISM

There is some evidence that these and other measures have helped to stimulate a more robust training culture in some British firms. By 1994 some half million people had attained National Vocational Qualifications, many within employment; over 800 firms have won the Investors in People awards with 6000 more working towards them; and the general level of in-company training activity appears to have improved over the past decade (HM Government, 1994, p. 81).

However, the TECs are still far from fulfilling their mission of creating world-class levels of training and skills (Coffield, 1992; Bennett et al., 1994). The vast majority of firms are still not training their employees to NVQ levels; two-thirds of graduates from Youth Training schemes do not attain NVQs; and only 41 per cent of young people gain qualifications at the 'A' level or NVQ/GNVQ level 3 standard, compared with over 65 per cent in France and Germany (Green and Steedman, 1996). The demand-led or voluntarist approach has still not delivered Britain's long-awaited skills revolution.

The current British government policy on training has been described as the triumph of ideology over experience (Coffield, 1992). Two overarching sets of problems still bedevil Britain's approach to training and these both relate to the historical preference for *laissez-faire* or voluntarist policies. Firstly, there is still no concerted national approach to training underpinned by the necessary statutory framework governing the roles, rights and responsibilities of different parties. Secondly, there is a marked and growing absence of effective collaboration between social partners and of institutional arrangements to promote this.

There are still no legal obligations on employers to train, to provide paid leave for training, or to contribute funds towards external training. While in other countries employers are bound to pay training taxes or to belong to employer organizations which exert pressure on them to invest in training, this option is still rejected in the UK. In the absence of these requirements and without the restraints of sectoral agreements on wages, it is relatively easy still for employers to avoid training by paying a wage premium to poach trained employees from other firms (Marsden and Ryan, 1995).

TECs have limited means for dealing with these problems. They only have at their disposal the power of persuasion backed up by their control over the allocation of public funds for training. However, these funds represent only a small proportion of the total costs of training in companies and thus do not necessarily provide great leverage (Meager, 1990).

As far as young people themselves are concerned there are no statutory rights to receive training and, given the prevalence of unregulated occupations, less requirements to qualify to find employment than in other countries where the majority of jobs require specified qualifications for entry. Training credits will do little to improve the supply of training since providers are already funded on a per capita basis and the possession of a credit will do little to 'empower' young people. At the age of 16, they are not necessarily in a position to use it to negotiate effectively with future employers about training options, especially in a recessionary labour market (Felstead, 1993).

There is also a concern that the uptake of the new opportunities may be very uneven and that those who are least qualified and less able to make informed choices will fare worst in this kind of training market. Outcome-related funding of training schemes under the Job Training Partnership

Act in the USA has often discriminated against the most disadvantaged as training providers have naturally tended to select trainees who are likely to meet the targets and thus ensure payment (Green and Mace, 1994). Unless great care is taken with the specification of performance measures in the UK the same distortions are likely to arise with Training Credits.

Lack of collaboration between the social partners has also become an increasing problem in British training. TECs were specifically designed as business-led bodies not as partnerships. They not only under-represent unions and education; they also under-represent small business, the public sector employers and sectors without regional headquarters like retailing and finance and insurance (Meager, 1990). They are unelected, unrepresentative bodies which do not have to account to a local electorate or, even, to local business. Recent research suggests that the lack of a sense of ownership in TECs by small and medium-sized firms limits the influence exercised by the TECs and their capacity to provide strategic leadership in local economic development (Bennett et al., 1994).

Trade unions, meanwhile, have been largely removed from any effective role in determining and implementing training policy. They are only minimally represented on the TECs and the Industry Lead Bodies (ILBs) which set standards in training, and have only a minor impact on the examining and awarding bodies like BTEC and City and Guilds. Educational representation has been similarly curtailed with the TECs generally having few educational representatives and with the removal of LEA representation on college governing bodies.

This breakdown in social partnership may have serious consequences for VET provision. Effective training policy cannot be devised without the active collaboration of the unions, since training cannot be divorced from other issues where unions have legitimate bargaining rights, like the implementation of new technology and labour processes, the definition and grading of jobs and the determination of pay (Rainbird, 1990). Unions can play an essential part in persuading employers to provide more training opportunities and in monitoring the quality of training provided. Where their influence is restricted to the individual firm and to local bargaining this can only encourage the continuation of the historical pattern of uncoordinated and uneven provision (Winterton and Winterton, 1994).

Union representation is also important at the level of national standard-setting for training. Without significant educational and employee representation the ILBs have frequently defined occupational competencies in the narrowest fashion to meet the immediate needs of employers rather than the longer-term needs of individuals and the economy.

## THE STATE AND THE SOCIAL PARTNERS IN CONTINENTAL SYSTEMS

Historically, the central state has played a much greater part in VET systems in continental Europe, both in terms of setting up and financing provider institutions and via the regulation of curricula and examinations. This continues to be the case today despite the trend towards devolution of power towards regional levels and to bodies representing the social partners. Continental European and Scandinavian VET systems clearly vary considerably, from the relatively centralized school-based systems of France and Sweden, to the more pluralist, employment-based systems of the German-speaking countries. In each case, however, the social partners play important roles in the system, represented at national, regional and local levels and participating in policy-formation and implementation with respect to various functions, including finance, training delivery, standard-setting, quality monitoring and assessment.

In Germany, France, Denmark and the Netherlands there are tripartite national standard-setting bodies in which unions are fully represented, and a number of countries, including Denmark, France and Italy, impose statutory training taxes on firms. It is also common to see national sectoral agreements between employer and employee organizations which regulate pay levels, link grade levels to qualifications and which seek to distribute the costs of training between different firms. Typically, in all these countries, the state is ultimately responsible for regulating the system and for determining the precise roles and responsibilities of the different social actors in the system.

## GERMANY

Unlike the French System, the system of initial VET in western Germany is relatively decentralized and predominantly work-based. However, as in France, the overall framework is tightly governed by federal legislation and the concept of social partnership underpins the entire system. Wolfgang Streeck (1987) characterizes its organization as 'neo-corporatist' to denote its typical admixture of market and public regulation and the intricate and subtle network of partnership bodies which determine policy and administer the system.

Initially based on the traditional apprenticeship model, the German Dual System has evolved into a highly organized national system of mass VET. The basic structure of the system is easily described. The majority of young people (over 60 per cent) enter an apprenticeship when they leave school which they do at ages varying between 15 and 19 depending on whether they have been studying at the *Hauptschule*, the *Realschule* or the *Gymnasium*. They sign an apprentice contract with a firm licensed to provide training and thereafter, for between two and four years, spend part of their week (usually three days) in work-based training under the guidance of trained instructors (*Meisters*) and part of their week in the *Berufsschule* studying general subjects and learning the theoretical aspects of their vocation. The vast majority of these (over 90 per cent) obtain their certificates of vocational competence at the end of the training period and are then qualified to enter full employment either with their initial employer or elsewhere.

The system is administered through a variety of corporate bodies operating at national, regional and local levels. At the national level, the Federal Institute of Vocational Training (BIBB) advises the Federal Minister of Education and Science (BMBW), who has ultimate control over training. The BIBB is a public body authorized by the state, whose central board gives equal representation to unions, employers and the *Länder* (11 members each) and includes five federal representatives with 11 votes. The DGB, the German equivalent of the TUC, nominates the employee representatives and the KWB, which brings together the peak organizations of the main chambers of commerce and the main confederations of employers, nominates the employer representatives. At the regional level the main power lies with the chambers of commerce (*Kammern*) and the *Länder* governments. Under the 1969 Act all the chambers have established vocational training committees made up of six representatives for each of the social partners (employers, employees, instructors, colleges). All *Länder* have tripartite training committees representing employers, employees and instructors. At the local level, power lies with the works councils which must exist in all firms with over 200 employees and whose roles in VET are enshrined in the 1976 Works Constitution Act and the Coordinate-determination Act (CEDEFOP, 1987b). The social partners are involved in all of the main functions of the VET system. These include: the setting of objectives, standards and regulations; finance; administration, monitoring and assessment. They each involve the national, regional and local levels.

Objectives, standards and regulations are determined largely at the national level. The main responsibility lies with the Federal Ministry which is advised by the BIBB. Most decisions require a consensus to be reached among the social partners represented on the BIBB's central board, although this is often only by a bare majority. Federal law frames the entire system, defining the roles and responsibilities of the different social partners; the obligation of firms to join chambers; the obligation of firms to train all their young employees according to the standard terms of the apprentice contract; the obligation of firms providing training to be licensed by the chambers and to employ qualified instructors (*Meisters*); the qualification requirements for entry into classified jobs; training regulations on the duration, content and minimum standards for different classified occupations. At the regional level the *Länder* committees are responsible for coordinating these training regulations with the regulations for vocational college provision which they control.

The responsibility for financing the system is also spread between the social partners. The state (federal and *Länder*) finances the vocational colleges and the employers finance the on-the-job training. Trainees make a contribution through their reduced apprentice earnings. Federal government also provides large sums in incentives for employers to train and for special training programmes. National agreements are also reached by the employers and unions in some sectors for training levies on firms. At the regional level the *Land* governments also provide financial incentives for employers to train. The chambers charge dues to their members and they often levy firms for funds for external training centres.

Administration, monitoring and assessment occur largely at the regional level. The chambers (under BIBB guidelines) are responsible for training instructors; operating external training sites; approving training firms and monitoring their performance; arbitrating in disputes between employers and trainees; and examination setting and assessment. Monitoring and assessment are conducted by specialist training counsellors employed by the chambers and expert juries comprising vocational instructors and others. At the local level the works councils play an important role in ensuring that training regulations are followed and that the company meets or exceeds the standards laid down. At the national level the performance of the training system is evaluated in the annual BMBW vocational training reports over which the social partners have been consulted through the BIBB. National employee and employer organizations also have training research departments which monitor training for their sectors (CEDEFOP, 1987b).

The Dual System has a number of drawbacks, most of which are endemic to all work-based training systems. The training is relatively narrow and job-specific, particularly in the smaller firms which provide most of it, and this is arguably a disadvantage at a time when new technology and reorganized work processes in leading-edge enterprises increasingly require multiskilled and flexible employees (Casey, 1990). It is also a system which divides the academic and vocational students into different tracks, reproducing within the vocational system the usual hierarchies of labour within which women and migrant workers are confined to disadvantageous positions. However, it is undeniably successful in ensuring that a very high proportion of young people receive training to reasonable standards and attain recognized national qualifications at the end. Despite the additional problems caused by reunification, as the new *Länder* struggle to bring their training into line with the western states, the system still appears to operate effectively, although there has been a drift in recent years away from apprenticeships to full-time academic courses.

A number of factors can be adduced as responsible for the relative success of the system, including the historical and cultural traditions in Germany which place great stress on the importance of education and training and which maintain the high social status of the skilled worker (Hayes, 1984; McLean, 1995). However, roles played by the social partners are also key. Although unions and employers are frequently at odds about aspects of policy, there is a level of basic agreement over objectives which in part accounts for the relative prestige, stability and longevity of the system. The close involvement of employee and employer organizations in policy-formulation and implementation undoubtedly increases the commitment of all parties to making the system work, while at the same time helping to ensure that no pool of expertise is lost to the system and that no interest group can manipulate it to its own exclusive advantage. Regulation through the collective actions of the social partners is also vital for ensuring the effective articulation of training and labour market policy which is critical to the working of the system. It is the national agreements reached between the partners which ensure that apprentice pay levels are set at a level which encourages employers to train, which discourages firms from using additional pay incentives to poach trained employees, and which ensures that the costs of training are fairly spread across a wide range of employers. Equally critical to the success of the operation is the strong regulative role played by the federal state in setting the overall framework and defining the roles of the different parties. The Dual System is a work-based model of training but it is definitively not a free-market one.

## THE IMPORTANCE OF THE SOCIAL PARTNERSHIP MODEL

The historical and comparative analyses pursued in this chapter suggest the fundamental importance of collaboration between the social partners in the effective provision of VET. Such collaboration can only be effective where the state, at national and regional levels, intervenes to coordinate the roles and responsibilities of the different partners. Voluntarist policies, which minimize such interventions, have not generally been successful. This is due to the underlying limits of the market as a means of regulating the supply and demand for training (Finegold and Soskice, 1988; Streeck, 1987).

Training is a collective public good from which all social actors benefit. Individual actors, however, may frequently make rational choices not to train. Employers often prefer to poach rather than to invest in training, especially, as in the UK, where there is no strong training culture and where employer associations lack the power to enforce a common code of practice. Furthermore, it is in the employers' interests to provide narrow, job-specific training to minimize the risk of losing their trainees and forfeiting their investment, even though this may not be in the best long-term interests of the firm, let alone the individual or the national economy. Employers tend to think short-term about their training needs and consider training as a cost rather than an investment for the future and this tendency is exacerbated, as in the UK, where the structure of company ownership and the threat of mergers and takeovers puts a premium on showing short-term profit (Hutton, 1995). The supply of training in a market system consequently tends to be insufficient both in quantity and in quality and the costs are not fairly distributed between employers.

There are reciprocal problems on the demand side. Employers may well not seek to employ well qualified people or pay the rates to attract them because they have grown used to a shortage in the supply of skills and have organized their labour processes accordingly. This is the vicious circle of the 'low-skills equilibrium' for which the market has no answer (Finegold and Soskice, 1988). Likewise, young people may decide not to train because they have insufficient information and life experience to see the long-term advantages (Streeck, 1987) or because they calculate that the pay rewards resulting from the acquisition of qualifications do not warrant the opportunity costs incurred during the process of training. Relatively high wage rates for unqualified young people and poor differentials for those with skills and qualifications have, historically, provided a disincentive that has perpetuated low levels of training in the UK. These and other manifestations of market failure will virtually guarantee the limited effectiveness of a voluntarist training policy.

The foregoing analysis does not provide arguments for the superiority of any particular system or for the advisability of any one country trying to adopt the system of another. What it does attempt to show is that any mass system of VET must have certain properties in order to be effective. These might be defined as coherence, transparency, multi-determination and multi-agency.

Coherence and transparency in institutional structures, curricula and qualification systems are essential in order to promote access and progression for users of training provision and to ensure a close articulation with the labour market. Multi-determination and multi-agency are essential because VET systems are complex organisms, charged with carrying out multiple functions which touch on the vital interests of many different parties and require the investment and expertise of various different groups to operate with maximum efficiency.

Employers, unions and educationalists must all be intimately involved at all levels for VET to be successful. VET without employer input is bound to lose relevance to the world of work which defeats one of its objects. VET without educational inputs will be narrow and inflexible and dangerously divorced from other areas of education. Without the active involvement of the trade unions VET is unlikely to achieve high quality and will not achieve any functional fit with other aspects of labour market and employment policy relating to job entry requirements, job definition, wage determination, labour mobility and so on.

The pluralist representation of interest groups in the design and implementation of VET systems does not, however, obviate the need for strong central coordination and control. Systems based on the principle of social partnership only work when one of the partners, the state, defines the roles of the others and determines the shape of the system as a whole.

# 5 Education and Cultural Identity in the United Kingdom[1]

The United Kingdom is a multinational state with a single monarchy and parliament and shared language, but four constituent parts: England, Scotland, Wales and Northern Ireland. The term 'British', which is often used as an adjectival synonym, is somewhat anomalous, for the United Kingdom is composed of Great Britain *and* Northern Ireland. Each of these four parts has distinctive cultural, linguistic, religious and national identities. Northern Ireland is further divided along sectarian, religious and political lines, with a substantial minority who would welcome the creation of a single state for Ireland once more. The four parts have distinctive educational traditions, and three boast separate educational systems. This results from the different ways in which each country, historically, was incorporated into the United Kingdom.

Education in England and Wales forms a single system. In 1536 the Act of Union between England and Wales made Wales subject to English law and this has subsequently continued to apply in the field of education. Consequently, while education in Wales is administered separately through the Welsh Office, and despite some variations in the law, for example in relation to the teaching of the Welsh language, education in Wales is essentially governed under the same statutes as in England. Scotland, on the other hand, has a separate education system under its own statutory framework. The Act of Union between England and Scotland in 1707 left Scotland with its own legal system, Church and structures of local government. The United Kingdom Parliament has continued to frame separate legislation for education in Scotland, which is now administered through the Scottish Education Department. The situation in Northern Ireland is again different, as a result of the long and tortuous history of Anglo-Irish conflicts, and rather too complex to be dealt with here in any detail. Suffice to say that since the culmination of English colonization of Ireland in the 1800 Act of Union, Irish education has been subject to separate legislation from Westminster. This continued to be the case for Northern Ireland after the creation of the Irish Free State in 1921 left those six counties as part of the United Kingdom. Northern Ireland, therefore, has separate education statutes, although one of the most salient features of the current system, the tendency for Catholic and Protestant children to go to different schools, depends less upon legislation and more upon the current sectarian divides.

Thus different histories have created distinctive educational traditions in the four parts of the United Kingdom. A full survey of education and cultural identity in these separate parts would need to consider not only the historical role of each of these educational systems in the formation, and re-formation, of regional (indeed national) identities, but also their contributions to the construction of overall ideologies of British nationhood.

## EDUCATION AND NATIONAL IDENTITY

The role of education in the historical construction of British national identity is a complex issue. In his 1922 work on *Nationalism and Education since 1789*, Edward Reisner argued that 'England seems to have used ... schools hardly at all as a means of nationalist propaganda' (Reisner, 1922, p. 317). This, no doubt, was overstating the case, for example Victorian and Edwardian schools were certainly not reluctant to celebrate the glories of the British Empire, but it does point towards a distinctive aspect of British educational development. By comparison with such continental European states as France and Germany, it would appear that education in Britain played a less coherent role in the formation of the nation state, and schools were less frequently seen as a major instrument in the forging of national identity.

Such lack of clarity in the relationship between the state, education and national and cultural identity was in part a reflection of the lack of clarity within the education system itself. In addition to the complexities of the separate (yet loosely linked) nature of educational provision in the separate parts of the United Kingdom, the most distinctive feature of British education has been its voluntary character. Both in the eighteenth and nineteenth centuries this voluntary approach was held to be morally, and educationally, superior to compulsory schooling schemes in continental Europe. These were associated with despotism and subservience, in contrast to the freedoms enjoyed by British citizens, which were seen as being essential to British character. Voluntarism (or voluntaryism in its historical usage) meant freedom for pupils from compulsory attendance, and freedom for schools from state interference. When, in 1870, elementary schools funded from local rates were introduced in England and Wales, such schools were intended to supplement the existing voluntary system. Indeed, the voluntarists were granted a period of grace, and increased grants from central government, to fill the gaps if they could, and thus avoid the necessity for 'state' schools. Similarly, at secondary level, in 1895 the report of the Bryce Commission celebrated the English educational tradition for its 'freedom, variety and elasticity'. English education, in particular, has been quite singular in the extent to which it has prioritized the individual school over the system and the personal development of the individual pupil over the collective educational needs of society. Although, since 1979, a concerted effort has been made by central government to promote a greater sense of national unity and an enterprise culture, independent schools have been excluded from the legislation, and are still held up as models to be copied by state schools.

Why, in modern times, has the British state adopted such a *laissez-faire* attitude towards education? Britain was exceptional in its early achievement of territorial and cultural unification as a nation state. It was favoured by its insular geography, and ability, at least since the Norman Conquest, to avoid foreign invasion. The Tudor monarchs hammered England into a national mould with the suppression of baronial and church independence, the successful early centralization of state power and the establishment of English as the sole official language. The English Reformation and the break with Rome helped to consolidate a native Protestant identity and culture. As Seton-Watson wrote in his classic text on nationalism and nation-building: 'By the end of Elizabeth's reign the process of formation of English national consciousness had been virtually completed' (1977, p. 33). Of course, the British state as it exists today was still not an established entity. England had been united with Wales in 1536, but the union with Scotland was not consolidated until 1707, while Ireland was to undergo a long and bitter process of colonization. National and ethnic divisions thus remained, but there was nothing of the order of those protracted national conflicts which, in continental Europe, propelled absolutist monarchs into deliberate efforts of nation-building in which education played such an important part (Green, 1990).

Early national state formation and the maintenance of stable national boundaries thus had a lasting effect on English and Welsh attitudes towards nationhood and education. Nationalism and educational development in England and Wales were fused during the English Reformation, but thereafter there was no basis for a fervent indigenous nationalism, and no impulse from the central state to link nationalist aspirations with educational development. As an ideology, according to Seton-Watson, 'English nationalism never existed since there was no need for either a doctrine or an independence struggle' (1977, p. 34). Given the relative ease of the assimilation of Wales, a poor and sparsely populated country with no obvious centre and difficult internal communications, it could be said that by the end of the sixteenth century the nation and the state already co-incided within stable territorial boundaries. This fact provided the bedrock for a national identity which was subsequently constructed around the myths of those long-standing and relatively stable institutions of Church, Crown and Parliament. The diversity of ethnic and regional cultures in England and Wales provided no serious impediment. As Eric Hobsbawm has noted 'the English were quite exceptional in boasting of their mongrel origins and glorying in the philological mixture of their language' (1990, p. 108). Wales, though the Welsh language was still widely spoken, shared in this national identity, if not on equal terms. Between 1540 and 1640, 2004 Welshmen became students at the English universities of Oxford and Cambridge, compared with 420 during the whole of the Middle Ages (Webster, 1990, p. 143). Ambitious Welsh parents of all social groups wanted their children to learn English, and in nineteenth-century elementary schools a placard, the Welsh 'Not', was hung around the necks of those children who lapsed into the vernacular. Higher education of the Welsh continued of necessity to take place in England, for not until the 1870s was there a university college in Wales.

The construction of a British identity after 1707 required more deliberate efforts. The Scots remained highly ambivalent about the Union, which had only been foisted on them to prevent Catholic resistance to the Protestant succession by Hanover, and against which the Jacobites continued to rebel. Scotland itself had no uniform national identity, divided as it was between Lowlanders and Highlanders, and its population being no more uniformly Celtic in origin than that of Wales. It did, however, have strong indigenous traditions, including more universities than England and a system of parochial schools, and was not so easily assimilated into a Great Britain of England, Wales and Scotland. What part Scottish education has played in this assimilation is hard to say. On one level the distinctive Scottish system would appear to have functioned more as a source of continuing Scottish cultural autonomy. Its strong roots in the community, fostered by the active role of the Kirk, have continued to mark it out. So, too, have the strong traditions of science, engineering and medicine in higher education, an early product of the Scottish Enlightenment and cultural affinities with continental Europe, which came to form a marked contrast with England in the nineteenth century. These traditions are still seen as a valued part of the Scottish cultural inheritance. The quality of that inheritance was appreciated south of the border. In the early years of the nineteenth century some English parents, even members of the aristocracy, sent their sons to the universities of Edinburgh or Glasgow in preference to Oxford and Cambridge. For example, the future prime minister, Lord John Russell, was a student at Edinburgh University, 1809–12. The University of London was promoted by Scotsmen, including such Edinburgh graduates as Henry Brougham and James Mill.

Linda Colley has suggested that at the beginning of the eighteenth century Great Britain 'was like the Christian doctrine of the Trinity, both three and one, and altogether something of a mystery' (1994, p. 13). During the course of the century, however, and particularly during the wars with America and France, a more visible British identity was gradually constructed. To a large extent this identity was created out a sense of difference from the 'Other', which was usually France. Protestantism was the common cement between the English, the Welsh and the Scots, and this was underlined by continual conflict with Catholic Europe, and, of course, Catholic Ireland. Beyond this the Empire provided a sense of common identity, offering opportunities for advancement, particularly for Scots in the army and colonial services, and affording a sense of common national superiority. As Colley has written 'in the half-century after the American war, there would emerge in Great Britain a far more consciously and officially constructed patriotism which stressed attachment to the monarchy, the importance of Empire, the value of military and naval achievement, and the desirability of the strong, stable government by a virtuous, able and authentically British elite' (1994, p. 145).

Though foreign wars, foreign in both senses in that they were not fought on British soil, were the most important single ingredient in forming this national identity and culture, education also played a part in this process. In the nineteenth century the great majority of public elementary schools were controlled by the Anglican Church through the National Society, or by the Nonconformist churches through the British and Foreign School Society. Both societies stressed religious values which, despite denominational divisions, were part of a shared Protestant culture. Schools also promoted nationalist and imperialist values, particularly towards the end of the century, as the cult of Empire gathered force. In 1878 the Education Department 'directed HMIs to excite interest "in the Colonial and Foreign Possessions of the British Crown"' (Horn, 1988, p. 40). The tradition of celebrating 24 May, Queen Victoria's birthday, as Empire Day, began in Canada. The Empire Day movement spread to Britain and in 1905 5540 elementary schools and six teacher training colleges celebrated Empire Day. By 1919 only the two Welsh counties of Anglesey and Merioneth and the three boroughs of Colne, Darwen and West Ham had failed to support the celebrations, which usually involved raising and saluting the Union Jack flag and singing the National Anthem and other patriotic songs

(Horn, 1988, pp. 48–9). Boys' public schools promoted the ideology of Britain's imperial mission, and the qualities of leadership, honour and integrity which Kipling would later famously associate with 'the white man's burden'. The Boer War of 1899–1902 fostered imperialist sentiments in public schools, as immortalized in Newbolt's poems eulogizing the heroism of the public schoolboy dying in some far-off field defending the Empire and dreaming of his school. At this time, both in elite and elementary schools, the doctrine of National Efficiency placed great emphasis upon health and drill as a means of producing healthy young people worthy of taking their place in the greatest empire the world had ever seen. The Code of Regulations for Public Elementary Schools, introduced in 1906, brought moral instruction into the curriculum, and urged the promotion of courage, self-denial and 'love of one's country'. As Horn has shown, 'Publishers, especially those concerned with history and geography textbooks, responded to these initiatives by producing works stressing what has been called the "Holy Trinity" of "Citizenship", "Empire", and "Patriotism"' (1988, p. 43).

## HISTORY AS A SCHOOL SUBJECT

History has been a prime subject for the promotion of cultural and national identity. In the nineteenth century almost all the history studied in British schools (apart from that taught in support of the study of the classical languages of Greece and Rome) was British history. In the first half of the twentieth century European history was added, but although there was a broadening of the ancient civilizations to include Egypt, the history of the rest of the world only intruded as part of the British imperial story.

In a pioneering study Valerie Chancellor (1970) showed how nineteenth-century history textbooks conveyed strong messages to their readers about social class, politics, morality, religion and Britain's place in the world. The purpose of history teaching, as of education more broadly, was to promote law-abiding citizens, contented with their lot, who would be able to distinguish right from wrong, and who were inspired by a love of their country. Thus in many textbooks clear distinctions were made between the deserving and the undeserving poor, while the landed aristocracy were portrayed as a declining influence. True British values, both in politics and in economics, were to be found in the rising middle classes (the classes to which most of the authors themselves belonged). All was suffused by a general optimism and sense of progress, a Whig history which celebrated the existence of a constitutional monarchy and a reformed Parliament. History was used as a source of moral examples. The brave and wise ranged from Alfred the Great to William Wilberforce; the wicked and foolish from 'Bad King John' to George IV. The superiority of Christianity over other beliefs and faiths was upheld and, within Christianity itself, the superiority of Protestantism over Roman Catholicism was conveyed. These messages from domestic British history helped to confirm the cultural identity of British children in the nineteenth century, but they were strongly reinforced towards the end of that century and in the early years of the next by the increasingly imperialist and jingoist historical treatment of Britain's place in the world. For example, the widely-used *A School History of England* by C.R.L. Fletcher and Rudyard Kipling, a work first published in 1911 but still on sale in the 1950s, promoted racial stereotypes and patriotic fervour. The population of the West Indies was described as 'lazy, vicious, and incapable of any improvement, or of work under compulsion' (Glendenning, 1973, p. 34). In contrast Fletcher and Kipling concluded their book with a call to arms: 'I do not think there can be any doubt that the only safe thing for all of us who love our country is to learn soldiering at once, and be prepared to fight at any moment' (Glendenning, 1973, p. 33).

Though in the later years of the twentieth century a variety of influences – for example the internationalism which succeeded the two World Wars and the curriculum initiatives of Local Education Authorities whose schools included substantial numbers of children from minority backgrounds – moderated the worst excesses of British history textbooks, the basic self-congratulatory message continued. As Rob Gilbert observed of the 1980s:

> In history texts, the common goal is to explain the process by which individual agents and social change have addressed and largely solved the problems of equality, opportunity, mobility and material welfare. This has been achieved by the working out of general ideas of justice and welfare by historic groups and individuals through traditional institutions and procedures....The interaction of these elements of change has occurred within or produced a continuous and apparently inevitable process of improvement, which will continue as long as the need for harmony and a concern for national interest are observed. (1984, p. 177)

While special events, such as Empire Day, and the messages conveyed in history, geography and civics textbooks and lessons were obvious means of promoting cultural and national identity, national cultural values were also conveyed through the hidden curriculum of games and school rituals, and through such associations as the Boy Scouts and Girl Guides. British, and particularly English, education has traditionally elevated character formation above intellectual development, and notions of national identity were as likely to be instilled in schools through the covert and affective processes of personal development as through the more overt and cerebral procedures of inculcating ideologies.


SINCE 1979

In 1979 Margaret Thatcher and the Conservative party won the first of four electoral victories which have kept the party in power for a longer consecutive period than any other has enjoyed this century. During these years successive Conservative governments sought to purge British culture of what they perceived as its major weaknesses – state monopolies and state socialism – and to promote the 'traditional' values of private enterprise, thrift and personal responsibility. This resulted in the privatization of public services, the reduction of trade union power and the removal of professional privileges. In education there was an assault upon one set of 'producers', Local Education Authorities, and upon teachers' associations, and a concentration of much greater power in the hands of central government. Nevertheless, such power was used in part to promote greater diversity and competition within the system: the opting out of schools from local control, an increase in the powers of governing bodies, as well as a national curriculum and national testing to provide the data for competition between schools, an ending to teachers' pay bargaining rights and the abolition of tenure for university staff. Such reforms brought considerable changes in the culture of education, changes which, as in the national culture more broadly, reflect the promotion of a more competitive, market-driven ethos.

In a political sense these four electoral victories of the Conservative party since 1979 may be viewed in part as a victory of English culture within the United Kingdom. The Conservative party dominates in England but wins very few parliamentary seats in Northern Ireland, Scotland and Wales. The last five leaders of Labour, the main opposition party, have included two Welshmen in James Callaghan and Neil Kinnock, one representative of a Welsh constituency, Michael Foot, and a Scot, John Smith.

Nevertheless, the limitations of the nationalistic element in the national curriculum introduced under the 1988 Education Reform Act must be acknowledged. Neither the national curriculum nor national testing has been implemented uniformly across the United Kingdom, nor even across England and Wales. They have not even been applied to independent schools in England. In the summer of 1993, moreover, the basic lack of authority at the centre of English education appeared to be confirmed when a combination of teachers and parents forced the government to abandon part of its testing programme. Subsequent retreats have seen a further scaling down of the national curriculum, of national testing and of the publication of pupils' test results. Government recognition of cultural diversity within the United Kingdom was shown by the appointment of separate working parties (and hence separate syllabuses) both for history and for mathematics in England and Wales. The requirement that the Welsh language must be a subject for study in all parts of Wales, whether traditionally Welsh-speaking or not, represented a considerable break with tradition. For centuries central policy had been to promote the English language in Wales, as for example under the Revised Code of 1862 which prescribed reading and writing in English rather than in Welsh.

In 1988 Kenneth Baker, then Secretary of State for Education, explained how the new national curriculum would further national identity when he declared that in future all children in English state schools would learn the key events in British history. These included: the establishment of the Anglican church in the sixteenth century, the development of Parliament in the seventeenth, the industrial revolution of the eighteenth, the extension of the franchise, and imperialism, which he defined as 'the spread of Britain's influence for good in the world'. 'We should not be ashamed of our history,' he concluded; 'our pride in our past gives us our confidence to walk tall in the world today' (Aldrich and Dean, 1991, p. 95).

Such language may be interpreted in various ways. Traditionalists and cultural restorationists have tended to see it as employing history, quite properly, to give all children some sense of the nation to which they belong, and as a useful antidote to a creeping multiculturalism that despises and rejects all things essentially British. Others have interpreted such historical emphases as a continuation of education as cultural imperialism. Since the Second World War the cultural, linguistic and religious diversity of the United Kingdom has been substantially increased by the advent of settlers from the Commonwealth and from other countries. National curricular emphases upon traditional British history and English literature may be seen as a continuation of the cultural imperialism which began in the British Empire and Commonwealth, and now has been returned to the United Kingdom itself.

WHOSE CULTURE?

During the period of Empire Britain had a nationalism of the 'great power' variety (Nairn, 1981). Conservative, celebratory and frequently complacent, it was more prone to seek legitimacy in the past than to forge new national identities for the future. Secure in the inert appeal of centuries of tradition and institutional legitimacy it had little need to develop an overt ideology or to adopt a strident language and no concerted institutional effort was required to promote it. Schools often did so, according to their own inclinations and traditions, but there was no national curriculum to foist it on them. Ironically, it is only in the recent past, with the end of Empire, that the debate about schooling and national identity has raged more fiercely in England and other parts of the United Kingdom.

Since 1945, however, as the nation has sought to find a new post-imperial role and identity, education has become, paradoxically, more obviously a battleground for different versions of national and ethnic identity. As elsewhere in Europe, economic globalization, the decline of traditional cultures and communities and the increase of supra-national political integration have led to revived regionalist movements, as in Welsh and Scottish nationalism. Additionally, the cultural claims of postwar Asian, Afro-Caribbean and other settled minority communities have raised intense debates about the merits of multicultural and intercultural education, and have led to growing demands for separate schools for minority communities (Gundara and Jones, 1990). It has been pressure from this quarter, rather than from the rather weaker movement for a greater European dimension in education, which has led to the reactive growth of new lobbies committed to a 'little England' notion of traditional culture and arguing for the reassertion of a narrowly defined national culture in British schools. Recent Conservative governments have been influenced by the 'cultural revisionists' on the Right of the party, and the creation in 1988 of the first national curriculum for schools in England and Wales led to sharp subsequent conflicts over the concept of culture embodied in the curriculum. Generally speaking, the cultural revisionists in the government have won out over the multiculturalists in the critical debates about the English and history curricula. This has led to the implementation of a more narrowly defined national culture in schools, with a predominance given to British history and English literary texts, and with a requirement for compulsory religious education to reflect predominantly Christian values. In general the outcome of the national curriculum debates has been in favour of a more monocultural curriculum, dominated by a narrow conception of English culture to which minority ethnic groups are meant to assimilate. This resolution, however, remains fragile, since it is clearly in tension with the multicultural realities of many urban schools and with other government policies which attempt to make education more market oriented and schools more responsive to the wishes of parents. One current focus of this tension is to be seen in the requests from non-Christian religious communities for government financial support for their schools. Another is the reaction of minority parents to a national curriculum which appears to diminish or exclude other cultural identities (Gaill, 1993).

Contemporary controversy about schooling and national identity has not arisen primarily as a reaction to the development of European federalism, nor has it been driven essentially by movements for Scottish, Welsh and Irish autonomy. The most potent stimulus has come from reactions within the white English population against the increasingly pluralistic and multicultural nature of English cities and their schools. The first portents of this movement came in the 1950s with the beginning of the racist backlash against Asian and Afro-Caribbean communities in London and other large multiracial cities. Those in the white population who saw urban black communities as a threat to their traditional culture and way of life found an eloquent voice in the Conservative politician Enoch Powell who, having finally abandoned his visions of a restored British Empire, now began to preach a new 'little England' cultural nationalism. It was not until the 1980s, however, that influences such as these began to reverse the general movement towards multiculturalism in schools which had grown in the teeth of racist opposition throughout the 1970s.

During the ten years to the mid 1990s there was an increasingly overt opposition to multiculturalism in education, not only among the racist fringes who were always opposed to it, but also among sections of the political establishment, particularly members of the so-called 'New Right'. In 1977 Edward Norman argued in a widely read volume of the 'Black Papers' that 'England is not a pluralist society except in the most qualified sense. It is, on the contrary, a society whose leaders of opinion have lost confidence in their own traditional values and who represent the resulting chaos as reasoned diversity' (Jones, 1989, p. 44). Since then political lobbies like the Hillgate group and the Centre for Policy Studies have consistently campaigned against multiculturalism in education, and for the restoration of a curriculum based on a narrower definition of English culture which stresses the dominance of Christian values, British history and the English literary canon (Jones, 1989). In their 1987 Pamphlet, *The Reform of British Education*, the Hillgate authors railed against what they saw as the 'pressure for a multi-cultural curriculum' which 'goes hand in hand with a tendency to denounce as "racist" all teachers who count the English language, British history and our national culture as things which it is their duty to impart' (Hillgate Group, 1987, p. 3).

The 1988 Education Act, and the national curriculum which resulted from it, represent to some extent a victory for the Conservative cultural restorationists against the multicultural movement in education. Through various controversial revisions to the orders, the English and history curricula have increasingly come to represent a narrow monoculturalism focusing on a specifically white English heritage. Furthermore, the national curriculum is now bound by law to reflect predominantly Christian values. The message to minority communities is that their children should assimilate to the dominant values in schools.


CONCLUSION

Schooling, as Eric Hobsbawm once remarked, has been a potent weapon in the forming of nations (Hobsbawm, 1977). In the historical formation of the British state, however, education has arguably played a lesser role than in some other European states, and nationalism has often taken a relatively muted form in the school curricula. The early consolidation of the British state, which occurred centuries before the development of national education, pre-empted any major role for education in British state formation. The distinctive education systems which grew up in England, Wales, Scotland and Ireland in the nineteenth century played a role in shaping cultural identities in those regions, and no doubt also played a part in forging a loose kind of Great British identity, particularly in the period of Empire, but only in respect to the turn of the century would it be possible to argue that schools have been the primary sites for the formation of national consciousness.

In other ways, however, the picture is more complex than this and the settlement less stable. Scottish education has been subject to many pressures to conform with English norms over the past century and has converged in some areas, but in others it is still quite distinctive and likely to remain so. Despite the migration of some English measures, like the new vocational qualifications, across the border, Scotland is still exempted from the national curriculum, and the Scottish Education Department curriculum guidelines pay some respect to Scottish culture and traditions. European Union policies still emphasize the importance of intercultural education and the rights of non-native speakers, and its programmes have lent support to minority initiatives in the United Kingdom. Furthermore, some aspects of government education policy may have different and contradictory effects. While the national curriculum promotes cultural restorationism, policies on vocational education adopt a modernizing rhetoric that has little to do with restoring a traditional culture which is often represented as an impediment to enterprise and change. Similarly, policies which emphasize parent power and choice may yet afford minority parents opportunities for promoting their own cultures in the educational experiences of their children.

# 6 Educational Achievement in Centralized and Decentralized Systems

School decentralization arguments have been widely adopted in the rhetoric (if less in the practice) of educational reform in many countries around the world, and particularly in the English-speaking states. Claims that decentralization will enhance the effectiveness of school systems have formed the central plank in the work of many prominent school reform advocates (Chubb and Moe, 1990; Sexton, 1987). However, the logical arguments advanced to support these claims are much contested (Ball, 1990a; Carnoy, 1993; Green, 1994; Whitty, 1992) and the empirical evidence, such as it is, has yet to substantiate the case. Decentralizing measures, such as 'school choice' and 'local management' policies in England, New Zealand and the USA, are too partial and too recent in origin to permit any definitive analysis of their effects on aggregate national outcomes; and the evidence proffered by advocates from within-country cross-school comparisons only weakly supports their case, if at all. Chubb and Moe (1990), for instance, find that private (i.e. less centralized) schools in the USA rate higher than state schools on school effectiveness traits but this could be simply the result of their ability to select pupils with whom it is easier to display effective schooling. Comparative studies have not adequately established that they can achieve higher levels of 'value-added' than the supposedly more centralized schools in the public systems (Carnoy, 1993). Furthermore, international comparisons, which decentralization advocates rarely cite, provide more evidence, if anything, for the effectiveness of more 'centralized systems', depending on what one means by these categories.

The purpose of this chapter is to review some of the evidence from international comparisons on the relative effectiveness of 'centralized' and 'decentralized' education systems in the advanced industrialized nations and to construct a number of hypotheses, relating to characteristics of centralism and decentralism, to explain variations in educational outcomes between countries. This will entail comparing outcomes for a sample of nations for which we have comparable data, isolating certain 'clusters' of institutional (and cultural) characteristics which seem to be common to a number of high achieving systems, and analysing how these may be affecting aggregate national levels of attainment as measured by qualifications.

This procedure is clearly highly provisional and the hypotheses cannot be fully tested empirically since we have insufficient data currently to do this. To perform any statistical analysis of the factors underlying variations in national outcomes we would need a large sample of countries for which we had reliable comparative data on outcomes and institutional and cultural characteristics. The latter would need to be precisely defined and susceptible to valid measurement by proxy indicators. At present none of these conditions are met. Data sets on national outcomes for a wide range of countries are not entirely reliable either because the outcome definitions used are insufficiently precise or not fully comparable (as with the ISCED levels in OECD, 1995) or because the national survey samples used are not always representative (as often with the IEA studies). Fully comparable quantitative data on national institutional characteristics are scarce. The OECD has begun to define indicators and assemble comparative data for a range of characteristics but the work is still in its early stages and the indicators will require a great deal more refinement before they can be used for these purposes.

However, for a small sample of countries we do have quite robust comparative data on educational outcomes and a wealth of analytical comparative work on institutional structures. The comparative data set on outcomes relates to qualifications and has been constructed by benchmarking the major qualifications in each country at given levels and collecting data on the stocks and flows of these qualifications for a series of years. It affords the most reliable comparisons for a group of countries which have national qualification systems, reliable official records of qualifications awarded by year and age of recipient, and labour force survey data on highest qualifications held. The countries include France, Germany, Singapore and the UK. Although they have less comprehensive national systems of qualifications and thus present greater problems for comparison, a number of other countries have been extensively studied in terms of their achievement levels and these can also be included in our comparisons. These include Japan, Sweden and the USA.

Comparative studies of these countries have consistently shown that France, Germany, Japan, Sweden and, in recent years, Singapore achieve relatively high average levels of educational qualification, whereas the UK and the USA seem to lag somewhat behind. France, Germany, Japan, Sweden and Singapore are traditionally accredited with having relatively centralized educational systems, although in the German case it is more proper to talk about centralization at the regional level (Archer, 1979;

Boucher, 1982; Gopinathan, 1994; Prost, 1968; Passin, 1965; Samuel and Thomas, 1949; Schoppa, 1991). The UK and the USA have traditionally been seen as classic examples of educational decentralization, although their systems are now changing (Archer, 1979; Green, 1990; Lauglo and McLean, 1985).

## EDUCATIONAL OUTCOMES IN FRANCE, GERMANY, JAPAN, SINGAPORE, SWEDEN, THE UK AND THE USA

Data for educational outcomes for the seven countries are taken from three sources: the International Evaluation of Achievement Studies (IEA, 1988), the recent International Adult Literacy Survey (IALS) (OECD/Statistics Canada, 1995), and the author's own research with Hilary Steedman (Green and Steedman, 1993; and forthcoming).[1] These studies are based on different methodologies and compare different things among different age groups. The IEA studies used here are based on tests of knowledge and skills in Maths and Science administered between 1981 and 1986 to sample school populations aged 10, 13/14 and 18 years in a wide range of countries. The IALS study was based on various tests of literacy administered in 1994 to samples of adults in Canada, Germany, the Netherlands, Poland, Sweden, Switzerland and the USA. The Green and Steedman studies are based on analyses of the stocks and flows of qualifications in the sample countries for various years. These disparate methodologies limit the degree to which the results of the different studies can be compared. The national comparisons made here, therefore, will be largely based on the qualifications evidence. However, where this is less conclusive, as with the data for Japan, Sweden and the USA, the survey/test evidence will also be used.

The Green and Steedman research on national qualification attainment has included France, Germany, Singapore, the UK and the USA, with Japan included in the earlier study (Green and Steedman, 1993). The methodology involved benchmarking the major national qualifications awarded in each of these countries against UK levels and subsequently comparing the stocks and flows of these qualifications in each country using official data sources on qualification awards and labour force survey data on highest qualifications held by different age groups in the 16–65 populations. The focus of the research was on qualifications normally taken at the end of compulsory education (i.e. at about 15 or 16 years) and at the end of upper secondary education, including foundation training (at between 17 and 19 years) and which were judged to be equivalent to the

UK NCVQ qualification levels 2 and 3 respectively. NCVQ level 2 represents attainment of 5 GCSEs at grades A–C or better, a General National Vocational Qualification (GNVQ) level 2, or a National Vocational Qualification (NVQ) level 2. NCVQ level 3 represents attainment of two or more A levels or a (G)NVQ level 3. These levels are roughly equivalent to the OECD's ISCED levels 3 and 4, although the latter are only defined in very general terms and utilize equivalences based on reports made by individual governments rather than through any benchmarking of standards as employed here.

For each country the major national (i.e. state-recognized) qualifications were selected and benchmarked against the UK levels. Judgements about levels of qualifications were made by subject experts drawn from each of the countries and through analysis of syllabuses, test criteria and examination papers. Level judgements were based on a range of criteria including: (a) the position of the qualification in the relevant national hierarchy of qualifications; (b) the duration and mode of study of the course concerned; (c) the typical age of students entering and qualifying; (d) the entry requirements for admission to the course; (e) the range and level of the contents specified for the course; (f) the types of assessment used and standards required; (g) the rights of access to other courses conferred by the qualification; and (h) the typical destinations of graduates in employment or further education or training. The survey was not able to include qualifications awarded by private bodies and not recognized by the state, and nor could it assess skills acquired but not certificated. Consequently in countries where skills are frequently acquired informally and not certificated, or where they are attested in certificates not recognized by the state, the data on qualifications may underestimate the true prevalence of skills. Inevitably, establishing level equivalence between qualifications in different countries involved making normative judgements, as for instance where the range and breadth of knowledge attested in one qualification had to be balanced against the depth and complexity of knowledge in another. The final evaluations thus represent judgements made against a range of criteria and agreed among a body of expert assessors.

The results of the evaluations for qualifications deemed equivalent in level to the UK NCVQ level 2 were as follows: for France, the *Brevet*, the CAP (*certificat d'aptitude professionnelle*) and the BEP (*brevet d'études professionnelles*); for Germany the *Hauptschulabschluss* and the *Realschulabschluss* (and assuming this level for those with the *Abitur* who have bypassed the earlier qualification); and for Singapore, 5 O levels, the Certificate of Office Studies and the National Trade Certificate level 2. The level 3 equivalents were: for France, the *Baccalauréats* (including the general, technological and vocational *baccalauréats*); for Germany, the *Abitur*, the *Fachhoschulreife* and the Apprenticeship certificate (excluding those completed in two years or less); and for Singapore, two or more A levels, the Certificate in Business Studies, the Industrial Technician Certificate, and the National Trade Certificate level 1. In each country, these qualifications represent the vast majority of awards made to young people at this general level.

Japan and the USA present a greater problem for comparisons since there are few national qualifications at this level in either country. The High School Certificate in the USA, awarded by individual schools, attests completion of a number of courses, but does not guarantee the attainment of a given level in a range of subjects and cannot therefore be used for these comparisons. In this case we can only use data for degrees and associate degrees, which, although also issued by individual institutions, are deemed to involve a more consistent standard. Like the USA, Japan also uses high school completion certificates as the measure of attainment at the end of upper secondary education. However, although these are issued by individual schools without external moderation and also involve variability in standards between institutions, the latter appears to be less pronounced than in the USA. Furthermore, a study of vocational upper secondary schools in Japan in 1982 by the NIESR compared textbooks and syllabuses with those for vocational courses in similar areas in the UK and came to the conclusion that the standard and range of studies (in vocational areas and Maths) were close to those in the National Diploma, a level 3 qualification (Prais, 1987). Data for high school graduation in Japan are thus presented but must be treated with caution. On the basis of this set of qualification equivalences, and with particular caution in relation to two of the countries, we can now compare qualification levels for seven countries using data on flows and stocks for recent years.

Information on stocks of qualifications held is contained in the annual labour force survey reports for France, Germany, Singapore, the UK and the USA (the Japanese LFS data is available but has not yet been analysed). These reports generally contain data on the highest qualifications held by the adult population, down to the level of the major individual qualifications. The data for Singapore cannot be disaggregated to the level of individual qualifications and the broad 'secondary' classification does not correspond directly with our level 2 category and therefore cannot be used for comparisons. However, the higher 'post-secondary' classification is comprised of precisely the same qualifications as were designated to be level 3 equivalent and can be the basis for valid comparisons. For the USA the only categories which can be used are those described as 'degree' and 'associate degree'.

The LFS data allow comparisons across countries for levels of qualifications of the active, inactive and total population by age band, gender and occupation. Taking the data for 1994 for the 25–28 year olds in the total population (the youngest age band capturing the majority of awards made at this level), we can see that there are marked differences in the proportions of the age group in each country having obtained at least level 2 and at least level 3 qualifications (Table 6.1). Compared with the UK and Singapore, both France and Germany would appear to have a considerably higher proportion of their 25–28 year olds qualified at level 2 or higher and at level 3 or higher. However, in the Singapore case, the younger 19–24 age group is considerably better qualified than the older age group, reflecting the speed of improvement in rates of qualification in recent years. The overall German advantage against the other countries is considerable due to the large numbers gaining the apprentice qualification through the Dual System and it may be objected that not all of these apprentices have attained a level 3 standard. However, even if we exclude those apprentice graduates whose highest previous qualification was the *Hauptschulabschluss* (i.e. from the lower-ranking secondary schools) still 52 per cent of the age group could be said to have reached level 3 compared with 36 per cent in the UK.

Data on stocks are perhaps the most straightforward basis for comparisons of national qualification levels. However, they have the disadvantage that they are always presenting a historical picture of the rate at which a country is generating qualified people. The persons included in the data for 25–28 year olds would normally have gained their level 3 qualifications at

*Table 6.1* Proportion of 25–28 year olds qualified to levels 2 and 3 or higher in 1994

|  | Level 2 or higher | Level 3 or higher |
|---|---|---|
| France | 79 | 42 |
| Germany | 80 | 75 (52) |
| Singapore (25–29) | — | 35 |
| (19–24) | — | 41 |
| UK | 53 | 36 |
| (USA) | — | (32)* |

*Degree and associate degree only.

18 or 19, i.e. between 1980 and 1984. Comparative data on qualification flows, on the other hand, can generally be assembled for last year: at the time of writing for 1994. This allows us to see more clearly the results of recent changes in policies and rates of qualification in different countries. The data are also based on total body counts, not sample surveys, and therefore avoids the potential errors associated with the latter.

However, there is no one agreed method for calculating qualification flows as a proportion of a county's relevant age cohorts. The simplest method is probably that used in the French national statistics which involves dividing the total number of qualifications awarded in a given year by the size of the most typical year group taking them (i.e. 18 year olds for level 3 qualifications). This so-called 'age cohort qualification rate' is a statistical abstraction. It does not refer to the rate of qualification of actual people of a given age in a particular year. However, it does offer a reasonable proxy for the accumulated qualification rates of actual people in a given year cohort. (If the quantity and age spread of awards remained stable over a number of years equal to the year span of the spread of awards, then the rate would be the same as the accumulated qualification rates for each individual age group within that age span at the end of the period.) The measure can also be used as a fair basis for comparison providing that each country uses it in the same way and that care is taken to include individuals who have bypassed a given level of qualification and attained a qualification at a higher level, and to avoid double-counting individuals who have gained two qualifications at the same level.

This method is applied here but with some modifications necessitated by the different kinds of data available in each country. For Germany we include as level 3 qualifications the *Abitur*, the *Fachhoschulreife* and the (higher) apprentice qualifications. For the *Abitur* and *Fachhoschulreife*, a figure is used which is based on the proportion of those leaving school in a given year with particular levels of qualification. For the apprenticeship figure, discounts are made for those passing who already have a level 3 qualification or whose previous qualification is the *Hauptschulabschluss* or less. For Singapore we include as level 3 two or more A levels, level 3 equivalent vocational qualifications and polytechnic diplomas gained by those who do not already have a level 3 qualification. In each case the rates are calculated by dividing total awards by the age cohort number for 18 year olds. For England we use the official DFE A level qualification rate which is calculated in terms of the proportion of those reaching 18 in a given year who gain two A levels in that year or a previous year. This method will give a somewhat deflated age cohort qualification rate since it excludes those over 19 gaining two A levels. However, these are few in number in England, as compared with France for instance, where, due to frequent grade repeating, some 30 per cent of *baccalauréat* candidates are over 18. To minimize the comparative discrepancy for the total level 3 rate for England we have included 19 year olds gaining GNVQs and NVQs in the English figure.

For Japan and Sweden, for which we have no national qualifications at this level, we can only present rates of matriculation from upper secondary high schools. This is not a very safe basis for comparison since standards at matriculation from high schools in these countries will vary between vocational and general streams and, to some extent, between institutions. However, for Japan, at least, we have some evidence that the standard expected in the vocational high schools (which are generally ranked below the general high schools) is generally at least as high as that for our benchmark level 3 vocational course in the UK (Prais, 1987).

Using these methods we find that the level 3 age cohort qualification rates vary considerably by country (Table 6.2). Again, Germany and France come out with high rates of qualification at this level, and this time Singapore comes close behind France. England (and Wales for vocational qualifications) lags considerably behind. If we accept high school graduation as level 3 equivalent, Sweden and Japan would both come out with high rates compared with all the other countries.

Further comparisons of national attainments can be made using the data from the IEA studies and the recent IALS survey on adult literacy. The IEA study, *Science Achievement in Seventeen Countries* (1988), was based on tests carried out on samples of children aged 10, 14 and 18. The national results for the 18 year olds cannot really be compared since the populations in school at this age are more highly selected in some countries than others. However, the average national results for the 10 and 14 year olds can be compared and Table 6.3 shows the ranking of each country for each age group in terms of all the countries in the survey. Japan and Sweden come out with high average scores for both age groups whereas Britain and the USA have relatively low average scores for both age groups. Singapore also comes out low which is consistent with the picture emerging from the stocks and flows data about the relatively recent improvement in rates of qualification. What is also notable from the IEA study is that there was a high degree of dispersal in the scores recorded for the UK and the USA, with the bottom 25 per cent doing particularly badly in both those countries. This confirms the conclusions drawn by Postlethwaite from the 1965 IEA Maths study that England showed the largest differences between students' attainments of any country in the study (Postlethwaite, 1982).

*Table 6.2*    Age cohort qualification rate at level 3 in 1994

| | | |
|---|---|---|
| **England** | | |
| Two or more A levels | (England) | 28.0 |
| GNVQ Advanced | (England, Wales and NI) | 0.34 |
| BTEC National Diplomas | (E, W and NI) | 7.36 |
| BTEC National Certificates | (E, W and NI) | 1.16 |
| BTEC level 3 NVQs | (E, W and NI) | 0.07 |
| City and Guilds level 3 | (UK) | 2.28 |
| Other[1] | (UK) | 1.05 |
| Total | | 40.26 |
| **France** | | |
| Baccalauréat[2] | | 58 |
| **Germany (western *Länder*)** | | |
| *Abitur* or *Fachhochschulreife* (1993) | | 31.7 |
| Apprenticeship[3] | | 31.6 |
| Total | | 63.3 |
| **Singapore** | | |
| Two or more A Levels | | 23.5 |
| Higher Technical[4] | | 5.3 |
| Diploma[5] | | 21.7 |
| Total | | 50.5 |
| **Japan (1992)[6]** | | 92.2 |
| **Sweden (1992)[7]** | | 83 |

1. This includes NVQs, City and Guilds and other occupationally specific qualifications judged to be at level 3. The figures are stocks figures for the 19–21 population taken from the LFS (see Helm and Redding, 1992).
2. Includes general, vocational and technological *baccalauréats*. Data from Ministry of National Education, Notes d'Information.
3. Excludes those passing the apprenticeship who already have an *Abitur* or *Fachhoschulreife* (20 per cent) or whose previous qualification was below the *Realschulabschluss* (25.7 per cent). Data from Statistisches Bundesamt.
4. This includes the Certificate in Business Studies, the National Trade Certificate level 1 and the Industrial Technician Certificate. Data collected from Singapore Ministry of Education and Institute for Technical Education. Data on polytechnic awards to those without prior level 3 qualifications from individual Singapore polytechnics.
5. These are polytechnic diplomas normally taken at 19. The figure excludes all those who already had a level 3 qualification.
6. This is the upper secondary graduation rate for 1992 from OECD, *Education at a Glance* (1995, p. 214).
7. This is the upper secondary graduation rate as in ibid.

Table 6.3   Rank order of countries for achievement at each level

| Country[*] | Rank for 10 year olds | Rank for 14 year olds |
|---|---|---|
| England | 12 | 11 |
| Japan | 1 | 2 |
| Singapore | 13 | 14 |
| Sweden | 4 | 6 |
| USA | 8 | 14 |

[*]From IEA, *Science Education in Seventeen Countries, A Preliminary Report*, Pergamon Press, 1988, p. 3.

The IALS study was based on tests of literacy carried out on adult populations in eight countries including Germany, Sweden and the USA. The tests were designed to ascertain proficiency in three areas (defined as: Prose Literacy, Document Literacy and Quantitative (arithmetic) Literacy) and were scored against a scale with five ascending bands: from level 1 to level 5. The report of the study does not produce a national rank order but one can be produced by averaging, for each country, the percentages scoring at each level. On this basis it is calculated that 36.96 per cent of the Swedish sample were scoring at levels 4 and 5 (the highest levels) across the range of criteria compared with 29.44 per cent for Germany and 26.26 per cent for the USA. On the other hand, 21.83 per cent of the US sample only scored at an average of level 1, compared with 9.98 per cent for Germany and 6.75 per cent for Sweden.[2]

The relatively low ranking of the UK and the USA in aggregate level of attainment, as compared with a range of countries (including, variously, Germany, France, Japan and Sweden) is confirmed by other studies which have reviewed the available evidence (Ashton and Green, 1996; Finegold and Soskice, 1988; Reynolds and Farrell, 1996).

## FACTORS INFLUENCING EDUCATIONAL ACHIEVEMENT IN HIGH-ATTAINING COUNTRIES

The data presented above suggests that one group of countries (France, Germany, Japan, Sweden, Singapore), whose education systems have been traditionally characterized as 'centralized' (Archer, 1979; Boucher, 1982; Gopinathan, 1994; Green, 1990; Schoppa, 1991), appear to obtain better aggregate attainments than another pair of countries (the UK and USA) which are traditionally characterized as 'decentralized' (Archer, 1979; Green, 1990; Kaestle, 1983; Lauglo and McLean, 1985). Does this demonstrate that centralized education systems generally achieve better average educational results than decentralized ones? Clearly, the answer to this is no. Firstly, the sample of countries is too small for deriving any general rules: a larger sample would no doubt include some counter-examples of more centralized systems which performed relatively poorly and some more decentralized systems (the Netherlands?) which obtain relatively high average standards. Secondly, the terms centralization and decentralization are themselves too vague to yield much insight into the system factors that affect national rates of achievement. The countries traditionally designated as centralized in our sample here differ considerably in the ways in which central control is utilized. In Germany, 'central' control over the school system (as opposed to the apprentice system) is exercised at the level of the individual *Länder* and not at the federal government level, although the policies of the *Länder* are coordinated with each other by inter-state bodies. In Japan, there is indeed strong central government control over the school system – Monbusho controls the curriculum and textbooks – but there is a large number of private schools, including Juku, high schools and universities. The Juku are fully independent and the private high schools and universities, although part financed and regulated by the state, have a greater degree of autonomy in certain areas than the public institutions. Historically, Sweden and France have both had highly centralized educational systems but this is now changing to some extent, although too recently to have had much impact on the outcomes reported above. Both operate a degree of 'school choice', although this is still limited in France. Sweden has given more discretion to schools concerning the curriculum, and France has transferred some responsibilities from the central to regional and municipal levels (although not much to individual schools). Each of these countries may still be reckoned to have relatively 'centralized' systems but saying so does not tell us very much. So what can be deduced about the factors affecting achievement in the higher attaining countries?

The causes of educational attainment among nations, as with individuals, are complex. Comparative researchers have sought in vain for particular characteristics of education systems which might explain the different average levels of attainment between countries, but the only factor which systematically correlates with national educational outcomes appears to be the time spent studying by children (IAEP, 1992; Inkeles, 1982). Many of the factors which appear to dominate national debates about standards, like school organization, class size and levels of finance, seem to have little explanatory power in relation to the causes of differences in national standards, at least among countries at similar levels of development.

No significant statistical relationship has been found between levels of educational expenditure within advanced industrial nations and national educational outcomes (Lynn, 1988). Of the countries in this study, Japan has the second lowest public expenditure per student after Singapore and, arguably, the highest educational outcomes. The USA has the highest public expenditure per school student and among the lowest educational outcomes (data for educational expenditures in OECD, 1995).

High average levels of achievement in different countries are not consistently associated with any particular form of school organization. Some countries with comprehensive schools during the compulsory years have very high average outcomes (Japan, France and Sweden); others do not (the UK, USA). Equally there are examples of both successful and less successful selective systems. The IAEP study found no consistent relationship between average national attainments and policies on streaming (IAEP, 1992). It would appear that in high-achieving countries teachers generally have high public esteem, but there is no statistically significant correlation between national educational outcomes and levels of teacher pay relative to other professions in the same country. Nor can any statistical correlation be established between average class sizes and national standards of attainment (Lynn, 1988). Japan has considerably larger average class sizes than most of the other countries in this study, apparently without negative effects on its levels of achievement.

The outcomes of the educational process in different countries would seem to be the result of a host of factors, some relating to the internal features of the education system (institutional structures, curriculum design, teaching methods, forms of assessment and certification), and others relating to the social context in which it is set (societal and parental attitudes and expectations, employment opportunities and the nature of the labour market, etc.). It is the interaction of these factors, rather than any particular practices in education, which would seem to determine the levels of achievement characteristic of different systems (IAEP, 1992; Altback et al., 1982).

The countries which achieve higher standards in education and training, like Germany, France, Japan and Singapore (in recent years), would appear to have one fundamental thing in common: as nations they place great emphasis on educational achievement, engendering high educational aspirations amongst individual learners. They tend to have a 'learning culture' in which parents and teachers have high expectations of their children's educational achievements, where the education systems are designed to provide opportunities and motivation for learners of all abilities, and where the labour market, and society in general, rewards those who do well in education.

Education has played a particularly important role in the historical development of Germany, France, Japan and Singapore as modern nation states. It was a critical factor in the industrialization of each of these countries: in France after the Revolution; in Prussia after the Napoleonic invasions; in Japan after the Meiji Restoration; and more recently in Singapore. In Japan and Germany it was also seen as crucial to the process of political and economic restructuring after the Second World War. For these and other historical reasons these societies place an exceptionally high value on education both for its potential contribution towards national development and for its enhancement of individual opportunities.

The effects of this cultural stress on education are now manifested in a number of different ways in each of these countries: the majority of young people are willing to defer wage earning until 18 and beyond in order to extend their education and gain higher qualifications; parents are willing to maintain their children through extended secondary education and, in the Japanese case, to devote considerable resources to paying fees for Juku and upper secondary schools; and employers are willing to invest heavily in training and to reward young people who gain qualifications.

High expectations in these countries are also institutionalized within the education systems. Prescribed curricula govern the content of education in different types of school and for different ages. These establish norms and expectations for all children and give clarity and purpose to the educational process. Curriculum development and pedagogical research have been more systematically organized and focused than in countries like Britain, and this, together with prescribed curricula and teaching methods and the extensive use of professionally designed materials and textbooks, has tended to encourage a more uniform practice within education, with shared understandings of aims and objectives among teachers, parents and students. In his evaluation of the IEA data Postlethwaite has concluded that the importance of systematic curriculum development and evaluation could not be overemphasized (1982).

In each of these systems, whether comprehensive or selective in structure, there is a clear identity and purpose for each institution and at each stage children appear to know what is expected of them. Norms are established for all children, in whichever stream, and they are reinforced through regular assessment and reporting. The practice of grade repeating, which is widespread in Germany and France, serves to underline the expectation that certain standards are required at each level for all children. The practice has been criticized for the supposedly damaging effects that such 'labelling' may have on pupil confidence and motivation. However, recent research in France indicates that at the secondary stage *redoublement* does not noticeably damage pupils' self-esteem and that for a proportion of those repeating a class, subsequent progress is better than for those of similar attainments who do not repeat (Robinson, Taylor and Piolat, 1992). Grade repeating may be seen, therefore, as a practice which embodies an important and empowering educational principle: while some children may take longer than others, all are capable of achieving. Japan, and other East Asian states, tend not to practise grade repeating, but their cultures and school practices, perhaps even more than in the continental states, embody the belief that all children can achieve given motivation and effort (White, 1987).

Tightly regulated structures and institutionalized norms would also seem to have effects in classroom practices. British and US observers of classrooms in Germany, France, Japan and Taiwan (HMI, 1986, 1991 and 1992; White, 1987) frequently note the relative orderliness and purposefulness of lessons.[3] This may be partly a result of teaching methods which tend to stress whole-class activities. However, it may also be attributable to the clarity of aims and purpose afforded by the structures described above. In either case it would appear that the teachers' work in these countries may be made easier through the use of whole-class teaching and by the supportive structures provided by national curricula, standardized assessment procedures, recommended methods and textbooks and so on. Where less energy is expended on planning lesson content, producing learning materials and organizing individualized learning in class, more time and effort can be given to the learning process (Reynolds and Farrel, 1996).

In support of this Postlethwaite's review of the IEA data (1982) suggested that there was some evidence of a correlation between the average proportion of lesson time spent 'on task' in different countries with both aggregate national attainments and the dispersal of attainments. He cites Japan, using Cummings' evidence, as an example of a country with high levels of attainment where students tend to be actively engaged for a high proportion of classroom time. According to Cummings, the average proportion of actively engaged classroom time in Japan was 90 per cent compared with about 65 per cent in some Chicago schools tested. Higher rates of time spent 'on task' is one of the effects one might expect to be associated with the relative orderliness of 'whole-class' lessons as reported by observers of classrooms in Japan and Germany (Postlethwaite, 1982).

High aspirations are encouraged for all students in these systems not only by the institutionalization of shared norms and standards but also by the structure of incentives and rewards offered to students. At the end of compulsory schooling there are appropriate examinations or awards for all children in whichever type of institution or stream. These are invariably grouped examinations and awards requiring passes in all major subjects and they have the effect of encouraging children to do well in all subject areas. Even in Singapore, where the single-subject British O and A level exams are taken, these are offered to students in groups whereby each student is required to take a prescribed combination of subjects. Qualifications tend to form part of a well-understood hierarchy, having genuine currency in the labour market or giving rights of access to higher levels of education and training. (The system in Japan works somewhat differently and will be considered later.) Each educational track, therefore, has progression possibilities built into it, so the majority of children have incentives to achieve. This is reinforced, typically, by the structure of the labour market which rewards those who gain qualifications.

## THE FAILURE TO INSTITUTIONALIZE HIGH EXPECTATIONS IN ENGLAND AND THE USA

Compared to the higher achieving countries discussed above, both England (and Wales)[4] and the USA have been relatively unsuccessful in institutionalizing high expectations for all their pupils. They have both been consistently successful in educating their elites to the highest international standards, but have failed to generalize the high aspirations of their elites to the generality of their populations. In recent years commentators in both countries, including governments, have frequently bemoaned the lack of a 'learning culture' throughout society and have made unfavourable comparisons on this between their own countries and other countries like Japan and Germany (Ball, 1991; National Commission on Excellence in Education, 1984; National Commission on Education, 1993). Not only do their cultures appear to fail to generalize sufficiently the desire to excel in education, their education systems would appear to lack many of the features which in other countries appear to institutionalize high expectations.

In accordance with their common liberal traditions – and in the US case also because of its federal structure – neither country has traditionally favoured giving central government too much power in education. This has made it difficult to enforce common structures, practices and standards across the whole of each system. Uniquely among European education systems, England did not have a national curriculum until very recently. In the USA, there are mandatory school curricula prescribed by some state Boards of Education but there is still no national curriculum. Nor does either country have a national system of qualifications in the continental European sense of the term. The UK has recently developed a national system of vocational qualifications (overseen by the National Council for Vocational Qualifications) but its academic qualifications are awarded by numerous private examining boards which have only recently become subject to significant levels of government regulation and this falls far short of a state guarantee of the standards of individual awards. The awards are also for elective single-subject examinations which make no requirements on students to perform to a given standard over a range of core subjects, as in the typical continental grouped awards. The USA has no national awards guaranteed by the state at all. High school graduation requirements typically allow a large degree of choice in subjects taken, and diplomas may be gained without reaching any specified standard (National Commission on Excellence in Education, 1984).

There are other important areas where light central regulation has allowed a diversity of practices. Neither country can claim to have a common institutional structure of schools across its entire territory, as is the case in countries like France, Germany and Japan. Arrangements vary by state in the USA and by Local Education Authority in the UK. In both countries there has been a tradition of relatively low levels of central government regulation and intervention as regards teaching styles and materials and modes of assessment, although at certain periods in the USA State Boards have been quite active. While this is now changing to some extent in both countries, it would seem likely that there is a greater variety in pedagogic practices across schools in England and Wales and the USA than is the case in some of the more regulated systems like France and Japan (HMI, 1990).

Lastly, but by no means least significant, school funding systems in both countries involve degrees of discretionary local funding which lead to considerable regional disparities, particularly in the USA where the federal share of primary and secondary funding is only 6 per cent of the total (Reich, 1991; Winkler, 1993). In affluent Belmont, north-west of Boston, average schoolteacher pay was $36 000 in 1988 and only 4 per cent of students dropped out before graduating from high school. In nearby Sommerville, a less affluent area, average teacher pay was $29 400 and a third of students failed to complete high school. Two years later the average teacher salary in Arkansas was even lower at $20 300 (Reich,

1991, p. 27). Such enormous regional disparities in resources may not entirely explain differential outcomes but they are symbolic of a host of other factors and attitudes which may be highly significant.

While in some areas, as in the prescription of textbooks, there may be powerful democratic and human rights objections to overly strong central regulation (see Horio, 1988, on Japan), it is not hard to see that a low level of regulation across a number of fields is likely to increase the variability of practices and standards across schools and regions within a given country. As we have seen, there is evidence from the IEA studies that this is the case for the UK and it is a common perception from observers both inside (National Commission on Excellence in Education, 1984; Moore, 1990) and outside the country (HMI, 1990) that this is also the case for the USA. This may, of course, result from other social and cultural factors in these countries – both for instance have relatively high levels of inequality of wealth and income as compared with the majority of European and, indeed, developed Asian states (as measured on the Gini scale). However, it would seem highly plausible that low levels of regulation also contribute to this effect. It is in the nature of markets, if unregulated, to produce differentiation. As recent research has suggested (Adler, Petch and Tweedie, 1986; Carnoy; 1993; Moore, 1990), the adoption of school choice policies in both the UK and the USA already shows signs of exacerbating the differences in quality and standards across schools.

The essential difference between the compulsory school systems of the high achieving countries as compared with the lower achieving countries would appear to be that the former have both a culture and certain institutional mechanisms which encourage high aspirations and achievement among a wide majority of children whereas the latter are successful only with their elites, whether they are the children with the higher abilities or those from the higher social groups. Whereas in all countries you will find some low-status schools and educationally marginalized social groups, in the lower achieving countries this is relatively more widespread. As every teacher in the USA and the UK knows, the gap between the schools in deprived inner city areas and schools in the prosperous suburbs and rural areas can be immense. The argument here is that this is exacerbated by the liberal or *laissez-faire* traditions which have prevailed historically in these countries. While the affluent schools, drawing on deep pools of cultural and social capital among their constituents, have prospered when left to their own devices, others schools, less well advantaged, have not. There seems, as yet, to be little in the policy armoury of the liberal states that can counter this effect.

The irony is that it is these systems, which traditionally pride them-selves on their concern for the individual student, which seem to leave so many without hope or self-confidence, whereas in some other systems, which are often characterized as less humanistic because of their more regimented and uniform nature, fewer students are so marginalized. Robinson and Taylor (1989) report on a survey of attitudes to self, school and school work by samples of English, Japanese and French low-attain-ers. They found that 'the depressed level of self-esteem is most pro-nounced for the English' and comment that 'the [English] system, which explicitly claims to be child-centred rather than curriculum-led, and which is concerned "to meet the needs of individual children" and to match the subject, level and methods to these needs, is in fact the system which shows the greatest gradient in general self-esteem and in commitment to school.'

## FACTORS AFFECTING ATTAINMENT IN POST-COMPULSORY EDUCATION AND TRAINING

By the end of compulsory schooling some of our seven countries are already quite clearly differentiated in terms of average levels of attain-ment. However, it is during the post-compulsory phase of education and training (PCET) that the differences in qualification rates become most apparent. This is because PCET is the most critical phase as regards qualification attainment. The 15–20 years phase of PCET is where most young people gain their terminal and highest qualification and it is where they transport this qualification to their differential positions in the labour market. It is also the phase where the different levels of participation in different countries begin to impact on rates of qualification. Although in all our seven countries the majority now stay on into PCET, it is a smaller proportion in the UK, for instance, than in the other six countries (Green and Steedman, 1993; OECD, 1995). What happens in the PCET phase should therefore be relatively important in explaining differential national rates of attainment.

At first sight there would appear to be no obvious institutional charac-teristics which are common to the higher attaining countries and not shared by the lower attaining countries. Institutional structures in PCET fall into three broad types. There are systems which are based primarily on the apprentice model with a minority set of elite educational institu-tions running parallel. Germany offers the preeminent example of this (and the only one in our sample) with its Dual System of apprentice training representing the dominant mode of PCET and with the *Gymnasien* reserved for a minority (although a growing one). There are predominantly school-based systems with a variety of institutions offering different kinds of provision. France, Japan and Singapore fall into this category: France with its general, technical and vocational *lycées*; Japan with its general and vocational high schools; and Singapore with its academic junior colleges, vocational polytechnics and technical training centres. England and Wales is also now a predominantly school-based system, although the different institutions – school sixth forms and further education colleges – are not clearly differentiated in their curriculum offer. Each of these systems maintains a residual form of apprentice training. Lastly, there are the predominantly school-based systems where there is one dominant type of institution, offering a comprehensive provision. The USA with its high schools exemplifies one version of this, and Sweden, with its comprehensive *Gymnasieskola*, another (OECD, 1985). Whatever their institutional structures each of these systems incorporates different tracks, some of which are academic and some vocational. The balance between the two varies by country. In the USA and Japan general or academic education is dominant. In the other countries the majority of participants are on vocational courses, although in France, Germany and Sweden these contain a large element of general education (OECD, 1990). England and Wales, and Singapore, which adapts British qualifications, are somewhat unusual in having relatively little general education in their vocational programmes (Green and Steedman, 1996).

These different institutional models show no obvious correlations with national outcomes. Clearly, it is possible for systems which are predominantly employment-based, like Germany's, to achieve high average outcomes, just as some school-based systems (Japan) can do. The highest achieving systems tend to place a great stress on general education in all the tracks (except perhaps Singapore), but then so does the system in the USA, at least in quantitative terms, and this appears to perform less well. It is still, of course, true that the higher achieving systems are mainly distinguished by having curricula largely specified by central or state government, whereas in the UK and the USA there is still no national curriculum for the post-compulsory phase. However, it is more difficult to argue for this phase that the institutionalization of normative expectations is crucial for high average attainments because education and training provision are here necessarily more specialized and differentiated, it being the stage where young people are beginning to make choices about careers. In PCET it is the labour market which begins to exercise the predominant influence on determining norms and expectations and it is to this which we should now turn.

The most obvious feature which is common to the higher achieving systems (and not to the USA and the UK) is the high degree of articulation between education and training (ET) systems and labour markets. In each of the higher achieving countries there are mechanisms which ensure that job entry and pay are tightly linked with qualifications held or educational levels attained (in those countries without national qualifications). How these mechanisms function varies between countries. France and Germany are both historically highly credentialist societies. A large number of jobs in each country are reserved by law for those with particular qualifications. In Germany this extends beyond the normal range of professional occupations to craft work as well since federal legislation forbids those without Dual System qualifications to employ others and provide services in areas such as plumbing, building maintenance and so on (CEDEFOP, 1987). Even where statutory regulations do not apply, in both countries national sectoral agreements between employer organizations and unions determine entry requirements and pay levels for a wide range of jobs where these are explicitly linked to qualifications.

In Japan, as in several other Asian countries, the system works somewhat differently. Job attainment is governed not by qualifications but by the networks of association which link different educational institutions to different firms. Access to high status positions in prestigious firms is dependent, to a large extent, on gaining access, by competitive exams, to the best high schools and the best universities, and then on being recommended by them to the best firms. The prevalence of internal labour markets in Japan, at least in the large firms, means that promotion depends less on qualifications than on seniority and job performance. The latter involves performing well in training and showing the ability to acquire new skills, all of which may be facilitated by earlier educational success. Singapore, with its large proportion of foreign multinationals, tends to have more occupational labour markets, as in Europe, and here too the labour market is becoming fiercely credentialist.

Both Britain and the USA diverge markedly from the above patterns. Although there is a degree of credentialism and network influence operating in both countries, neither display the same degree of articulation between education and training and the labour market. Historically, both countries have been relatively less credentialist than continental Europe, having relatively more open labour markets, where employers often place greater stress on experience than qualifications. Criteria for job entry and pay determination are less pervasively regulated by government and national and sectoral agreements between unions and employer organizations. Qualifications clearly count in both countries, but there are other avenues open for building successful careers which are not so dependent on qualifications and formal schooling. Succeeding at school and acquiring qualifications figure highly for a proportion of young people in the UK and the USA. However, there is a large proportion who appear to give up on aspiring to these things at a relatively early age. In France, Germany and Japan, there is also a marginal group who give up but it would seem to be smaller. One reason for this may that in these countries there is practically no secure employment available to those who do not graduate from high school or gain formal qualifications. In Britain and the USA, with their more open labour markets, there are more second chances for those without qualifications (Wolf, 1992).

The close articulation between ET attainment and the labour market in the higher achieving countries is to a large extent the result of statist and corporatist influences which have historically played a greater role in continental European countries than in Britain and the USA (in Asia we may talk of statism but less of corporatism). These influences have also affected the supply of work-based training, whose relative prevalence has also contributed to differences in national levels of qualification. In general terms, the higher achieving countries, with their higher level of state or corporatist regulation, have tended to achieve higher levels of employer and individual investment in training than countries, like Britain, which are less regulated and more prone to market failure in training (MSC, 1985). The reasons for this have been exhaustively analysed in a number of studies (Carnoy, 1993; Finegold and Soskice, 1988; Marsden and Ryan, 1995; Streeck, 1987).

Put simply the argument is as follows. Society benefits economically from a well trained population, above and beyond the gains captured by individuals and their families. These social gains, or economic externalities, accrue, as Carnoy writes, 'through the lower costs of social and economic infrastructure, a better social environment (higher public consumption), a more effective political system, and even, under certain organizational arrangements, higher productivity' (Carnoy, 1993, p. 166). However, because many of the gains are 'external' to individuals, in unregulated market situations both employers and individuals are likely to under-invest in training. Employers may make rational choices not to train because they fear the loss of their investment due to the likelihood of other employers poaching the employees they have trained, or because they calculate they can make better profits in the short term by operating a low-cost, low-skill business strategy (Finegold and Soskice, 1988). Individuals may also under-invest in training for a number of reasons. They may lack sufficient information and maturity to calculate the long-term marginal benefits of training or they may lack access to funds to invest in training (Carnoy, 1993; Streeck, 1987).

The higher achieving countries in our sample have generally used some form of regulation to overcome these problems of market failure. In France, Singapore and Sweden training taxes are levied on employers to encourage them to train. This either takes the form of a payroll tax which can be recouped by employers who demonstrate sufficient effort in training (France) or a punitive tax on firms employing people on low wages (as in Singapore). The latter provides an incentive for employers to pay higher wages and thus to train to recoup their costs through higher productivity (Ashton and Green, 1996). In Germany training levies only apply in a few sectors although there are small compulsory levies payable to the chambers (*Kammern*) which play a major role in regulating the apprentice system. However, more importantly there are national sectoral agreements which keep apprentice wages low (thus reducing employer training costs) and which govern pay at different levels. The latter prevents firms paying higher wages for the same job and thus being able to poach employees trained at another employer's expense (CEDEFOP, 1987; Marsden and Ryan, 1995). Japan operates none of these forms of regulation. However, it does not need to because its system of internal labour markets and life-long employment in the larger companies ensures that firms are unlikely to lose their training investments through trained employees moving to other companies. In each of these countries the individual's incentive to train is enhanced by the tight linkage between achievement in formal education and training and access to jobs.

The USA and the UK are exceptional in our group of countries since they neither have pervasive internal labour markets nor forms of regulation to stimulate training. This has allowed the perennial problem of employers free-riding by poaching trained employees rather than training themselves. In addition to this both countries have traditions of short-termism in business decision-making. The nature of company ownership law and financial markets in both countries tends to place great pressure on firms to deliver short-term profits and dividends to shareholders or face takeover (Hutton, 1995). This has also increased the disincentives to train. The result is that in both countries company training tends to be wide-spread and systematic only in the larger companies. Individuals are like-wise less inclined to invest in training where they know that the labour markets allow employment opportunities, at least in the short term, which do not involve personal costs of training.

CONCLUSIONS

Comparisons across a small range of countries clearly cannot provide any definitive answers regarding the causes of national differences in average levels of attainments. Even with a larger sample of countries and with adequate empirical measures of system characteristics, this would be difficult because of the sheer complexity of factors which affect outcomes. However, the comparisons made above do indicate certain factors which are common to a range of more successful countries and not shared by the less successful ones and this may be suggestive of certain avenues for fruitful investigation.

What emerges from the above is that there are certain very broad cultural characteristics which seem to underlie national education achievement and that these can be seen to be manifested in a set of related institutional characteristics. Put at its most simple (and arguably simplistic) level, the high achieving countries appear to have an 'inclusive learning culture' which is characterized by the high premium which society places on learning *for all groups*. High aspirations for the majority are reinforced by the way in which the education and training systems institutionalize norms and expectations for everyone, and not just the elites, and the way in which the labour markets reward those doing well in education and training. To achieve inclusive norms and opportunities, systems generally have to employ a number of devices which act to standardize certain practices which would otherwise, in an unregulated market situation, become highly differentiated as a result of unequal market endowments. These typically involve, *inter alia*, the specification of fairly uniform institutional structures and standardized funding systems; the use of national curricula and a degree of prescription in methods of assessment and teaching; and the existence of national systems of qualification (or some alternative means for recognizing attainment and allocating rewards which is transparent and predictable). In the PCET sector it also involves means of articulating education and training with the labour market which provide incentives for individuals and employers to train.

Such structures and practices do not necessarily require all decisions to be made at the central government level and nor, indeed, do they require that it is the state alone which makes all the decisions. Germany has a federal system of education which devolves power down to the state level, and a corporatist system of training and labour market control which gives the social partners substantial control. Japan allows semi-private bodies substantial roles in its education system. However, it does seem to require a high degree of state 'regulation', where government acts in a concerted fashion at different levels to define and operationalize the system, including defining and enabling the roles of the different social partners within it. Although not invariably 'centralized', the most effective systems do indeed all appear to show signs of 'tight regulation' in the critical areas, with high levels of policy coherence, institutional systematization and close articulation between levels of the ET system and between the ET system and the labour market. Such systems are clearly not 'market' systems or even 'quasi-market' systems.

Coherent structures and 'concerted' social action in education and training have been achieved in recent years in a number of countries with quite different cultural traditions and political systems. However, their state forms, broadly speaking, seem to fall into two types. There are the 'corporatist' continental European states like France, Germany and Sweden which have combined high levels of state regulation and intervention (at different levels) with encompassing institutional structures for integrating the social partners in decision-making. And there are the more purely 'statist' countries in developed Asia which have a relatively low density of corporate organization in 'civil society' and where the only 'partner' of big government is 'big business'. Each state form can be associated with certain common institutional characteristics as regards education, although there are, of course, also myriad differences resulting from different national cultures and histories. Both types of state seem capable of generating high achieving educational systems in ways that the 'neoliberal' states, like the UK and the USA, are not.

# 7 Education, Globalization and the Nation State

Globalization has become a topic of great interest to social scientists, not only in the field of economics, but also in political and cultural studies. Despite the volume of theoretical work in this area, however, the issues it throws up have only recently begun to be taken up by educational theorists and, even here, somewhat one-sidedly within the postmodernist tradition. The final chapter in this book examines theories of globalization, their use by education theorists, and the implications for education of recent global trends in economics and politics. Specifically, it seeks to assess the arguments put forward by postmodern educational theorists, such as Usher and Edwards (1995), that globalization portends the demise of national education and the national education system as we know it.

In its full-blown form (Reich, 1991; Ohmae, 1996; Waters, 1995), globalization theory predicts the end of the national economy and the end of the nation state as the primary unit of political organization and loyalty. It also argues the emergence of a borderless world (Ohmae, 1990) where national cultures are transformed by global communications and cultural hybridization. The implications of all this for education are potentially immense. National governments would cease to control their education systems, which would gradually converge towards some regional or global norm, divested of any specific national characteristics. The historic functions of national education systems, to transmit national cultures and to reproduce national labour power, would become obsolete. The national education system, the historical product and key institutional support of the nation state, would effectively cease to have a function in the new order.

The theory of globalization is based on revolutionary notions of time and space and how these dimensions are changing in the postmodern world. Its claims, logically, can only be assessed through an approach which is both global and historical, although sadly much of the theorizing to date has been somewhat wanting on both these counts. This chapter therefore attempts a comparative and historical analysis of the changing role of the nation state and the national education system since their simultaneous inception in Europe in the late eighteenth century. It seeks to highlight how the form and functions of education systems have changed with the different phases of state formation associated with the rise and consolidation of nation states in different regions of the world. The examples are drawn from Europe, Asia and America, a geographical selection which reflects the limits of the author's knowledge and provides its own theoretical limitations. The final arguments are inevitably provisional, given the very early stage of research on many of the questions at issue here. However, its main objective is simply to offer some historical perspective on the question of national education and its future in a more global era. If it can achieve this it will have served its purpose.

## EDUCATION AND THE FORMING OF EARLY NATION STATES

National education systems were first created as part of the state-forming process which established the modern nation state. Their archetypical historical moment was the period of nation state formation in the century following the French Revolution in Europe. They belonged quintessentially to that period when the sovereign, territorially bounded state, based on absolutistic or monarchical rule, gave way to the modern nation state, legitimated by the people or the nation, and where the nation was formed by national education. However, their origins go further back than this, to the central European absolutisms which first created compulsory and state-funded schools. The history of national education is thus very much the history of the nation state in formation – not just the record of its achievements.

Absolutism in Europe marked the beginning of the modern state-forming process with its development of the principles of sovereignty, bounded territoriality and administrative integration. The Reformation had signalled the independence of monarchs from the transcendent authority of Rome and the Catholic Church and the arrival of Protestantism as the first protonationalist ideology. However, it was warfare, both internal and external, which gave the spur to absolutism. War, and the preparation for war, as Giddens has written, 'provided the most potent energizing stimulus for the concentration of resources and fiscal reorganization that characterized absolutism' (Giddens, 1985, p. 112). It was also in the development of military technology and organization that absolutism developed prototypical forms of industrial production and administration, anticipating the Taylorist routines of the mature industrial capitalism (Tilly, 1990). Out of war also came the 1648 Treaty of Westphalia, which marked the beginning of the modern European system of independent states, standing diplomacy and international recognition of the sovereign rights of states, albeit the smallest princedoms (Cooper, 1996).

Absolutism developed many of the features of the modern state. It replaced the weak and often non-contiguous frontiers of traditional dynastic kingdoms and states with more defined and significant territorial borders; it enshrined the concept of a single sovereign authority over defined territories; and it began to consolidate systems of integrative administrative control over these territories, replacing the uneven and limited central controls of the feudal state with its poor communications, overlapping jurisdictions and parcellized sovereignty (Anderson, 1974). Absolutism pioneered the first national fiscal policies through taxes raised to support military expenditures; it developed standing armies, and laid the basis of rational administration with more formalized procedures, enlarged bureaucracies and the collection of national statistics. It also, in certain areas, advanced the capitalist process by creating free waged labour and developing fledgling industries through the central initiative of mercantilist states.

In all of this education played a growing, if still limited, role, particularly in countries like Prussia and Austria where late absolutist rulers began to intervene in the process (Green, 1990). Schools not only furnished the administrators and engineers for the burgeoning bureaucracies and emergent industrial and civil projects; they also, at the elementary level, prepared reliable military recruits and loyal subjects. At their most ambitious, as in Prussia under the Elector Frederick the First and then Frederick the Great, they were conceived as a means of reconstituting labour discipline and social control among youth, peasants and industrial workers, where traditional forms of social authority had declined. As James Van Horn Melton has effectively argued, the efflorescence of state-sponsored Pietist education in Prussia in the late seventeenth and early eighteenth century can be seen as a response to the weakening of traditional forms of control and the onset of proto-industrial production in the countryside. With the breakdown of the traditional apprenticeship in the towns, and the proliferation in rural areas of absentee landlords, the masterless, landless poor and the proto-industrial labourer, traditional social bonds had been significantly weakened. The Pietist education revival was supported by the state as a useful instrument for regenerating social authority, uniquely adapted, so the mid-century cameralists argued, for creating the kind of voluntary submission and self-discipline which was needed for the new industrial workers and the peasantry as they were granted more independence (Melton, 1988).

However, it was in the post-revolutionary period of nation state formation that the project of national schooling came into its own, for it was during this period that the people – the nation – were brought decisively into the equation of the sovereign, territorial state. In the absolutist, Hobbesian meaning of the term, sovereignty had resided in the person of the absolute ruler, as supreme authority over the territory and the subjects within it. The impact of the Enlightenment and the French Revolution was to transform the notion of sovereignty so that the nation itself became constitutive of that authority. The nation became the body of citizens whose collective sovereignty constituted them as a state which was their political expression (Hobsbawm, 1990).

The post-revolutionary nation state completed what the absolutist state had started (de Tocqueville, 1955). It consolidated national boundaries, creating defined borders around preferably unbroken territory; it continued to centralize authority, breaking down the old feudal particularisms and creating a more unified and integrated administrative apparatus; and it entrenched state powers in new civil codes and administrative procedures, with bureaux and statistics to make them effective and to extend the reach of official surveillance and monitoring (Giddens, 1985). However, what was most novel about the nation state was not the state but the nation. States had to create nations and the citizens which composed them since these did not come ready-made and since states now had to prove their legitimacy with reference to the people.

The old guarantors of popular loyalty – dynastic legitimacy, divine ordination, historic right and continuity of rule – had been severely weakened by revolution. New sources of legitimacy had to be constructed; new citizens and a new nation formed. The post-revolutionary state, as Hobsbawm argues:

> had a necessary organic relationship to 'the nation', i.e. to the inhabitants of its territory considered as, in some sense, a collectivity, a 'people', ... by virtue of the political transformation which was turning it into a body of variously mobilized citizens with rights or claims. Even when the state as yet faced no serious challenge to its legitimacy or cohesion, and no really powerful forces of subversion, the mere decline of the older socio-political bonds would have made it imperative to formulate and inculcate new forms of civic loyalty (a 'civic religion' to use Rousseau's phrase), since other potential loyalties were now capable of political expression. (Hobsbawm, 1990, p. 85)

States created nations of citizens in a multitude of ways. They conscripted and disciplined them in the national defence; they registered their births, marriages and deaths; they monitored and regulated their movements across borders and their political activities; they punished and incarcerated them; they enlisted them into new state rituals, convened them under national flags, and rallied them to the mobilizing sounds of anthems and national declarations; and they recorded their collective characters in a mountain of official statistics. But most of all they educated them. As Baron Dubin wrote in 1826:

> Practically all modern nations are now awake to the fact that education is the most potent means of development of the essentials of nationality. Education is the means by which people of retarded cultures may be brought rapidly to the common level. Education is the means by which small and weak nations may become strong through their cultural strengths and achievements. Education is the only means by which the world can be 'made safe' for the national type of organization. (Fuller and Robinson, 1992, p. 52)

Through national education systems states fashioned disciplined workers and loyal recruits, created and celebrated national languages and literatures, popularized national histories and myths of origin, disseminated national laws, customs and social mores, and generally explained the ways of the state to the people and the duties of the people to the state. At times they even reflected on the rights of citizens and the responsibilities of the state to the people. National education was a massive engine of integration, assimilating the local to the national and the particular to the general. In short, it created, or tried to create, the civic identity and national consciousness which would bind each to the state and reconcile each to the other, making actual citizens out of those who were deemed such in law by virtue of their birth or voluntary adoption.

It did not, of course, do this equally or disinterestedly. Civic rights were in theory universal, but citizenship in practice involved a hierarchy where each class and each gender had differential rights and opportunities both socially and politically (Marshall and Bottomore, 1992). Schools generally reflected this differentiation, educating each according to their station, except where the need for a meritocratic safety valve allowed a talented trickle through to careers and upward mobility. However, there was still a common notion of nationhood and national culture even where each class was apportioned a differentiated slice. Education was the pre-eminent author and guardian of this national identity and culture.

In practice, not all nations developed nationhood in the same way, and nor did they develop their national education at the same time or in the same forms. Generally speaking, the states in Protestant-dominated northern Europe created national education in advance of the Catholic nations of the Mediterranean, just as did the Puritan states of the northern USA relative to the slave-owning Anglican states of the South (Cipolla, 1969). Protestantism, with its culture of the book, its work ethic and its proselytizing mission, saw more use for education than the Catholicism of saints, martyrs and images (Stone, 1969), until, that is, the Counter-Reformation spurred the Jesuits into action as the 'schoolmen of Europe'. Significant also to the timing and character of national education was the nature and trajectory of state formation in the different countries. Where the process of state formation was particularly compacted and intensive, so too was the development of national education. Typically, where countries were forced into accelerated state formation, either by revolution as in France or America, or by territorial conflict and defensive nationalism as in Prussia, or simply by the desire to reverse a history of economic underdevelopment relative to some dominant power, education was pressed into service by the state as an essential vehicle of national development. In these cases national systems were developed early. On the other hand, where nation state formation was peculiarly protracted and retarded, as in Italy, or simply lethargic due to precocious state formation in earlier times, as in Britain, then the development of national education was fitful or delayed (Green, 1990).

In either event, it would seem to have been the nature and timing of the process of state formation which largely determined the course of development of national education systems. This process, more than theories of industrialization or urban development, would seem best to explain the uneven growth of national education across Europe and North America. It explains both why national education developed so early in predominantly pre-industrial and rural societies like eighteenth-century Prussia and Austria (and even post-revolutionary France which was still a land of small peasants and artisans) and why it developed so late in Britain despite the latter's early industrialization and early urban concentration. It also explains why Italy, heir of the Roman civilization and the Renaissance, and home of the great city states and the Papacy, did not develop a national education system until after unification in the 1870s.

National education systems were not a technical necessity of early industrialization, although they played their part in later industrial development. Nor were they exclusively a response to the divisions and conflict which emerged in anomic and class-divided urban environments. First of all, and in their chief aspect, they were a tool of central states for the forming of the nations of citizens which would give them legitimacy and ensure their survival, both at home and within the European interstate system. As Ramirez and Boli (1987) have summarized the process:

European states became engaged in authorizing, funding and managing mass schooling as part of an endeavour to construct a unified national polity ... Military defeat or a failure to keep pace with the industrial development in rival countries stimulated the state to turn to education as a means of national revitalization to avoid losing power and prestige in the interstate system. (p. 3)

## EDUCATION, NATIONALISM AND EMPIRE

The ideological work performed by national education in the early phase reflected the imperatives of nation state formation in the post-revolutionary era. The liberal ideal of the nation state, at least up to the second half of the nineteenth century, was aggregative and emancipatory, involving the integration of smaller units into larger states which might be both viable and progressive. New nations, according to the theory, had to meet a size threshold ensuring their viability as independent nations. Mazzini's map of a future Europe, which was drawn up in 1857, envisaged only 12 states, each of which would be considerable powers (Hobsbawm, 1990). This principle of aggregation meant, in practice, that nations were inevitably heterogeneous, both culturally and linguistically (as, in fact, they had usually been). Thus the nationalism of pioneers like Mazzini rested not so much on linguistic or cultural heritage and homogeneity, but rather involved the fabrication of new and, in a sense, synthetic national identities.

Nationality for the liberal nationalists, as for the Jacobins of the French Revolution, meant, essentially, statehood. It was not dependent on ethnicity or language so much as conferred by virtue of citizenship gained by birth or by voluntary adoption. The nation consisted of those who wished (and were eligible) to make a commitment to citizenship. Whereas in all states there might be a dominant ethnie, to use Smith's term (Smith, 1995), in countries where this citizen notion of the nation was dominant, as in France or the new nations of America and Australia, nationalism tended to take a 'civic' rather than a cultural or ethnic form. The constitutive myths of nationality tended to be forged from inclusive political principles of common purpose and values, rather than primarily from traditional and exclusivist principles of cultural and linguistic affinity. Education systems frequently tried to promote such inclusive civic ideologies. They embraced principles of secularism or *laicité* to avoid divisive confessional conflicts, and they emphasized the modern republican heritage and its future goals, as in France and America, rather than the traditional histories and characters of peoples and their cultures and religions.

The later nineteenth century, however, saw the emergence in Europe of a new kind of nationalism which stressed language, traditional culture and, at its extreme, race. This had its ideological roots in the romantic nationalism of Fichte and Herder, both products of a Germanic culture perennially prone to stress the defining principles of language and ethnicity in reaction to the historic dispersal of German speaking peoples across a territorially unstable diaspora. The distinction between this essentially ethnocultural concept of nationhood and the state-centred political concept bequeathed by the French Revolution is well brought out by Rogers Brubaker in his classic comparative study of *Citizenship and Nationhood in France and Germany* (1992). The opening paragraphs are worth quoting in full:

> For two centuries, locked together in a fateful position at the centre of state- and nation-building Europe, France and Germany have been constructing, elaborating, and furnishing to other states distinctive, even antagonistic models of nationhood and national self-understanding. In the French tradition, the nation has been conceived in relation to the institutional and territorial frame of the state. Revolutionary and Republican definitions of statehood and citizenship – unitarist, universalist, and secular – reinforced what was already in the ancien régime an essentially political understanding of nationhood. Yet while French nationhood is constituted by political unity, it is centrally expressed in the striving for cultural unity. Political inclusion has entailed cultural assimilation, for regional and cultural minorities and immigrants alike.
>
> If the French understanding of nationhood has been state-centred and assimilationist, the German understanding has been *Volk*-centred and differentialist. Since national-feeling developed before the nation-state, the German idea of the nation was not originally political, nor was it linked to the idea of citizenship. The prepolitical German nation, this nation in search of a state, was conceived not as the bearer of universal political values, but as an organic cultural, linguistic and racial community – as irreducibly part of the *Volksgemeinschaft*. On this understanding, nationhood is an ethnocultural, not a political fact. (p. 1)

During the latter part of the century, and in parallel with the rise of Germany as a unified and powerful state under Bismarck, it was the latter ethnocultural notion of nationhood which came to dominate in European politics. In the years from 1870 to 1918, the classic Age of Empire, this was developed into an often reactionary and aggressive nationalism of race and cultural exclusivism. Eric Hobsbawm has charted this transformation and detailed the numerous explanations given for it. Among these were the development of 'race science' by post-revolutionary reactionaries like Count Gobineau and later eugenicists like Houston Stewart Chamberlaine, the effects of large-scale migrations, the insecurity of petit-bourgeois populations caught in the cross-fire between capital and labour, and the growing alienation of some social groups from the standardization of the modernizing process. On top of this, of course, were the effects of empire and imperialist ideology. From the 1870s on, with the surge in German and American manufactures and agriculture, Europe faced a sustained crisis of overproduction manifested in price depressions and declining investment opportunities. Imperial expansionism provided no way out, and with a revival of trade protection Europe became engulfed in a wave of economic nationalism and resurgent militarism. In the face of rising democracy and popular agitation towards the end of the century, governments increasingly sought to secure their legitimacy by appeals to a nationalism which was both ethnic and exclusivist in its rhetoric and symbolism.

Towards the end of the century this more strident nationalism was reflected in different ways in schools across Europe and elsewhere. In Japan a national education system had been created following the Meiji Restoration of 1868. Initially developed to play its part in the reformers' drive to defend Japan through modernization and the adoption of Western science and technology, education soon became subject to a nationalist backlash which sought to resist westernization and to reinstate traditional Japanese values. This culminated in the Imperial Rescript on Education of 1890 which fused Shinto-statism, Confucian ethics and a modern attitude towards learning into a comprehensive statement on the patriotic purposes of education and the responsibilities of the citizen in the new state. The Rescript became, until 1945, 'the basic sacred text of the new religion of patriotism' (Dore, quoted in Burke, 1985, p. 349). In Germany, after unification in 1871, education was increasingly influenced by '*Volkisch*' ideas of national character and destiny. In the 1880s and 1890s, Nietzche Lange and Hugo Goering inveighed against the intellectualism of humanist education and called for a renewed emphasis on physical education and national pride (Samuel and Thomas, 1949). This was echoed in the growing popularity of the profoundly nationalistic school history textbooks by Friedrich Neubauer. Kaiser Wilhelm's campaign to reform the secondary curriculum was also inspired by the desire to infuse a stronger national spirit into education. The traditional classics curriculum of the *Gymnasium* was subordinated in favour of a renewed emphasis on German language and history (Albisetti, 1983).

In France, after the 1870 defeat by Prussia, there was also a drive to inculcate patriotism through education, although here, through the work of Jules Ferry and others, it was typically under the banner of a popular republicanism (Gildea, 1988). As Gambetta put it in 1871: 'We must put the gymnast and the soldier alongside the primary school teacher' to train 'a new generation, strong intelligent, as enamoured of science as of the fatherland' (Gildea, 1988, p. 71). The explicit aim of Third Republic education policy was to create a new type of Frenchman (Weber, 1979) who would make the Republic strong and capable both of defending itself against Prussian aggression and of reconquering the territories of Alsace and Lorraine lost after defeat in the Franco-Prussian war. New ideals of physical prowess and athleticism were adopted, displacing the earlier intellectualist Catholic disdain for physical activity. A standard history was promoted in classrooms through the common Lavisse textbooks 'to inculcate a shared sense of France's past greatness, of its heroes and virtues, and its preeminent place amongst nations' (Smith, 1995, p. 91).

In Britain, likewise, towards the end of the century, there was an upsurge of more aggressive nationalist sentiment in education. With the rise of the liberal imperialism of Rosebery, Haldane and Asquith, and the imperially inspired national efficiency policy of the Fabians, education was ripe for an onslaught of nationalistic rhetoric. The technical education movement was galvanized by, among other things, a powerful nationalistic response to the rise of German manufactures and trade, although Britain soon came to concentrate more on turning out clerks to staff the burgeoning offices of finance and colonial administration rather than engineers and scientists to promote manufacture. The new drive towards physical and paramilitary training in schools, and in the expanding Boy Scout Movement supported by the Webbs and others, derived from a fear of decline in the stock of the Imperial race, fuelled by reports of the poor physical condition of the recruits during the Boer War. In fact the whole Fabian argument about 'social efficiency', from which issued the policies for scholarship ladders into secondary education, had strong imperialist overtones. As Sidney Webb once said 'it is in the classroom ... that the battles of the Empire for commercial prosperity are being lost' (Simon, 1965, p. 174). All these came together most potently in the public schools which were going through a period of narcissistic self-adulation at the turn of the century. In them physical prowess, leadership, conformism and patriotic spirit found their apotheosis. In these schools, as in others, the curriculum increasingly encoded not only the virtues of patriotism, leadership and military prowess, but also the whole stock of colonial racial imagery and myth (Mangan, 1993).

The empire nationalism of the *fin de siècle* was of course only a prelude to worse things to come. Imperial rivalries brought on the First World War, whose settlement only intensified the rebarbative nationalisms which would lead to a further world war within two decades. The period from 1918–45 has rightly been regarded as the apogee of nationalism in its most reactionary racial and ethnocentric forms (Hobsbawm, 1990). The First World War ended with the break-up of the old empires, and the adoption by the West, as an antidote to Bolshevism, of the Wilsonian nationality principal, which endorsed the formation of small states and the concept of cultural nationalism. Versailles represented, perhaps, the fullest attempt ever made to redraw the map along ethnic/linguistic lines (Hobsbawm, 1990). But it did not work. Most of the new states which were built on the ruins of the old empires, like Czechoslovakia, Poland, Romania, Turkey and Yugoslavia, were as multinational as the old 'prisons of nationalities' they replaced (Hobsbawm, 1990, p. 133). Their irredenta, or national minorities, were often as oppressed in their new small states as they had been in the old empires. The rhetoric of cultural nationalism, which the Treaty encouraged, spread both among national minorities and majorities. Catalan nationalism in Spain grew under the Franco dictatorship as did Flemish nationalism, in this case with encouragement from Germany. Turkish nationalism led to the extirpation of Armenians in 1915 and this was followed, after the 1922 Greek-Turkish war, by the expulsion of some 1.5 million Greeks from Asia Minor, where they had lived since the days of Homer. At its most extreme, the principle of ethnic nationalism, with its impossible ideal of ethnically homogeneous states, led to Nazi plans to repatriate German irredenta and expel the Jews – and thence to the Holocaust.

Racism and ethnic nationalism found its way into the heart of education in a number of states during this period. Hitler used German schools to promote his Aryan supremacist doctrine and to fuel anti-Semitism. Japanese schools also became breeding grounds for an aggressive and militaristic nationalism. Army officers were stationed in schools where they trained teachers in military discipline and the use of weapons, students were exhorted to offer themselves courageously to the state, and textbooks, written and published by the Ministry, became increasingly nationalistic (Schoppa, 1991). In many countries, of course, neither governments nor schools succumbed to such virulent nationalisms, and indeed the popular fronts, as in France and Britain, promoted the idea of a civic nationalism working in international solidarity in opposition to Fascism. However, in the climate of the interwar years, dominated for the most part by economic recession and reactionary nationalism, it is hard to see that education prospered anywhere.

## EDUCATION AND POSTWAR NATIONALISM

The postwar world brought a new international order. While the Cold War was soon to divide the world into conflicting power blocs, internationalism, initially at least, was the official or ideal currency of inter-state relations. Reactionary ethnic nationalism was in retreat, and the association of nationalism with the Left, typical of the pre-1848 period, was at least partially restored (Hobsbawm, 1990). Following the atrocities of the war, the capitalist powers of the West, just like Japan and the communist powers to the East, wished to dissociate themselves radically from the nationalism of Hitler, Mussolini and wartime Japan. The growth of regional defence (NATO and the Warsaw Pact) and regional and world commercial and financial organizations (the World Bank and IMF) encouraged supranational affiliation and interdependence, weakening the hold of narrow nationalist ideas. In the Third World anti-colonial liberation movements, which could hardly use the rhetoric of Hitler, and which in any case often needed both to unite their populations and to court Soviet support, adopted the language of anti-imperialism rather than the discourse of ethnic nationalism. The new post-colonial states, like the older national states, were demonstrably multi-ethnic in character. Indeed, among the burgeoning number of recognized states in the postwar world few – less than 10 per cent according to Smith (1995) – could claim to be nation states in the 'pure', ethnically homogeneous, meaning of the word. The nation state had become the model for independent statehood worldwide and this, in practice, increasingly meant multinational statehood. The national identity promoted in these states tended, officially at least, to stress the civic rather than the ethnic notion of nationhood.

Education, in the postwar era, continued to be associated with nation-building and state formation. Although its typical official modality stressed civic integration and cultural pluralism, rather than the cultural nationalism of the previous period, the national education system was no less associated with the process of national development than before; in fact this association had if anything been strengthened by its prevalent adoption in newly independent states. However, arguably, there were important changes underway in the relations between education and state formation in the western world, as well as growing divergences between the older and newer states in the meaning they assigned to national education.

Among the older states during the postwar period there have been some clear examples of education being used as an explicit agent of state formation. Most obviously, in those countries faced with the task of political and economic reconstruction like Japan, Germany and France, education was often at the forefront of policies for national development. Germany elected to retain its traditionally segmented structure of secondary school after the war, against American advice to adopt a new high school model, but it made dramatic improvements in its system of apprentice training which soon became the envy of Europe, accredited with playing a major role in Germany's miraculous economic reconstruction. Japan, initially at least, followed the advice of the American occupying powers and created a modern, meritocratic and remarkably egalitarian (Cummings, 1980) system, based on the American 6-3-3 structure of primary, middle and high schools. These were comprehensive and mixed-ability up at least to the end of middle school. The government also enacted a new 'fundamental law of education' which put individual development and democratic culture at the heart of its educational project. Like both of these countries, at least from the late 1950s, France engaged in a massive modernization and expansion of its education system, creating the comprehensive lower secondary college in 1963, and then the mass *lycée* and higher education system from the 1970 onwards. As in Japan, and to some extent Germany, French educational development was at the heart of a long-term economic planning process.

Two changes, however, can be discerned in western states in the relation between education and state formation. Firstly, it was increasingly the case that where education was identified with the national interest, as it has been repeatedly in the rhetoric of all western governments in the 1980s and 1990s, this was in terms of the national economy and economic competitiveness, and not in terms of citizenship and national cohesion. Secondly, among some of the older nation states, there was a sense in which education was no longer so explicitly part of the cultural process of nation-building. To be sure, there were national crises which, as with the First and Second World Wars, brought with them waves of educational reform across a number of countries. Most obviously, the Sputnik scare and the imagined threat of Soviet technology in the late 1950s spurred the US into a massive expansion of its community colleges and universities, just as the fears of Japanese manufacturing supremacy and trade surpluses inspired extensive reforms in the 1980s. The 1984 National Commission on Excellence in Education report, *A Nation at Risk*, was a classic of crisis-inspired educational polemic with its claims that the US, with its relatively poor standards, was committing an act of 'unthinking, unilateral educational disarmament' (pp. 5–6). However, there was a sense, in some countries, in which education was suffering from a crisis of identity and purpose, unable to meet all the conflicting demands made on it by sundry lobbies and interests, and so far committed to the philosophy of individual advancement in a pluralist society that it no longer quite knew what its collective or public purpose was.

As western countries, somewhat reluctantly, began to acknowledge the growing diversity and cultural pluralism of their populations, they found themselves uncertain of what their nationality meant and what kind of citizens should be produced by their schools. In England education policy oscillated between periods of advancing pluralism and multiculturalism, followed by right-wing 'little England' reaction and cultural 'restoration'. In some countries like France, with its republican and integrationalist notions of civic nationality, a concept of education as citizen-formation endured, although this was increasingly under stress with the proliferation of youth unemployment and social exclusion, and the demands of minority groups. Asian children wanting to wear traditional headscarves in school ignited a national controversy, challenging the very principle of *laicité* on which republic education was anchored. In the USA, Germany, Canada and the Netherlands, each with strong minority communities, governments found themselves equally confused about what kinds of citizens their schools were meant to produce.

In the developing world, however, there has been an ever more explicit link between education and state formation, with education unequivocally linked with both citizen-formation and national economic development. Developing states have directed an increasing proportion of their revenues to public education (Inkeles and Sirowy, 1983) and have been expanding their administrative structures to control it. Empirical studies comparing dates of independence and dates of compulsory education laws for a range of countries show that new states are setting up national education systems more rapidly than before (Ramirez and Boli, 1987). As Bruce Fuller and Richard Robinson have written:

> Third world states ... hold the school institution as sacred; they regard it as being the organizational mechanism for delivering mass opportunity, economic growth, and national integration. The state education system is the cornerstone of the state's drive to construct and reinforce modern institutions. Third world governments, nudged by their international bankers and benefactors, must build more classrooms, hire more teachers, enrol more children. The heretical nation-state that chooses not to expand mass schooling quickly becomes the object of criticism within the international press and diplomatic circles. The state allegedly plays a pivotal role in expanding mass education and ensuring that the school

yields miraculous economic and social benefits. (Fuller and Robinson, 1992, pp. 3–4)

New states have not been invariably successful in using education as an instrument of nation-building. What is striking, however, is the frequent coincidence of successful nation-building and planned educational development. As in nineteenth-century Europe, rapid educational growth today is often associated with countries undergoing peculiarly intensive periods of state formation. In many cases this has been induced by crises of national identity born of war, national division and social transformation. It has also been linked with concerted national drives for economic development, usually aimed at catching up with some more advanced regional power, which acts as a role model. The East Asian 'tiger' states have provided the most dramatic example of this in the recent period. Each has experienced crises of national identity, born of regional conflicts or internal strife (Castells, 1992): South Korea forced to reconstruct after civil war and in the face of continuing hostility from its communist northern neighbour; Taiwan, like Korea, at the heart of regional and Cold War tensions with its sovereignty still disputed by mainland China; and Singapore, cast adrift by the British and Malaysia, and thereafter struggling to create a state which no one had thought viable. Each has sought rapid economic expansion, both for its own sake and to catch up with the regional champion and former occupying power, Japan. In all of these countries nation-building has been seen as a question of national survival, with education at its heart.

Of all these countries Singapore represents the most classic case of nation-building as the politics of survival. While in many ways atypical – being a small and historically internationalized city state – it also provides a striking example of education as the politics of nation-building in its civic, republican form. As such it can serve here as a useful case study of one particular route for national education in the modern global world.


EDUCATION AND STATE FORMATION IN SINGAPORE

Singapore was a state born, unwillingly and despite itself, in crisis and trauma, an independent city state with a national infrastructure, but a state without a nation and without a national identity. Given limited self-government by the British in 1959, Singapore was led by a party (the People's Action Party: PAP) whose longstanding objective was to subsume it into a larger federal union. In 1963 it was duly incorporated into the Malaysian Federation only to be expelled two years later amidst political acrimony and racial strife. It was now granted full independence and its government found itself leading a country of multiple nationalities, languages and creeds and which it had previously thought non-viable as an independent state. In was in these unpropitious circumstances that the Singapore state set about constructing itself a nation. Education was central to this task.

The national identity to be forged had necessarily to be multicultural and multilingual, just as it had to contain a strong civic ideology to bind it together. There was, as Michael Hill and Lian Kwen Fee (1995) have argued, probably little choice in this. Singapore had a Chinese majority with, among its working class at least, strong national sentiments and close connections with mainland China. It was also a country with a significant Malay minority and one surrounded by Malaysians with whom it wished to retain good relations. Its majority spoke Chinese, including the dominant Chinese business community, but its political and professional elites, both Chinese and Malay, spoke English, which was also the language of international business. Alongside these were the Tamil, English and ethnically mixed populations, adding to the plethora of religions, languages and loyalties (Quah, 1984).[1] It was the complex nature of supra-national political loyalties, as well as the diversity of cultures, which made anything but a concertedly non-ethnic concept of nationhood untenable. To have privileged any one community would have immediately risked relations with two important neighbours: one, mainland China, which some had feared would launch a communist takeover of Singapore and which was soon to become an important trading partner, and the other, Malaysia, which was considered by many of Singapore's leaders as well as its Malay population to be Singapore's natural ally and potential confederate nation (Hill and Lian Kwen Fee, 1995). Under these circumstances, a traditionalist, ethnic-revivalist nationalism was not an option and never had been.

From its inception, in fact, the dominant regional independence movements had adopted resolutely cosmopolitan politics. The Singapore-based Malayan Democratic Union was led by middle-class, English-language-educated non-Malays who had been trained in British universities and exposed to left-wing politics. They were anti-colonial and committed to a united, independent Malaya, including Singapore, where nationality would be bestowed upon those who wanted it and who were prepared to renounce other citizenships. Their People's Constitution of 1947, which attempted to construct a Malayan civic identity as multiracial and with equality for all groups, set them clearly in opposition to other groups wanting to promote *bangsa Melayu* (exclusivist and primordial Malay culture and values) (Hill and Lian Kwen Fee, 1995, p. 46). Likewise, the Malayan Forum, the London-based group formed in 1949 which included future Singapore leaders like Lee Kuan Yew and Goh Keng Swee, had learned from the struggles over Malaysian Union the importance of non-racial politics, and sought a broad-based coalition for a socialist Malaya, including Singapore. Lee's subsequent People's Action Party, formed in 1954 and taking power in 1959, was also a broad coalition seeking to take Singapore into a multiracial Malaysian Federation (Hill and Lian Kwen Fee, 1995, p. 160). In pursuit of this, and despite their desire to maintain Chinese and Communist Party support, they sought to allay Federation Malay fears about the inevitable influx of Chinese on incorporation by emphasizing Malay culture and declaring Malay as the national language. However, once accepted into the Federation the leadership remained steadfast on their multicultural concept of Malaysian nationality and it was this that finally led to their expulsion. This experience, and the race riots between Singapore Chinese and Malays in 1964, left a deep impression on Lee, confirming his belief in the necessity of a non-ethnic policy which would now be applied in the building of an independent Singapore.

In power, the PAP were faced with the twin tasks of galvanizing the ailing and limited entrepôt economy and of creating a cohesive citizenry ready to work together towards building the new multiracial state. In pursuit of the first, the government abandoned the rhetoric of socialism (although not the commitment to central planning) and adopted a pragmatic policy of courting foreign multinational companies and overseas investors to create jobs and stimulate manufacturing industries (Soon Teck Wong, 1992). In pursuit of the second, it adopted a dirigiste and interventionist social policy aimed at winning consent to its programme and to its vision of a cohesive, multicultural nation under a strong central state (Gopinathan, 1994). State power and effectiveness were pursued through judicious cooption of key professional and ethnic constituencies and with the help of a loyal and efficient civil service. Social integration was promoted by a variety of means, including a non-segregationist housing policy, measures to create larger, multiracial electoral constituencies, and numerous public campaigns to promote good citizens and neighbours, stable families with growing birthrates and, most recently, the revival of community associations and civil society generally. In the first instance the emphasis was strongly on the non-ethnic civic conception of citizenship, with cultural issues depoliticized and consigned to the realm of the family and the private (Hill and Lian Kwen Fee, 1995). However, in the second phase, from the late 1970s, there has been an attempt to revive traditional values and cultures as an antidote to fears of deculturation and westernization. Throughout national identity has remained consistent with the civic republican tradition, stressing common political values and the public virtues of a common citizenship. But, of late, this has begun to incorporate more publicly what are taken to be the positive features of the different ethnic cultures and traditions.

In all this education has played a key part, not only instrumental in Singapore's miraculous economic development, but equally as a vehicle for promoting a cohesive civic identity, based on the ideological tripod of multiculturalism, multilingualism and meritocracy. The first two of these had been at the centre of debates about education since the colonial period.

Prior to the Second World War education had been linguistically divided, with English language education in the Christian Mission schools, Chinese language education in community-based and private schools, Tamil education in estate-run schools and Malay education in government-supported schools. The political elite spoke English, the Chinese business elite Chinese, and there were sharp divisions between the Anglophone Chinese elite and working-class Chinese speakers (Hill and Lian Kwen Fee, 1995). Since early in the century Sun Yat-sen's nationalist politics had a strong appeal to the Straits Chinese and nationalist sentiment was increasingly taken up in the Chinese schools. By the 1950s the Chinese schools were more organized and financially independent than the other vernacular schools, and there was a growing radicalization of students within them. Chinese graduates were frustrated by the absence of career opportunities open to them given that Chinese was not the official public language and Chinese students became increasingly influenced by the Communist Party of Malaya, which had retained strong support since its resistance to Japanese occupation during the war. Increasingly alarmed by this, the colonial authorities had initially sought to encourage English-language education in schools as a multiracial solvent and to cultivate a loyal English-educated elite.[2] However, resources were inadequate to achieve this effectively. In 1955, the All Party Committee on Education proposed a new multicultural policy involving bilingual education in primary and secondary schools, equal treatment for Malay, Chinese, English and Tamil, as well as a new common curriculum emphasizing civics and encouragement for more ethnic integration in schools (Hill and Lian Kwen Fee, 1995). This was supported by the MDU, and reflected in the policies of the PAP in power after 1959.

Despite its initial, tactical support for the Malay language when first in office, the PAP began to develop bilingual, integrated schools throughout the 1960s with English/Chinese and English/Malay as the most common combinations. Malay schools were integrated most rapidly but by 1973, 25 per cent of all schools had been integrated (Hill and Lian Kwen Fee, 1995, p. 77). English language education gained rapidly in popularity as a passport to opportunities. The net result of these changes was that Malay, Chinese and Tamil vernacular education declined sharply; by 1978 English-medium students outnumbered Chinese-medium students by 9 to 1 (Hill and Lian Kwen Fee, 1995, p. 81). In terms of everyday usage, English and Mandarin gained ground while Malay and Tamil lost out.

In 1979 the policy was to change again. The Goh report of that year found that the bilingual policy was failing since most students were taught in two languages, English and Mandarin, neither of which was spoken at home by 85 per cent of them. This was held responsible for the high rate of attrition in the primary school leaving exam, where 60 per cent failed in one or both of these languages and where only 71 per cent did well enough to continue in secondary education (Hill and Lian Kwen Fee, 1995, p. 85). Wishing not to abandon bilingualism, but also recognizing the difficulties many students experienced, Goh recommended the creation of three different routes for students: English and a mother tongue as first languages for the most able; English and mother tongue as a second language for the average students; and English and mother tongue as a spoken second language only for those with most language difficulties. Although it faced some opposition, not least from parents of children allocated to the third stream, this policy was subsequently adopted and appears to have worked, or at least not to have hindered increasing retention and success in the Singapore education system (Soon Teck Wong, 1992).

By 1994, 57 per cent of Singapore students were achieving five or more GCE O levels and over 50 per cent were achieving two A levels or an equivalent or higher vocational qualification, a rate well in excess of that achieved, for instance, in the UK (Green and Steedman, 1996). The policy also retains the commitment to multilingualism in the Singapore state, although both it and the government's simultaneous 'Speak Mandarin' campaign are in effect promoting a *de facto* bilingualism, which may in the long run prove less unifying than a wholesale shift towards English monolingualism (Hill and Lian Kwen Fee, 1995). That the latter is resisted is due to the Singapore government's continuing belief in the importance of retaining its indigenous cultures, which brings us on to the question of civic education, the other primary theme in educational debates.

Civic identity in Singapore has tended to stress the common social and political values of meritocracy and equal opportunities, material advance and welfare, and active and responsible citizenship. This has generally involved an emphasis on what Breton (1984) has called the civic-instrumental, rather than the cultural-symbolic dimensions of nation-building. However, since the 1970s, with the emerging social problems of drug abuse, crime, divorce and abortion, there has been a strong government-led movement to stem deculturization and avert the dangers of western individualism by reinvigorating community cultures and associations and rekindling adherence to 'Asian' values, or at least those which are seen as positive and amenable to development within modern Singapore. Education has been seen as important in this. As Goh wrote in his 1979 report: 'One way of overcoming the dangers of deculturization is to teach children the historical origins of their culture' (Hill and Lian Kwen Fee, 1995, p. 196). The policy on civic and cultural education has, in fact, been through several phases reflecting these changing priorities.

Civic education was introduced into the school curriculum in 1974 in the form of a subject called 'Education for Living'. This combined Civics, History and Geography and was taught in the mother tongue, with teachers able to make use of the history textbooks which had been made available in four languages by the Ministry. By 1979, Lee Kuan Yew and others were pressing for a further strengthening of the moral aspect of education. The aims of this can be seen quite clearly from Lee's public letter to Goh regretting the lack of emphasis on moral education in his 1979 report. It is worth quoting at length. A number of issues were raised by the report; he wrote:

> The first subject concerns good citizenship and nationhood. What kind of a man or woman does a child grow up to be after 10 or 12 years of schooling? Is he a worthy citizen, guided by decent moral principles? Have his teachers and principals set him good examples? ... Is he loyal and patriotic? Is he, when the need arises, a good soldier, ready to defend his country, and so protect his wife and children and his fellow citizens? Is he filial, respectful to elders, law-abiding, humane and responsible? Does he take care of his wife and children, and his parents? Is he a good neighbour and a trustworthy friend? Is he tolerant of Singapore's different races and religions? Is he clean, neat, punctual, and well mannered? (Hill and Lian Kwen Fee, 1995, pp. 89–90)

Soon after this letter a report on moral education – the Ong report – was issued, calling for a renewed stress on Asian values. This led in 1981 to the piloting of a moral education course, called 'Being and Becoming', for children up to 15 years old. The course emphasized loyalty to the country and social responsibility and was designed to curb the perceived growth of western individualist values which it was believed would promote such social ills as a decline in the work ethic, parents being sent off to old people's homes and corruption among bankers (Hill and Lian Kwen Fee, 1995). Religious education was also introduced for older children, and then, in 1984, as a compulsory subject for third and fourth year secondary students. This was broadly based, including Bible knowledge, Bhuddist Studies, Hindu Studies, Islamic Religious Knowledge and, at Lee's behest, Confucian Ethics. The programme was not, however, a success. Bhuddist Studies proved to be much more popular than Confucian Ethics, and, amidst alarm over a growing militancy among Islamic and Catholic groups, the government became concerned that the programme was contributing towards social divisions. The Religious Harmony Act of 1990 was introduced to establish clear parameters regarding religious activities, and a new initiative was undertaken to establish a set of shared Singapore values which would be secular and civic in orientation, while still drawing on traditional cultures.

The Shared Values White Paper of 1991 emphasized five key themes: (a) nation before community and society before self; (b) family as the basis of civil society; (c) regard and community support for the individual; (d) consensus instead of contention; and (e) racial and religious harmony. The initiative has been seen by a number of commentators (Rodan, 1993; Clammer, 1993) as an attempt to head off the growing pluralism and westernization of Singapore society, and to buttress government legitimacy, through a renewed emphasis on national unity and distinctiveness. Aware of the potential divisiveness of emphasizing cultural particularities and individual religions, the government sought to articulate a set of common values which draw discretely on the different religious traditions, but present them in a typically instrumental and pragmatic fashion (Hill and Lian Kwen Fee, 1995, p. 218). In this sense it is an attempt to reconcile a contradiction of globalism articulated in 1989 by government minister George Yeo: 'We must balance this contradiction between being cosmopolitan and being nationalistic. We cannot be a trading nation, if we are not cosmopolitan. We cannot be nation, if we are not nationalistic. We must be both at the same time' (Hill and Lian Kwen Fee, 1995, p. 215).

Singapore is a strong state and a highly cohesive society (Gopinathan, 1994). It has achieved this, despite its unpromising beginnings, through an intensive effort of nation-building led by a determined government and competent civil service which has used all the powers of coherent long-term planning to achieve its goals. Despite an overbearing and often authoritarian level of government intervention in everyday life, including unpopular limitations on civil association and dubious measures to encourage fertility among professional women, the government has apparently retained high levels of support, being overwhelmingly re-elected in each election since 1959. Poor access to the media for opposition groups may have contributed to this but much of it has been due to the government's extraordinary economic achievements which have led to the highest standard of living in Asia after Japan (Ashton and Sung, 1994). Growth in GDP has averaged at around 9 per cent per annum over the past 30 years and by 1993 Singapore led the world in its savings rate (47 per cent of GDP) and its level of official foreign reserves per capita (Gopinathan, 1994). The effects of this economic development have been felt by all layers in Singapore society and this has vastly augmented the legitimacy of the government.

Education and training have played an important role in this economic development (Soon Teck Wong, 1992), both in raising the levels of general education among new generations of young people, and in providing specific skills required by the economy at different phases of its development (Green and Steedman, 1996; Soon Teck Wong, 1992). Particularly notable have been the repeated and successful initiatives by government (in conjunction with the multinational firms) in retraining the adult workforce, many of whom had previously only a basic primary education (Ashton and Sung, 1994), and the formidable success of the four polytechnics. These now qualify in excess of 20 per cent of the population at subdegree levels in technical subjects, for the majority within three years of completing compulsory education (Green and Steedman, 1996).[3] However, the contribution of education has gone far beyond this. It has also been a primary force for generating modern, meritocratic values among Singaporean youth and for promoting a cohesive society with a strong civic identity (Hill and Lian Kwen Fee, 1995). It provides an example, not easily explained by globalization theory, of the survival of a manifestly *national* education system, even in a very cosmopolitan country fully wired up to the global market.


EDUCATION AND GLOBALIZATION

Singapore, like the other advanced East Asian countries, still seems a resolutely 'national' society, not only in its strong sense of national identity but also in the distinctiveness of institutional structures and cultures. However, according to many of today's economists and social scientists, the Asian 'tigers' are at the centre of a process of global transformation which will render national economies and national cultures marginal and obsolescent. Theorization on the question of globalization has proliferated in recent years, not only in the field of economics (Dunning, 1993;

Ohmae, 1990, 1996; Reich, 1991; Waters, 1995) but also in the realms of political science and cultural studies (Featherstone, Lash and Robertson, 1995; Hall, Held and McGrew, 1992; McGrew and Lewis, 1992). The arguments put forward are wide-ranging in their implications for all areas of economic, political and social life and fundamentally challenge our received notions of the nature and role of the nation state. By extension they also have major implications for the forms and function of the state education.

One of the leading proponents of the theory of economic globalization is Robert Reich. His celebrated book, *The Work of Nations*, while based exclusively on US evidence, has become a standard point of reference for debates in the field. His basic argument is compellingly simple. With the advance of modern technologies, the transportation of materials and goods has become quicker and cheaper, and the transfer of information instant-aneous. A global market has now developed in goods, services, capital and ideas which makes the whole concept of the national economy redun-dant. Multinational corporations (MNCs) are becoming transnational cor-porations (TNCs); they can relocate their operations without respect to national boundaries as economic advantage dictates, typically having mul-tiple national bases and international workforces. Their investors are drawn from across the world, their goods and services are sold in many national markets and their products are composed of elements conceived, designed and produced in a multiplicity of international locations. Financial capital is equally fluid and mobile. International flows of capital are faster and less regulated than ever before with an increasing preva-lence of Foreign Direct Investment (FDI) and the volatile and speculative trade in bonds and futures. So powerful are these international market forces that national governments can no longer control their national economies, although they still engage in what Reich considers to be futile attempts at protection and regulation.

The key to the globalization process, according to Reich, is the transna-tional corporation. The most profitable companies, he claims, are trans-forming themselves into 'global enterprise webs' constituted by numerous international subsidiaries, spin-offs, franchises and affiliates. They owe no particular allegiance to any one country, although they may maintain a national headquarters; their shareholders are based around the world and their employees are paid and work in similarly disparate locations. According to Reich, in 1990, 40 per cent of IBM's employees were foreign, while Whirlpool, another US-registered company, employed 43 500 people in 45 countries. Bell South, the largest provider of basic telephone services in the US, had operations in more than 20 countries, developing telephone networks in Argentina and France, cable systems in France, management software in India, voice and data system designs in China and digital network technical assistance in Guatemala (Reich, 1991, p. 121). Even service sector enterprises have gone increasingly global. The advertising conglomerate, WPP Group, has 21 500 employees in 50 countries, Morgan Stanley 6000 in 18 countries. Altogether, in 1990, more than 20 per cent of the output of American-owned firms was produced by foreign workers outside the US, and the percentage was rising fast (Reich, 1991, p. 121).

Not only are firms operating in numerous national locations, argues Reich, but each of their products and services are increasingly cosmopolitan in origin:

> Precision ice-hockey equipment is designed in Sweden, financed in Canada, and assembled in Cleveland and Denmark for distribution in North America and Europe, out of alloys whose molecular structure was researched and patented in Delaware and fabricated in Japan....A sports car is financed in Japan, designed in Italy, and assembled in Indiana, Mexico and France, using advanced electronic components invented in New Jersey and fabricated in Japan. (Reich, 1991, p. 112)

So nationally hybrid are the inputs into the products of the transnational enterprise that it is increasingly difficult to determine how much of what was made where and which country gets the profits. When a Pontiac Le Mans is sold, for example, of the $10 000 paid to General Motors, about $3000 goes to South Korea for routine labour and assembly, $1750 to Japan for advanced components, $4750 to West Germany for styling and design engineering, $400 to Taiwan, Singapore and Japan for small components, $250 to Britain for advertising and marketing services, and about $250 to Ireland and Barbados for data processing. Only 40 per cent of the total price remains in the USA (Reich, 1991, p. 113). Such is the international mix in inputs to products that, ironically, if you want to invest in US products you are better off buying a Honda than a Pontiac Le Mans.

Reich's dramatic conclusion is that this global transformation will 'rearrange the politics and economies of the coming century':

> There will be no more national products and technologies, no national corporations, no national industries. There will no longer be national economies at least as we have come to understand that term. All that will remain rooted within national borders are the people who comprise

the nation. Each nation's primary assets will be its citizens' skills and insights. (Reich, 1991, p. 1)

Where regional economies come to be dominated by transnational corporations which have no national allegiance and which are beyond national government control, there can be no such thing as a national economy. The nation's wealth and the standard of living of its citizens no longer depends on the profitability of its nationally registered corporations, nor even on the success of its investors, since all this wealth is internationally mobile. What will count is how many of the nation's citizens can sell high-value skills and insights in the world market. The only assets which remain nationally rooted are human skills and the most valuable of these in the advanced global economy are the conceptual skills of problem-identifying, problem-solving and problem-brokering – the skills of those whom Reich calls the 'symbolic analysts'. It is these symbolic analysts who are the main financial beneficiaries of global enterprise. The nation's task is to maximize the number of its citizens who can sell these services on the global market and reap the reward for them.

Economists like Robert Reich have provided some of the most powerful arguments and evidence in favour of a theory of global transformation. However, the globalization debate does not stop with them. Political scientists and cultural theorists have also argued their own versions of the globalization thesis. In political theory the debate has been largely about questions of national sovereignty and autonomy and about how both have been eroded in the new global order. For David Held (1989) it is not only that the internationalization of production is 'unquestionably eroding the capacity of the state to control its own economic future' (p. 230); it is also that there is strong evidence that 'transnational relations have eroded the powers of the modern sovereign state' (p. 237). There are normally held to be three dimensions to this, in addition to the issue of economic sovereignty. Firstly, as Robert Cooper (1996) and others have argued, the nation state no longer exercises autonomous control over defence and international relations. Nuclear weapons have reduced the scope for military action; many countries are increasingly tied into regional and international defence and security agreements which include supra-national rights of inspection and notification of military activity; and some are party to regional defence organizations, like NATO with its integrated supra-national command structure. International relations between the advanced states are said to have 'cooled out': countries no longer aspire to settle their political differences through war, and international diplomacy is increasingly a matter of negotiation and accommodation. Inasmuch as military conflict has historically been a major stimulant of national consciousness and identity, this new 'peace' can been seen as removing a major source of national cohesion and state legitimacy.

Secondly, so it is argued (Hobsbawm, 1994; Smith, 1995), national governments are losing control and authority internally. They are unable to meet the mounting demands for quality welfare services because of social, demographic and technological change and the escalating costs arising out of these; and they have difficulty sustaining the credibility of their democratic institutions in the face of increasing electoral cynicism and volatility. Most damagingly, faced with the privatization of the means of war and violence, the state cannot even maintain its most basic internal functions of security to people and property. As Hobsbawm has written, the state is 'losing its monopoly and its historic privileges within its borders, as witness the rise of private security services or protection and the rise of private courier services to compete with the post, hitherto virtually everywhere managed by a state ministry' (Hobsbawm, 1994, p. 576).

Lastly, and perhaps most vociferously, it is argued that national governments are ceding sovereignty and autonomy to a new range of supranational organizations, both regional (EU, EFTA, NAFTA, ASEAN) and global (OECD, UN, IMF, World Bank, WTO). These have undoubtedly increased in number. As David Held has noted, whereas in 1909 there were some 37 international organizations and 176 non-governmental international organizations, these had increased by 1984 to 365 and 4615 respectively (Held, 1989, p. 232). Whether or not it is argued that national governments have exercised their national sovereignty by willingly ceding control to these bodies, or have had it wrested from them, it remains the case that national autonomy, if not sovereignty, is inevitably curtailed. To many commentators international politics have become so complex, with so many overlapping agreements and organizations and so much diffusion of power, that no state can really be said to be in control of anything. The danger, as Cooper says, is that 'we may all drown in complexity' (Cooper, 1996, p. 47).

In the domain of culture, globalization theory has been no less prolific, although it has been somewhat less consistent in its conclusions. Cultural theorists have generally agreed with the political globalists that the 'national', in its old form at least, is finished; what they cannot decide is exactly what globalization is putting in its place. 'The most common interpretations of globalization,' writes Pieterse (1995), 'are the ideas that the world is becoming more uniform and standardized, through technological, commercial and cultural synchronization emanating from the West, and that globalization is tied up with modernity' (p. 45). However, there are many who would not agree with this. Pieterse himself argues that global communications can be a force for both fragmentation and unification, engendering awareness of political difference as much as awareness of common identity and reinforcing both supra-national and subnational regional identities. He sees globalization 'as a process of hybridization which gives rise to a global mélange' – Thai boxing by Moroccan girls in Amsterdam; Asian rap in London, Irish bagels and Chinese tacos. For Roland Robertson, on the other hand, the globalization of communications and cultures has meant a process of 'glocalization'. 'Globalization', he writes, 'has involved the simultaneity and the interpenetration of what are conventionally called the global and the local, or – in a more abstract vein – the universal and the particular' (Robertson, 1995, p. 30). For both Pieterse and Robertson cultural globalization means both homogenization *and* heterogenization, both the universalism of the 'MacWorld' and the particularism of the 'Jihad world'. The net effect for both is, in fact, increasing cultural variety. Communications technology makes the world's cultural particularisms and localisms globally present as it does the dominant regional cultures of the West. However, in the reception these are reproduced and mutated into an infinity of cultural hybrids.

If even half of the above is true then the implications are enormous, not only in the realms of the economy but also in politics and culture. For education the implications would be radical indeed, since the very foundations for national education would have ceased to exist. Governments would no longer control their education systems, and the latter might lose their public and collective character altogether; schools would be enjoined to prepare young people for work not only in the national labour market but also in a global market, where skills demands are constantly changing; there would be increased international control over education forcing convergence and the disappearance of national education traditions; and there would be little scope left for education to reproduce 'national cultures' since these would have ceased to be recognizable. However, before examining these inferences, it is important to assess some of the evidence more carefully, since much of what is claimed by the globalists is still controversial and speculative.

The claims of globalization theory are hard to assess critically since, as with much of the post-Fordist analysis, they rest on extrapolations from trends that are observable, but local and uneven. Globalization theory hinges on the notion that current developments represent not merely an extension of long-established trends, but an acceleration of such an order that it becomes a qualitative shift. This is a relative judgement which requires a historical perspective. The problem with much of the writing by globalists is that there is insufficient historical depth and global reach, both in the evidence and arguments, to allow us to assess their claims properly. There are graphic and dramatic local illustrations but these are often subject to unwarranted generalization; recent trends are correctly identified, but tendencies are derived without consideration of likely counter-changes; the dialectic of history is missing. Furthermore, globalization theory often lacks historical depth; it is also unaware of its own past. As Hirst and Thompson have pointed out (1996), the origins of globalization theory lie in notions of the world-conquering capitalist market espoused by the nineteenth-century Manchester free-trade liberals, and also by Marx. And like *laissez-faire* liberalism, globalization theory has a strong tendency towards economism, reading the political off unproblematically from what it takes to be inevitable economic trends.

Another problem with globalization theory is that its claims are at various points both intuitively plausible and highly counter-intuitive. Few would doubt, or indeed even require to weigh the evidence, before agreeing that there is a more global market developing in goods, capital and communications. However, realists, and particularly historical realists, would find it instinctively implausible that the nation state was disappearing. Not only has the thing simply too much history to just disappear – even the most violent and comprehensive of revolutions fail to eliminate the traces of the past – but empirically it is clear that national states are still with us and, indeed, multiplying. More than 100 nation states have been established in the last 40 years and since 1991 18 new states have been officially recognized (Davies, 1993; Smith, 1995, p. 105). In one perspective at least the process of globalization can be seen as the global extension of the process of modernization initiated and epitomized by the (western) nation state – it represents precisely the generalization of the nation state (Giddens, 1985). Likewise, it seems to be intuitively plausible that countries like the UK and the USA are becoming increasingly globalized. However, it would seem far less obvious that this is happening in certain other European states, like Germany, and particularly in the East Asian states, all of which appear to remain quite 'national' in their outlook and institutions (Hutton, 1995). The challenge for globalization theory is to demonstrate that the phenomenon is both historically distinctive *and* truly global – or at least that it is likely to be so in time.

One of the most comprehensive critical assessments of the globalization debate is Hirst and Thompson's recent book, *Globalization in Question* (1996). Their general position is that while there is evidence of increasing internationalization in economic and political matters in some regions, the claims of the 'extreme' globalization theorists are overdrawn and conceptually 'thin'. They argue that internationalization of trade and investment has a long history and that its advance during this century has been both sporadic and geographically uneven. The post-1975 surge in indices of internationalization is neither unprecedented nor necessarily durable, since some of its causes have been highly specific and conjunctural. It has not in any case spread far beyond a small range of advanced countries. Arguing from a similar perspective in respect of political changes, they conclude that although its role may be changing, the nation state as such is not disappearing. It still has important functions to perform both internationally and nationally, and, at both these levels, that includes economic management.

Assessing the historical evidence of changes in international flows of goods, capital and labour during the century, Hirst and Thompson find that the recent levels are not so extraordinary. The volume of world foreign trade expanded at about 3.4 per cent per annum between 1870 and 1913, by 1 per cent between 1913 and 1959, by 9 per cent during 1950–73 and by 3.6 per cent between 1973 and 1985. In other words, despite a massive rise in world trade after World War Two, the recent trend has been down, back to its nineteenth-century levels (Hirst and Thompson, 1996, pp. 20–1). Using the current prices measure, the ratios of trade (imports and exports) to GDP for a range of major economies were higher in 1913 than in 1973 (although using a purchasing power parity measure gives a different picture (p. 27)). Likewise in terms of capital flows for a range of countries, Hirst and Thompson find little dramatic change over a century, concurring with Turner (1991) that capital account imbalances and capital flows, measured in relation to GDP, were higher in the pre-1914 Gold Standard era than they were in the 1980s (p. 28).

In terms of population movements Hirst and Thompson note that the greatest era for recorded voluntary migration was in the century after 1815. Some 60 million left Europe for the Americas, Oceana and South and East Asia; another 10 million left Russia for central Asia and Siberia, and around one million left Southern Europe for North Africa (Hirst and Thompson, 1996, pp. 22–3). In the half of the century from 1840, Irish famine, western price depression and eastern European pogroms produced some of the largest population movements ever. By comparison, postwar migrations have been relatively modest. Labour markets remain largely national affairs and opportunities for economic migration have been seriously curtailed, not only by the disappearance of the former 'frontier areas' of the globe but also by government barriers to immigration.

In many ways, as Hirst and Thompson conclude, the international economy was 'more open in the pre-1914 period than it has been at any time since, including that from the late 1970s onwards' (Hirst and

Thompson, 1996, p. 312). Much of the spectacular international market growth since that period has been due to specific circumstances which may not endure. With financial deregulation and the floating of exchange rates in the 1970s, there was an upsurge in financial activity through increased international lending, financial innovation and financial agglomeration. This led to the growth of volatile markets in bonds, futures and options. However, much of this capital flow is short term and there may be renewed efforts to establish exchange rate regimes which curtail it (although Hirst and Thompson are not sanguine about the prospects of European Monetary Union). As Hirst and Thompson show in their brief history for this century, monetary and exchange rate regimes have often been short-lived.

Foreign direct investment (FDI) and transnational corporations have been at the heart of debates about globalization and Hirst and Thompson concentrate much of their analysis here, drawing on datasets for MNCs in a number of countries at different time periods. Their argument is that by and large MNCs have not transformed into TNCs as Reich has claimed, although their stake in the world economy is enormous. There were an estimated 37 000 MNCs in 1990 controlling about 170 000 affiliated organizations (Hirst and Thompson, 1996, p. 55). Some 80 per cent of US trade in 1992 was conducted by MNCs. FDI stock in 1992 was US$2 trillion and the MNCs controlling this were responsible for sales worth US$5.5 trillion, more than the total world trade at US$4 trillion. A mere 100 MNCs accounted for about one third of total FDI stock and 14 per cent of total flows in 1990 (p. 53). Although its increase is now slowing down, FDI has grown faster than trade, with flows rising at 34 per cent per annum between 1983 and 1990 compared with 9 per cent for total merchandised trade (p. 55). The data conclusively demonstrate the massive weight of MNCs within the world economy, including both manufacturing and services.

However, as Hirst and Thompson argue, penetration of MNCs and FDI is far from global. Of the world's 37 000 MNCs in 1990, 24 000 were home-based in just 14 OECD countries. FDI is concentrated largely within three areas: 73 per cent of accumulated stock and 60 per cent of flows were located in America, Europe and Japan. Including only the six coastal provinces for China, it is estimated that only 28 per cent of the world's population receives 91.5 per cent of FDI (Hirst and Thompson, 1996, p. 68).

Furthermore, not only is the penetration of MNCs highly uneven globally, but their operations are generally fairly circumscribed to their home region, if not their country of registration, belying the claim than they have become transnational. Hirst and Thompson's data for 500 MNCs suggest that in each of their six countries, home sales accounted for over two-thirds of total sales, and more in services. Assets of companies in both manufacturing and service sectors were also concentrated in the home region. An analysis of profits distribution for the sample of MNCs also suggests a strong regional base. For US-headquartered companies, 69 per cent of profits were declared in the US; for the UK companies 67 per cent were declared in Europe; and for Canadian companies 80 per cent were declared in the US or Canada. (Hirst and Thompson, 1996, p. 87).

Multinationals, according to Hirst and Thompson, still have much to gain from being embedded in national economies. They 'benefit from being enmeshed in networks of relations with central and local governments, with trade associations, with organized labour, and with specifically national financial institutions, oriented towards local companies, and with national systems of skill formation and labour motivation' (Hirst and Thompson, 1992, p. 426). They are still manifestly keen to trade on the 'national' nature of their products, even where they are happy to see these produced abroad, and they invariably portray themselves for their home publics as national champions, loyal to the national economy (Reich, 1991). Typically they still retain the high value-added parts of the operations – the conception, design, R & D and technically advanced manufacture – in the home countries. As Hirst and Thompson (1992) conclude: 'The home-oriented nature of MNC activity on most of the dimensions looked at seems overwhelming. Thus MNCs still rely on their "home base" as the centre for the economic activities, despite all the speculation about globalization' (p. 95).

Hirst and Thompson are perhaps too ready to substitute 'home country' for 'home region' as the base of central MNC activities, and, arguably, they pay too little attention to the tendency among some MNCs to move parts of the high value-added work abroad.[4] However, many economists would agree with their emphasis on the national dimension of economic success. Leading analysts of global economic competitiveness, like Michael Porter (1990), still argue in terms of national economies and their national endowments. National infrastructures, institutions, skills and cultures are seen to be at the root of comparative economic advantage, both for individual firms and national economies. Indeed, as Hutton (1995) has argued, the success of companies in the leading economies, like Germany and Japan, is heavily dependent on the local infrastructures, including the quality of education and training provision, the stability of supplier chains, the vitality of research and development networks, the work culture, and the loyalty and commitment of financial institutions to national companies (Hutton, 1995). For theorists of flexible specialization (Piore and Sabel, 1984) and post-Fordism (Murray, 1988; Mathews, 1989) one of the key factors in the development of dynamic and flexible firms has been their location within industrial districts or enterprise zones with their high concentrations of research and development and their closely woven institutional networks providing both competition and cooperation. Hollywood and Silicon Valley in California, Emilia Romagna in Italy, Baden-Württemberg in West Germany, the Jura region in the Alps have all been singled out as exceptional areas of innovation (Murray, 1988; Piore and Sabel, 1984; Streeck and Schmitter, 1991). They form the hubs of global networks but they are clearly nourished and sustained by specifically local, and national, environments.

National infrastructures and cultures continue to contribute towards differences in national competitive advantage which have not been erased by the putatively equilibrating tendencies of the global economy. As Ashton and Green maintain in their new work (1996, chapter 5) 'there persists a substantial diversity in both skill formation systems and more generally in economic systems'. Reviewing the evidence on a range of national economic indicators they find relatively little support for the thesis of 'convergence' among national economies. The gap between the advanced economies and the non-advanced economies, broadly between the North and the South, has widened rather than closed, and even among the advanced economies there is continuing divergence on a number of indices. Rates of growth in wages have remained divergent with higher labour costs in Germany and Scandinavia and lower wage costs in Ireland, Greece, Portugal and the UK. Unemployment rates have shown quite different patterns in the advanced countries. Austria, Japan, Norway, Switzerland and Sweden maintained low levels of unemployment between 1970 and 1990 compared with considerably higher rates in other European states. Even with income distribution the picture has been mixed with steady or decreasing inequality in Canada, Denmark, Finland, Germany, Holland, Norway, Japan and Sweden, and increasing inequality in the UK and the USA.

Economic globalization, as the above accounts suggest, is a highly contested phenomenon. It is still too early to judge the long-term outcome of many of the recent trends, and the data are, as yet, insufficient to judge the pervasiveness of even current trends. The most that can be said here, in conclusion, is that while there are clearly new globalizing trends of great importance, we should be cautious, both on historical and current evidential grounds, in ascribing a new global order on the basis of developments that are uneven and of uncertain durability. The national economy still seems to have considerable substance, albeit that this is challenged in numerous ways by the global reach of multinational companies. But what of the 'global culture' and the globalization of politics?

In the domain of culture, globalizing trends are, in a sense, unambiguous. There can be no doubt that new information technology has exponentially increased the ease, economy and rapidity of communications and that this has given unprecedented access across the world to the global flow of ideas, information and cultural products. In the contemporary world no country is immune to the effects of international television, film and video, even where governments might wish that they were. Governments can no longer control access to the global flow of images and information within their populations and this is historically unprecedented. Both Lenin and Goebbels, earlier in this century, were aware of the ideological potential of film and radio, and made ample use of it. However, they could control it. Modern governments cannot. What is more, ideas and information are infinitely reproducible at minimum cost. So long as individuals or groups of individuals can afford TVs, videos or computers with modems, and this includes a large slice of humanity, they have an access to the international cultural pool which neither governments nor prices can do much to constrain. There can be no doubt either about the scale of impact this has had on national cultures. It would not be far-fetched, for instance, to ascribe the demise of communism in eastern Europe in part to the impact of modern media and cultural penetration. Populations exposed for years to images of western affluence and 'freedom' finally lost faith in the powers of the communist economy and polity to deliver the quality of life apparently available in the West (Hobsbawm, 1994). No amount of official dogma could hold sway against the ideological effects of such cultural penetration.

However, while we may agree that the means of modern culture are irrepressibly global, and that no nations – not even Albania – can remain cultural fortresses, we can be less sure about what global culture actually is and what effects it will have on national cultures in particular cases. Cultural theorists, as noted above, are divided as to whether globalization means cultural standardization or increasing diversity. The most plausible deduction seems to be that it means both at the same time. Cultural particularisms are more globally visible and present, leading to a greater diversity of cultural options for individuals and groups. At the same time, the dominant cultures of the West (and particularly those of the USA and the Anglophone countries) reach further across the globe, penetrating the national and local cultures of previously more isolated countries. The

double movement produces a international veneer of cultural homogenization but, at the same time, an infinity of cultural hybrids and mixes.
Cultures are transported across frontiers by similar means everywhere, but
they are received and assimilated in different ways.

This complex and differentiated dynamic of cultural transmission and
interpenetration underlies the divergent national cultural responses to
globalization. While European states all seem to develop diverse and cosmopolitan hybrids of American and European cultural forms, assimilating
the cultural artefacts of their migrant populations, the advanced Asian
states seem to evolve with more dichotomous cultural patterns, both
importing western styles and artefacts and strenuously preserving the
integrity of their national cultures. In other regions of the world, and particularly in Muslim fundamentalist states, cultural invasion has been met
with fierce cultural resistance and the reassertion of traditional national
singularity and exclusivism. Thus while we may say that the means of cultural transmission have become effectively globalized, we cannot say for
sure that there is a global culture. There are only different national
responses to what postmodernists have liked to call 'global culture' and
which, in reality, may be a very elusive and sometimes superficial phenomenon.

The question for students of national cultures is not whether global
cultural influences can penetrate the national cultural space but how far
they can actually take root. To many commentators, and particularly
those who stress the historical, ethnic and territorial continuity and
embeddedness of cultural forms, there may be distinct limitations to the
process of cultural globalization in many regions of the world. Smith
(1995, p. 21) has argued that: 'stripped of any sense of development
beyond the performative present, and alien to all ideas of roots, the
genuine global culture is fluid, ubiquitous, formless and historically
shallow.' Likewise, Vaclav Havel, in his 1994 speech on receiving the
Philadelphia Liberty Medal in Independence Hall (Havel, 1994) has
stressed the essential psychological limitations of a superficial global
culture:

Our civilization has essentially globalized only the surface of our lives.
But our inner Self continues to have a life of its own and the fewer
answers the era of rational knowledge provides to basic questions of
human being, the more deeply it would seem that people, behind its
back as it were, cling to the ancient certainties of the tribe. Because of
this, individual cultures, increasingly lumped together by contemporary

civilization, are realizing with new urgency their own inner autonomy and the differences with others.

While we may disagree with Smith and Havel on the historical and social inevitability of continuity among national and ethnic cultures, it would seem evident that there are still many countries where the national cultural element is highly persistent. Global culture, or, better, cosmopolitanism, like global economics, is a very uneven phenomenon. This is perhaps why it is so hard to assess whether nationalism is a more or less important force in the modern world.

In a volume written before the recent revolutions in eastern Europe, Hobsbawm argued, controversially, and against the 'ethnic' school of Smith and others, that nationalism 'is no longer a major vector of historical development' (Hobsbawm, 1990, p. 163). This can be accepted but only in the normative or (to use the jargon) historicist sense that it may no longer be considered a 'progressive' force. Whereas liberal nationalism in the early nineteenth century tended to be 'emancipatory' and 'additive', and thus emphasized the civic over the ethnic or linguistic aspects of nationhood, recent nationalisms have typically been secessionist and divisive, tending to emphasize ethnicity and traditional cultures. These may be seen, as Hobsbawm maintains, as a reaction against the homogenizing tendencies of the modern global order and, as such, often backward-looking.

However, it is not invariably, or even usually, the case that modern ethnic nationalisms emerge in underdeveloped states or among disadvantaged groups in developed states, as Hobsbawm sometimes suggests. Some of the most powerful movements of cultural revivalism have occurred within oil-rich Islamic states, in relatively prosperous areas of less developed states, like Croatia, and also within relatively prosperous sections of advanced states, such as Catalonia, Pays Basque and Quebec. When it comes to the crunch, as with the recent referendum on secession in Canada, regions with separation movements do often decide that their economic interests do not lie with secession. This, and the apparent contradiction between cultural isolationism and success in a global economy, would seem to suggest that nationalism in its ethnic form is unlikely to be a long-term motor of development.

However, since 1989 (and since Hobsbawm wrote his book), there has been an explosion of new nations and new nationalisms. Not all of these, and particularly not those in eastern Europe, can be seen as backward looking and merely reactive. Furthermore, there are many degrees and types of nationalism and it is not impossible that certain solidaristic forms of nationalism will prove to be a decisive advantage in the world economy for some states, as the recent success of the East Asian economies suggests (Hampden-Turner and Trompenaars, 1993; Hutton, 1995; Johnson, 1995). For the foreseeable future, at least, it would seem that there will continue to be a dichotomous pattern of increasing cultural globalization inducing deepening cosmopolitanism in some states and escalating cultural nationalism in others. The different responses depend to a large degree on the political forces in any given state.

Globalization theory hinges on the present and future role of the nation state as a political entity. Politics, in a sense, thus provides the limit case of the argument. We might well agree, for instance, that internationalization in the economic and cultural realms is such that globalist arguments must be treated very seriously. However, if globalization in the realms of politics cannot be demonstrated, then the qualitative shift argued by globalists must be disputed. This, it seems to me, is where globalization theory is at its weakest. The nation state has always coexisted with international markets. It has also always been party to international political ties. Indeed, arguably, the nation state was constructed from the start as part of an international system of states, each one bound by multiple ties and agreements. The role of the nation state today may be changing, but internationalization does not of itself necessarily reduce the scope or importance of its functions. This is true of both its external and internal relations.

In terms of external relations, it is certainly true that nation states have less autonomy than heretofore. In matters of defence, diplomacy, civil rights and regional and international economic management, a host of international agencies have acquired significant powers, and states have bound themselves, to some extent at least, to uphold and implement their decisions. As Hirst and Thompson have put it, world '[p]olitics is becoming more polycentric, with states as merely one level in a complex system of overlapping and often competing agencies of government' (p. 422). However, this loss of autonomy does not necessarily mean a net loss of sovereignty. National states have in many cases willingly transferred power to supra-national agencies and, as the history of UK relations with the EU demonstrates, can as easily opt back out of certain areas. Nor has this growth of international agencies necessarily reduced the functions of the nation state in international relations. On the contrary, nation states are the very building blocks of international governance. Without them international agencies would either not exist, or would have no legitimacy or means of enforcement. Among 'the central functions of the nation-state' in the future, as Hirst and Thompson have argued, 'will be those of providing legitimacy for and ensuring accountability of supra- and sub-national governance mechanisms' (p. 409).

Nor has the growth of supra-national agencies necessarily weakened the powers of the nation state internally. The rise of the European Union, for instance, has led to near hysterical reactions from Euro-sceptics and nationalists, particularly in England, who fear the erosion of national autonomy and identity. However, while it is clear that membership of the EU has meant loss of national autonomy in certain specific areas of domestic policy, and some voluntary 'pooling' of sovereignty, this does not necessarily equate to a net weakening of nation states, in terms of their regulatory and national decision-making capacities.

For all its attempts to develop a European structure of transnational governance and organized interest-group representation, the EU has been remarkably unsuccessful in embedding a transnational structure of neo-corporatist institutions, particularly as regards one of the social partners, the trade unions, who are most rooted in their national cultures and labour market regimes. As Streeck and Schmitter (1991) argue, the development of effective transnational corporate decision-making structures would have required the emergence of a strong European state. But this has not occurred, not least because of the attachment of national populations to their respective national institutions, because of clear perceptions of different national interests, and because of pervasive scepticism towards the manifest 'democratic deficit' in EU political institutions. With the continuing weakness of the European parliament, and despite 'qualified majority voting', EU politics and decision-making have remained primarily intergovernmental and not supra-national, its transnational interest groups pluralistic lobbies rather than organized systems of concerted interest group representation.

Supra-national sovereignty has been used more for the 'external reassertion of' rather than the 'internal intervention in' the European economy. As Streeck and Schmitter (1991) conclude, while Europe as a whole will continue to exist as 'a unified political entity of some as yet undetermined sort, the nation states that now constitute the European community will not disappear in that entity but will co-exist with it' (p. 151). The main change lies in the increasing complexity of political relations. Europe's future polity, they write:

> will be composed of traditional domestic relations within countries, tra-
> ditional international relations between countries, less traditional
> transnational relations between both individuals and organizations
> across national boundaries, and entirely nontraditional supranational
> relations between European-level public institutions, on the one hand

and, on the other, a European civil society consisting of domestic, international, and transnational forces and relations and including both national states and, in manifold national and cross-national combinations, their constituents. (p. 151)

The debate about European integration and its effects on national sovereignty has often been conducted at a relatively trivial level – as in the interminable debates about restrictions on the size of sausages and so on. However, looked at in a broader perspective, the net effect of European integration has not been to undermine the European nation states as such, but rather to set them on more secure foundations, as Alan Milward has persuasively argued in his historical assessment of the effects of European integration on postwar European states. In the introduction to *The European Rescue of the Nation State*, Milward summarizes his case as follows:

It is the argument of this book that there is no such antithesis [between the EU and the nation state] and that the evolution of the European community since 1945 has been an integral part of the reassertion of the nation state as an organizational concept. The argument goes, however, beyond this because the historical evidence points to the further conclusion that without the process of integration the western European nation state might well not have retained the allegiance and support of its citizens the way it has. The European community has been its buttress, an indispensable part of the nation state's post-war reconstruction. Without it, the nation state could not have offered its citizens the same measure of security and prosperity which it has provided and which has justified its survival. After 1945 the nation state recovered itself from collapse, created a new political consensus as the basis of its legitimacy, and through changes in its response to its citizens which meant a sweeping extension of its functions and ambitions reasserted itself as the fundamental unit of political organization. To supersede the nation state would be to destroy the Community. To put a finite limit to the process of integration would be to weaken the nation-state, to limit its scope and to curb its power. (p. 3)

One does not have to agree with Milward's full-blooded integrationalism to see that, taken in broad perspective, the nation states of Europe have become stronger and more secure than they were 50 years ago, and that European integration has contributed to this in both economic and diplomatic terms.

It is certainly the case that central governments, in many nation states, have reduced their direct control over certain areas of public life. Aspects of education, health, transport and security provision have been privatized in a number of countries. It is also true that, in the face of global market forces, governments have had less scope in the use of fiscal and monetary policies to direct national economies, and have had to tailor their labour market policies to the realities of global competition. However, taken over the longer term, the reach of governmental control has probably increased, not diminished. For every area where governments have ceded some direct responsibility, there are others, like the environment, information, copyright and air-traffic control, where they have become increasingly active. Furthermore, modern communications technology has, as Giddens (1985) has noted, vastly augmented the potential for state surveillance and monitoring.

In any case, much of what is interpreted as decreasing state control by globalists is more a change of form than of function (Blackstone et al., 1992). Under pressures of limited resources and interest group conflicts apparently beyond political mediation, the postwar Keynesian consensus on welfare capitalism has disintegrated. The old Morrisonian models of public ownership have lost credibility as neo-liberals have repeatedly sought to 'roll back the frontiers of the state', appealing as they do so to the 'unbuckable' realities of the global market. However, many of the ensuing changes in governance have modified rather than obliterated central state controls. Continental European models of social partnership and 'subsidiarity' have encouraged devolution and diffusion of powers and responsibilities, but central governments have not lost their pivotal functions in defining the roles and spheres of influence of the different partners, and in generally setting the rules of the game. Likewise in the 'contracting state' model of governance increasingly adopted in the UK (Ainley, 1993). Delegated management has given increasing day-to-day operational autonomy to local service providers, and financial allocations are increasingly controlled by the 5000 or so 'quangos' which now dispense around a third of all public spending.[5] However, central government has massively increased its strategic control in areas like education and health through new forms of contractual governance, with the whole apparatus of target-setting, quality control and performance-based funding.

The main argument against full-scale globalization, however, lies not in the assessment of this or that contemporary trend, but rather in an analysis of the 'functional necessities' of states. Despite the growth of supranational agencies and powers, it remains the case that the nation state is currently the only viable site of democratic representation, accountability and legitimation, and looks likely to remain so. Supra-national bodies currently enjoy only weak democratic legitimacy – indeed the democratic deficit in the EU is such that referenda on Maastricht and EU membership in several countries have produced either negative or only narrowly positive results. Even if they do acquire greater legitimacy in the future it will only be by virtue of the nation states which support and constitute them. Furthermore, the nation state still provides a crucial framework for social cohesion and solidarity. It is not the only level at which this can occur – local communities and international collectivities have important roles as well. But it continues to provide the vital relay between local and international attachments and loyalties. As Smith has written: '[N]ations and nationalism remain political necessities because ... they alone can ground the interstate order in principles of popular sovereignty and the will of the people' (Smith, 1995, p. 54). The question is, what type of nationalism?

It is undoubtedly true that many of the advanced western states find it increasingly difficult to maintain social cohesion and solidarity. Growing individualism and lifestyle diversity, secularization, social mobility and the decline of stable communities have all played a part in this. So too has the 'European peace', denying nations the unifying focus of a common enemy. In some countries, where markets and individualism have gone furthest in dissolving social ties, there is reason to wonder whether national solidarism has not vanished beyond recovery.

In *The Work of Nations*, Reich paints a frightening picture of social fragmentation in America. The affluent fifth of society, the symbolic analysts, 'are selling their expertise on the global market', enhancing their standard of living 'even as that of other Americans declines' (1991, p. 250). They no longer depend on the economic performance of other Americans and are increasingly unwilling to support them. They exist in a hermetically sealed world of privatized transport, communications, education and health care and are fast retreating into residential enclaves which are privately maintained and policed (there are now more private security guards than police in America) (Reich, 1991, p. 269). The affluent American is increasingly seceding from the rest of society, and so too, in their different ways, are other, less privileged, groups who no longer have a real stake. Where are the bonds of social cohesion here? As Reich says: '[t]he question is whether the habits of citizenship are sufficiently strong to withstand the centrifugal forces of the new global economy' (1991, p. 304).

However, the very question, in a sense, answers the debate about political globalization. As global forces in economics and culture create more fissiparous and more individualistic societies, so the need for countervailing sources of social solidarity grows. Arguably, nation states cannot refuse this role – or at least if they do, the result will be a chaos which finally invades even the enclaves of the privileged. As Hirst and Thompson put it in unambiguous terms:

> In an individualistic and pluralist society, where there are few common standards, where strong binding collectivities have declined and been replaced by communities of choice, and where informal social sanctions have weakened, then the role of law is more rather than less necessary (1996, p. 436).

Marx once wrote that 'socialism or barbarism' was the choice facing capitalist societies. Most governments in the advanced states today, needless to say, would not agree. However, under the impact of global capitalism, and despite the current neo-liberal vogue, governments may soon find themselves facing another dichotomy more redolent of Hobbes than Marx – between the state or barbarism. Let us hope that by then democracy is still part of the equation. The cohesive civic nation may still be the best guarantor of this.

## EDUCATION AND INTERNATIONALIZATION

How has education been affected by these globalizing trends in political economy and culture? Globalization theory, together with its twin postmodernism, has to date elicited a number of responses to these questions within the field of education research, most of them pointing towards a fundamental shift in the very nature of education as a national or state 'project'. Jane Kenway (1992) has argued that economic globalization and the information revolution augur radical changes in the very nature of the learning process, promoting a new commodification of education and an uncoupling of learning from its traditional institutional locations. Donald (1992) has contended that postmodern, globalized societies have gone so far in cultural diversification and fragmentation that the old educational goal of transmitting common cultures is now obsolete and beyond reclaim. Most recently, Usher and Edwards (1994), also from a postmodern perspective, have argued that global postmodernity has brought both a 'crisis in rationality' and a pluralization of cultures that fundamentally undermines the modernist goals of national education as a unified 'project'. Education can no longer control or be controlled; it can 'no longer readily function as a means of reproducing society or as an instrument of large-scale social engineering' (p. 211). With the progressive replacement of universal and standardized education systems by virtual learning networks, schools will cease to act as dispensers of rational, disciplinary knowledge, and socialization will be reduced to the development and certification of individual competence. National objectives in education will be limited to 'fulfilling the requirements of the economy under conditions of global competition' (p. 175).

The arguments in this book are against such extreme scenarios of educational transformation; rather than a full-scale globalization of education, the evidence suggests a partial internationalization of education systems which falls far short of an end to national education *per se*. National education systems *have* become more porous in recent years. They have been partially internationalized through increased student and staff mobility, through widespread policy borrowing and through attempts to enhance the international dimension of curricula at secondary and higher levels. They have also grown more like each other in certain important ways. However, there is little evidence that national systems as such are disappearing or that national states have ceased to control them. They may seem less distinctive and their roles are changing but they still undoubtedly attempt to serve national ends. The concluding sections of this chapter explore these themes.

Writers like Jane Kenway (1992) and Edwards (1994) have made much of the implications for education of new information technologies and the way these can interact with growing international markets. There is no doubt that the acceleration and enhancement of international communications through satellite, fibre-optic cable and the so-called 'information highway' opens up new possibilities for education. E-mail, internet, video-conferencing and the like now give access, to those who have the technology and the expertise, to the virtual school and the virtual college. Theoretically, learning need no longer be constrained by the limitations of time and space. Just as Gutenberg paved the way for the independent itinerant scholars of Renaissance Europe, so the global web can create a new generation of mental travellers, only this time they need not leave their terminals.

It seems unlikely that these developments will de-institutionalize education, at least at the compulsory levels. Minding, socializing and tutoring children still require physical proximity and contact and institutions which support these processes (Erault, 1991). Computer-based, interactive learning software has yet to be developed to its full potential, but even when it is, it seems unlikely that it can replace the role of the teacher in the classroom since children still have to learn how to learn (EU Commission, 1996). The notion that schools can be entirely replaced by 'networks of information' (Usher and Edwards, 1994), where children engage only in virtual learning, is no more probable now than when Ivan Illich first proposed the de-schooling of society in 1971. However, at the higher education level, information technology may well lead to a substantial decoupling of learning from institutional spaces. Already university distance learning courses are conducted within and across many of the advanced nations, greatly increasing the international cross-fertilization of university studies. There are certainly limits to this process of virtualization in higher education not least because modern scientific and technological research requires the concentration of enormous resources in equipment and laboratories which must be located in physical spaces. The humanities, however, do not require this since the only physical plant is the library and this, in time, can also be made virtual with access through the internet. Non-research student learning, moreover, can, and no doubt will, increasingly adopt distance modes, which are both cheaper and more convenient for many adult students, and this will add to the internationalization of higher education.

Another aspect of internationalization is student mobility. This has increased exponentially in recent years, not least through EU schemes such as ERASMUS, LINGUA, PETRA and COMETT, and more recently in eastern Europe and Latin America through TEMPUS and ALPHA. In 1987–88 3000 students received EC mobility grants. By 1995–96 this had increased to 170 000. The COMETT programme, which involves university–enterprise exchanges, increased its numbers from 4400 in 1990 to 8700 in 1994 (EU Commission, 1996). The new consolidated programmes of SOCRATES and LEONARDO will take this further, increasing the EU funds spent on student and staff mobility and exchange by some 40 per cent and doubling those spent on vocational education programmes (Sultana, 1995). Similar regional mobility programmes are now being developed in the Asian-Pacific, and elsewhere.

The international dimension of curricula has also been enhanced in secondary and higher education in many countries. The EU has pressed hard to broaden the European dimension in member states' curricula, to encourage international research cooperation, and to extend foreign language learning to a trilingual norm, although this has yet to make much impact in the UK. Japan has been moving in the same direction since the mid-1970s. The 1974 report, *Kyoiku, Gabujyutu, Bunka niokeru Koryu* (International Exchange in Education, Research and Culture), advocated educational exchanges, the enhancement of language education, cooperation with developing countries, the encouragement of foreign students and the preparation of Japanese students for living in an international environment. The National Council on Education Reform, an *ad hoc* advisory committee to the Prime Minister, which reported in 1987 on 'coping with internationalization', reinforced these aims and added proposals for improving facilities for Japanese language instruction to foreigners.[6]

Equally important as an agent of internationalization in education has been the proliferation of policy borrowing between states. This has a long history in education, which stretches back to the eighteenth century and beyond. Rousseau advised many eighteenth-century courts on education reform; Victor Cousin reported on Prussian education policies for the French July Monarchy; Matthew Arnold, Lyon Playfair and Sylvanus Thompson investigated and drew on French, Dutch and German secondary and technical education for reforms in mid-Victorian England; and Horace Mann scoured the Old World for educational ideas to adopt in the New World (Green, 1990). Even in formerly isolationist Japan, the Meiji reformers of the late nineteenth century were active in cultural borrowing, sending delegations to investigate European systems and bringing back experts to advise them on their own reforms (Schoppa, 1991). Virtually every educational reformer in Europe and America has been influenced by Pestalozzi, Montessori or Dewey or has borrowed some policy from somewhere (Green, 1990; McLean, 1990). However, policy borrowing has gone through distinct phases, with periods of intensive cross-fertilization (the late nineteenth century), followed by periods of relative isolationism (between the world wars). The last 20 years have been an exceptional period for international traffic in educational ideas (Keep, 1991).

There are a number reasons for this, including the work of international agencies such as the OECD, CEDEFOP, the World Bank and the EU, and also the proliferation of educational exchanges among staff and policy-makers. Perhaps most significant, however, has been the intensification of economic competition between nations and the perception by governments the world over of the importance of education and training for economic advance. The current wave of policy borrowing in the advanced nations appears to have begun in the mid-1970s just as governments were facing common problems of recession and mass unemployment. It has now advanced to the point where reform proposals are rarely presented without reference to foreign precedents and where thousands of international publications are devoted to explaining the structural intricacies and comparative performance of each national education system to policy-makers in other countries (and possibly their own).

During the past 20 years in the UK, for instance, there have been countless education reforms which have been derived from, or at least made reference to, other national policies. The first Youth Opportunities Programmes were derived from experiments with behaviourist work training schemes for juvenile offenders in Canada, and subsequent training reforms have invariably made reference to the Dual System in Germany (Low, 1988). Competence-based assessment had its origins in experiments in the USA in the evaluation of teacher competence in the 1970s (Wolf, 1995), just as ideas for specialist or 'magnet-type' schools have been derived from initiatives in New York and elsewhere. Also from America has come the idea of giving control over training to local enterprise groups: the UK Training and Enterprise Councils (TECs) were modelled on the American Private Industry Councils (PICs), the Employment Department being advised by Kay Stratton, a leading figure in the US work training movement (Bennett et al., 1994). The Employment Department has also derived its schemes for performance-based funding of training from the same US source (Green and Mace, 1994). Most, but not all, of the borrowings in the UK have come from the US. Reading Recovery Programmes were adopted from New Zealand, just as New Zealand has used the UK National Vocational Qualifications and the Scottish National Certificates as models for the modular system of vocational awards devised by the New Zealand Qualifications Authority.[7]

Policy transfer and diffusion represents one manifestation of internationalizing forces in education. But in reality it is only part of a broader process of international cross-fertilization in education brought on by global interpenetration. Policy-makers in the advanced nations (as in others) face similar economic and social problems; they seek educational solutions to these which inevitably draw their education systems closer together. In fact there is significant evidence of a general process of convergence in education systems across the world, at least as regards the broad structures and aims of education.

In their historical analysis of trends in a world-wide sample of national education systems, Inkeles and Sirowy (1983) found evidence of convergence in six areas including: the ideational and legal, the structural, the demographic, administration and finance, dynamics and curricula. The countries studied were broadly moving towards a common notion of education conceived as a social good and as an individual right and duty which should be vouchsafed by the state through legislation on free and compulsory schooling. Institutional structures were increasingly based on the model of a single ladder in compulsory education, with the development of formal – national – curricula now almost universal. Analysis of the trends in enrolments in primary and secondary education for a world-wide set of countries showed increasing convergence, with coefficients of variation declining from 0.44 and 0.91 respectively in 1955 to 0.21 and 0.51 in 1979 (pp. 312–13). For a European sample, although not for the world-wide sample, there was also a convergence in historical trends in pupil–teacher ratios from a variation coefficient of 0.41 in 1860 to 0.22 in 1960 (p. 316). In administration and finance, a number of features had become universal in the sample including a central ministry of education, regional and local structures of control and national systems of inspection. Trends also indicated greater convergence between 1955 and 1979 in spending on education (as a proportion of GNP), especially for the advanced nations, and some convergence, at least for western nations, around comprehensive education structures and increased equality of access (OECD data on HE access by social class for 11 countries for 1960 and 1970 (p. 325)).

Inkeles and Sirowy's study relates to a long timespan which predates many of the global changes discussed here. However, it is not difficult to discern patterns of convergence within European education systems within the recent period. Taking western Europe alone, it is clear that there has been a common trend towards the development of mass post-compulsory and higher education (OECD, 1995) in all EU countries, although some differences in enrolment rates are still evident (Green and Steedman, 1993). It is also clear that as upper secondary and higher education have expanded from elite to mass systems, they have also become increasingly diverse in their courses and curricula (Green, 1995b; OECD, 1990). As national systems have struggled to provide for their more diverse intakes, whilst seeking to avoid excessive differentiation, they have increasingly moved towards models of flexible tracking, where students pursue different types of vocational and academic courses, but with opportunities for transfers and progressions across tracks (Raffe, 1993). Typically, European post-compulsory systems now comprise three types of course: the general and academic; the broadly vocational or technical; and the vocational, which prepares students for particular occupations (OECD, 1990).

A number of European countries have sought to meet the anticipated need for more multiskilled employees through strengthening provision at the technician level with more theory-based, generic courses and fewer specialist occupational subdivisions. In France the occupationally specific CAP courses (some 250 types) are being superseded by the BEP courses (around 35) which have higher general education requirements and broader vocational studies based around families of occupations (Tanguy, 1991). The creation of the over 30 new *baccalauréat professionnel* courses alongside the existing *baccalauréat technologique* now provides a progression route for students on this new broad vocational track and this is taken by over half of the students who register on the BEP courses (Tanguy, 1991). Like the *Maturita Professionale* in Italy (OECD, 1990), the *baccalauréat professionnel* is a higher level vocational qualification whose prestige may be enhanced by its common title with the traditional academic qualification and by its concomant entitlements to HE entry, although it is seen primarily as a passport for direct entry to technician-level employment. Even in countries where vocational education is organized on an apprentice model of occupational training, there have been attempts to broaden the vocational programmes. In Germany Dual System training now normally involves two and a half days per week (or its equivalent) in studying general and theoretical subjects in the *Berufsschulen* and the number of classified apprenticeships were reduced from 465 in 1980 to 332 in 1988, with a concomitant broadening of content within each (Casey, 1990). In Switzerland the number of apprenticeships have similarly been reduced (OECD, 1990). In Sweden the vocational lines have been lengthened from two to three years, their general education content upgraded and provisions have been made for increased access to HE for those following these lines (Green, 1995b).

Other convergent trends in European systems are also readily apparent. In most countries there have been attempts to reinforce the institutional linkages between education and work, through the development of work-experience, work-shadowing, alternance and mentoring programmes. Employers have been drawn more systematically into the process of standard-setting under the *Commissions Consultatives Professionnelles* (CPCs) in France, the BIBB in Germany and the Industry Lead Bodies in the UK. Other manifestations of cross-sector collaboration include the numerous Education–Business Partnerships (EBPs) in the UK and the development, in the UK, Singapore and France, of modern apprenticeship schemes which rest on the collaboration of firms, employer organizations and education institutions. Governments in most EU states are also increasingly emphasizing adult continuing training and education and seeking to promote notions of lifelong or permanent education as a joint endeavour of the enterprise and the academy (Ruberti, 1993). The 'learning society' of the future, so goes the rhetoric, involves both the learning organization and the entrepreneurial school.

The rationale for increasing the linkage between education and enterprise derives in part from educational research (Streeck, 1987) which suggests high value-added, flexible production systems demand high levels of generic skills which cannot be developed exclusively in the academy where real-life learning experiences are necessarily curtailed and where equipment may be limited and out of date. It also owes to the emphasis placed by EU agencies on social partnership and subsidiarity, both of which suggest modes of delivery in education and training which bring together educators, employers and trade unions (EU Commission, 1996).

The EU has also encouraged member states to improve opportunities for lifelong learning by developing improved systems of advice and counselling, and new flexible systems of accreditation including competence-based modular approaches and the accreditation of prior learning (EU Commission, 1996). There are some signs that this is leading to a degree of convergence in assessment systems across Europe, at least as regards the main objectives of enhanced flexibility and access (Wolf, 1995b).

There are still marked differences in European education systems in knowledge traditions (McLean, 1990), in institutional structures (Green and Steedman, 1993), in modes of governance and control (Lauglo, 1995) and in outcomes (Green and Steedman, 1993). Most obviously, countries with rationalist, encyclopedic knowledge traditions, like France, tend to retain broad curricula to a late stage, whereas countries with more empiricist/humanist traditions, like the UK, have introduced specialization at an early age. Institutional structures still diverge between countries with divided secondary systems, like the German-speaking countries, and others with comprehensive arrangements. Likewise, post-compulsory systems can be divided into those which are predominantly work-based (Germany, Austria and German-speaking Switzerland) and those which are predominantly school-based (the USA, France, Italy, Spain, the UK, Sweden, the Netherlands). The latter can also be divided into those which are consolidated into single comprehensive institutions (the Swedish *Gymnasieskola* and the US high school) and those which have a diversity of institutions, as most countries still do (OECD, 1985). Among the pluralist systems there are some examples of moves towards greater institutional integration. English 'tertiary colleges' have brought together provision traditionally provided by school sixth forms and further education colleges, just as the French *lycées polyvalents* have combined the work of the general and technical *lycées*. Japan is now experimenting with some 20 combined high schools. However, this development is limited and most school-based systems still fall into either the comprehensive or the pluralist categories.

Arguably, these different institutional structures derive from significant national differences in labour market organization. Ashton and Green (1996) have argued that national labour market regimes and education and training systems combine, or articulate, to produce different national skills formation regimes. At least three models have been identified among the advanced states. In Japan, and some other East Asian states, traditional practices of lifetime employment for core workers in large enterprises give rise to a system of company-based, job-specific training, in which employers can invest large sums without risk of other employers poaching their trained workers. This elaborate system of occupational training in turn allows the education system to concentrate on general education and broad technical training (Ashton and Green, 1996; Green, 1995b; Koike and Inoki, 1990). A different model exists in countries like Germany which have tightly regulated and largely occupational labour markets and strong neo-corporatist structures. Here occupational training is largely delivered through the apprentice system which is jointly organized by the social partners. Employers are encouraged to invest in apprenticeship training because union agreement to low apprentice wages – in return for quality training – allows low costs, and because the extensive systems of sector-based wage bargaining fix rates for skilled jobs and thus discourages firms from paying wage premiums to poach workers other firms have trained. Young people are encouraged to train through federal regulations which require qualifications for access to skilled jobs (Green, 1995b; Marsden and Ryan, 1995). A third model of school-based training appears to dominate in countries like France, the UK and the USA where the absence of extensive, Japanese-style, internal labour markets causes problems of poaching and employer investment in training, and where weaker corporatist structures limit cooperative delivery of apprentice-style programmes (Green, 1995b). Although the trend towards school-enterprise cooperation mixes up some of the features of these modes, the systems are still readily identifiable and appear likely to remain nationally distinctive (Ashton and Green, 1996).

Other differences between education and training systems and their outcomes are also apparent. There continue to be important distinctions, for instance, between countries which have national systems, like France and Sweden, and those which have federal systems, where the region has autonomy in education, as in Spain and Germany. There are also long-standing and significant differences between countries with traditions of centralization in educational administration, like France, Sweden and Germany (at the *Länder* level), and those with traditions of greater decentralization, like the Netherlands and, until recently, the UK. Outcomes in terms of qualification rates at secondary and upper secondary levels also differ markedly between countries, as illustrated in the data presented in Chapter 6. Whether *the trend* here is towards convergence or divergence is not clear. Research has yet to be done to investigate this systematically.

Many of the differences in education and training systems derive from deep-seated historical traditions now institutionalized in structures, practices and institutional cultures which are peculiar to each nation. These are not readily surrendered despite the common efforts of the EU and other supra-national bodies. Efforts by the EU, for instance, to harmonize vocational qualifications and to enforce the opening of European labour markets to those with equivalent qualifications have failed dismally. Where countries have widespread national agreements and statutes governing qualifications and access to jobs, as they do in France and Germany, there has been enormous resistance to accepting foreign-qualified workers into regulated jobs, even where their qualifications have been deemed to be equivalent by European bodies. Germany has recently closed its doors to foreign construction workers in classified occupations in this manner. Such national regulations inevitably limit the effects of policy convergence. Sultana's claim, therefore, that 'the structural integration of the EU and the growth of pan-European consensus of European elites will lead to convergence of national policies in different fields, including education' (Sultana, 1995) would seem to be somewhat overstating the case. The net tendency within Europe, resulting both from supranational policy and, more importantly, from common responses to a common environment, is probably more convergent than divergent. However, further research needs to be done to establish these trends with any certainty.

The above arguments point towards greater international interpenetration of national education systems. But they do not point towards the demise of national systems as such. National governments still largely control their own systems and still use them for national ends. Supranational bodies like the EU have limited power to interfere with national education systems. The Treaty of Rome and the Single European Act, for instance, gave the European Community limited competence in the field of education, restricting it from direct provision and prescriptions about the details of school curricula. The main scope for action lay in the field of vocational education which the Commission has interpreted widely to mean all post-compulsory education. Articles 126 and 127 of the Maastricht Treaty provided the EU with a more explicit mandate for action but still largely within the post-compulsory sector and in relation to education and the economy (Sultana, 1995). Furthermore, the EU is still formally committed to retaining diversity among national education and training systems, maintaining that full-scale harmonization is both undesirable and impossible. As the recent White Paper on education and training argues: 'Given the diversity of national situations and the inadequacy of global solutions in this context, proposing a single model is not the answer. This would be doomed to failure given the pivotal role of the individual in the construction of the learning society and the social and cultural diversity of Member States' (EU Commission, 1996, p. 3). Other international agencies, such as the World Bank, have power over national education policy to the degree to which they control the purse strings. Their influence in the developing world cannot be underestimated. However, among the advanced nations financial inducements from supra-national powers have limited effects when it comes to their core educational aims.

Nor, generally, has national government control over education been weakened by international changes in state forms. It may be argued that the current neo-liberal fashion for marketizing education weakens central state control over national systems in certain respects. However, this has not led to a denationalization of education on a global level. In the first place, as argued in Chapter 1, market reforms have had an uneven impact across the world, penetrating deeply into the English-speaking countries and, for the moment at least, affecting the eastern European states in the wake of, and in reaction to, the demise of communism. However, much of continental Europe and, indeed, most of advanced East Asia has resisted any substantial marketization of education. Privatization policies have affected higher education and training provision in countries like Japan, but not as yet compulsory education to any significant degree. Likewise, measures to increase competition between state schools, as in open enrolment and school choice policies, have had limited impact in countries like France, Germany and Sweden, and practically none in Japan, South Korea and Singapore. In the second place, market policies do not necessarily, in any case, reduce overall central state control over education.

In continental Europe there has been a tendency towards devolving decision-making either to the regional and local state level or to the social partners at national and regional levels. However, it is still central government that determines the strategic aims of education and which fixes and monitors the roles and work of the key players in the game. In the English-speaking countries there has been a strong move towards devolving day-to-day management responsibility to the institutional level. But, whereas this removes government from detailed and direct administrative control over everyday matters, it rarely means a reduction in overall strategic control. Institutions have found themselves increasingly hidebound by indirect government controls exercised through 'earmarked' and performance-based funding, through additional reporting requirements in terms of inputs and detailed performance measurements, and through accountability to the numerous quality control bodies that tend to spring up where direct administrative controls are relaxed. In the UK, institutions are now accountable to a host of new quangos which set their targets, monitor the quality of their outputs and allocate their funds. Since 1979 the tally of new quasi-government agencies in the UK includes the Higher Education Funding Council, the Further Education Funding Councils, the

Funding Agency for Schools, the Schools Curriculum and Assessment Authority, the Higher Education Quality Council, the Teacher Training Authority, the National Advisory Council on Education and Training Targets, not to mention their various regional arms and the numerous local Training and Enterprise Councils. Governments committed to the 'marketization' of education have not been reluctant to increase the educational powers of the central state. In the UK, the 1988 Education Reform Act granted the Secretary of State for Education some 360 additional powers (Chitty, 1989; Simon, 1988). Few have doubted that the net effect of marketization and expanded central powers in education in England and Wales has been towards a general strengthening of government strategic control (Ranson, 1994).

Governments in the advanced states have invariably retained their control over the key areas of curricula, assessment and certification and have increasingly sought to steer their systems towards certain educational outcomes through the setting of targets. In those countries where there was formerly little government control over curricula and assessment this has been increased, as in England and Wales, where a national curriculum was introduced for the first time in 1988, and even in the USA, where the federal government has become more interventionist in relation to standards and assessment (Green and Steedman, 1993). In Japan, where there has been much talk about deregulation and diversification, the central education ministry, the Monbusho, seems to have lost few of its powers, and curriculum control is vigorously maintained through the national *course of study*, through the strengthening of the key areas of moral education, and through state controls over textbooks which have recently been simplified but not abandoned (Schoppa, 1991; Horio, 1988).

For all the postmodern protestations to the contrary, and despite the effects of globalizing trends, governments across the world still exercise considerable control over their national education systems and still seek to use them to achieve national goals. The nature of these goals, and the balance of priorities in different regions, has undoubtedly changed over time, as this chapter has sought to demonstrate. However, in the majority of countries governments still see education as a process of nation-building which involves both economic and social objectives. Education systems are still national institutions devoted, in varying degrees, to the preparation of future workers and the formation of future citizens.

Skills formation has been a major objective of education for governments both in the developing world and in the advanced nations. For the newly industrializing nations it is frequently seen as a condition of economic development. For the advanced nations it is seen as one of the principal means for maintaining high standards of living in the face of increasing global competition, particularly from the developing countries. The UK government 1994 White Paper, *Helping Business to Win* (HM Government, 1994), stated this in bald terms: 'The UK faces a world of increasing change; of ever-fiercer competition; of growing consumer power, and a world in which our wealth is more and more dependent on the knowledge, skills and motivation of our people.' This encapsulates a policy language now ubiquitous in official reports from governments in all advanced nations.

Economic 'globalization' has not only increased the pressure of competition but it has also changed its terms for the advanced states. As most developed nations now realize, in the face of increasing economic competition from low wage nations such as Vietnam, Thailand, Malaysia and China – not to mention the Latin American states as they come on stream – there is little mileage left in competing on wage costs for countries which seek to maintain a high standard of living. They have no alternative now but to move into areas of high value-added, knowledge-based production and services and these require, above all, high levels of skill and flexibility among their workforces (Finegold and Soskice, 1988). What is more, given the current difficulty of managing national economies through fiscal, monetary and trade regulations, where these are ever more difficult to impose, governments have found themselves increasingly interested in the area of skills formation because it is at least amenable to national control (Reich, 1991).

It may be said that the current obsession of western governments with education and training policy also owes something to political rhetoric and electoral pragmatism. As Avis et al. (1996) argue, education and training policy has been much hyped by governments because it is less contentious than employment and fiscal policies, because it allows them to make relatively risk-free election promises which few will oppose, and because it serves to mask the growing structural unemployment which is now endemic in most advanced economies (see also Ainley, Gokulsing and Tysome, 1996). Many economists see no proven link between skills and productivity and others argue that increasing the supply of skills is secondary to raising the demand for them, which is much more difficult (Keep and Mayhew, 1993). However, voters rarely question government claims that more education and training improves national economic competitiveness because they know that on an individual level, at least, human capital investment does pay dividends. Whatever the political calculations and however valid the economic reasoning, it remains the case that most governments see education and training as the critical factor in national economic performance and competitive advantage. As the CBI wrote in their influential 1989 report, *Towards a Skills Revolution*: 'Individuals are now the only sustainable source of competitive advantage' (CBI, 1989, p. 9). More perhaps than ever before, governments use education and training as an instrument for these – still very national – ends.

The situation as regards education and citizen formation is perhaps more complex. From a global perspective, it would appear that forming citizens and shaping national identities is still one of the primary functions of education in most countries. National curricula still tend to place great emphasis on national languages and cultures. History is used to popularize national myths and to promote national identities; literature to celebrate the national language and literary achievements; and civic and moral education to instil national values and notions of good citizenship. Many schools still incorporate into their daily rituals the symbolic paraphernalia of nationhood, with the flying of flags, the singing of anthems and the recital of pledges and declarations. In Japan children clean classrooms, prepare meals and monitor each other's behaviour to develop the qualities of social cooperation and individual discipline and persistence which are seen as central to the nation's values (White, 1987). Governments frequently call on education to promote national values and culture as a source of social cohesion and national solidarity.

In some countries, such as Singapore, the emphasis is on a kind of civic nationalism which aims to integrate multiple ethnic cultures and religions into a single, though diverse, national identity. In other countries, more strident and ethnically based notions of nationalism have prevailed. Schools have one-sidedly promoted the culture and language of the dominant group, enhancing its sense of common identity while marginalizing and excluding minority groups and cultures. With the demise of the former communist regimes in Eastern Europe, a host of new ethnic nationalisms have emerged in the successor states. Dominant groups have frequently adopted exclusivist policies in education emphasizing particular languages and cultures at the expense of others, or – at the extreme – promoting ethnically segregated schooling, as in Latvia and Lithuania.

In the main, this use of education for national identity-building has been most prevalent historically among emerging nation states, and states reconstructing after wars and revolutions. As Christie Davies has written:

Generally, we find a strong national focus in education in most early nation building processes as educational systems are established *pari passu* with the development of modern nation states, for example in

Europe, the USA and Japan. In such periods education is not only organized and geared to national traditions and state interests, but is also expected to support national identity and expand national manpower resources. (1993, p. 332)

As argued throughout this chapter, in the postwar period nation-building through education has been most evident in the new states which have emerged through decolonization, the collapse of former 'empires' and other forms of national transition. Most conspicuously, it has been among the new nation states undergoing periods of accelerated economic development and state formation that education has been used most deliberately as an instrument for forming citizens and forging new national identities.

Among some of the older, advanced nation states this process has also been visible in the postwar period, particularly where countries have been engaged in major reconstruction as with Germany and Japan after the Second World War. However, these cases aside, there is a sense in which education systems in the advanced western states in the recent period have ceased to be so centrally concerned with questions of citizen formation and national identity. As Robert Cowen has recently written, there is an 'atonishing displacement of "society" within the late modern educational pattern' (Cowen, 1996). The reasons for this are complex. In part they derive from the overwhelming policy priority given by governments to questions of skills formation and economic performance, and this, as we have seen, is one consequence of the spread of global markets. However, they go beyond this. In all western states there has been a steady rise in individualistic and consumerist values and identities, and with it a gradual erosion of collective and community identities and beliefs. This has been enhanced, in many states, by the advance of neo-liberal ideologies and the encroachment of the market into every area of life. As national services and resources are increasingly privatized and subjected to the competitive forces of the market, so the public domain is diminished and the legitimacy of collective goals reduced (Ranson, 1994). Education has remained a public service, for the main part, and governments have continued to exercise powerful control over it. However, the scope of government ambitions in education has reduced in many countries. National economic goals are still held inviolate and education is instrumentally geared towards these ends. However, broader national educational objectives in terms of social cohesion and citizenship formation have become increasingly confused and neglected, in part because few western governments have a clear notion of what nationhood and citizenship mean in complex and pluralistic modern democracies.

The poverty of social vision in education in western countries does not necessarily imply, as some postmodernists have claimed, that education can no longer act as an integrating social force. Indeed in many ways, the conditions in modern western states are more conducive to this now than they were in the last century when this was the explicit and dominant function of the national education system (Durkheim, 1977). When national education was first developed in Europe it sought to integrate societies that were multiply divided not only by class, religion, gender and ethnicity, but also by geography and language. The gulf between urban and rural populations in early nineteenth-century Europe was massive both in spatial and temporal terms (Weber, 1979). Rural populations lived, quite literally, in different historical times from their modernizing urban counterparts. Of no less significance were the divisions of language, not only among populations in the immigrant societies like America, but also within Europe. At the time of the revolution in France, when national education was already firmly on the agenda, only 50 per cent of the population spoke French. At the moment of unification in Italy, when national education was first introduced, less than 3 per cent of the population spoke Italian (Hobsbawm, 1990, p. 60).

Modern western societies have in some ways, as postmodernists claim, become more pluralistic. In terms of lifestyles and values, there is greater individual diversity inasmuch as individuals are freer to make their own choices. However, in other ways contemporary societies are less structurally fragmented than their predecessors. Religion, language and geography do not divide them as much as they did formerly and there is now a common social experience provided by a ubiquitous consumer and media culture. The latter, to be sure, do not provide any clearly defined structure of moral values or national identities. They do, nevertheless, provide a common language for communication.

The postmodern world is, generally, both more diverse *and* more homogeneous than modernity. Globalization, as cultural theorists contend, has not only provided new means for local and particular cultures to express and identify themselves; it has *also* made them more present and more visible to other cultures, thus enhancing the opportunities for common discourse. The sharp divides between communities based on region, class, religion and language have arguably decreased leading to greater social uniformity. On the other hand, with the demise of these community and group identities, there has also been a loss of the solidarity and moral bonding which obtained within them. This leads to greater individuation and thus greater diversity at the individual level.

The scope for education to act as a socially integrative force in contemporary society is not necessarily diminished or impeded by the forces of globalization and postmodernity. What has diminished perhaps is the political will of governments, at least in the West, to pursue the goals of social cohesion and social solidarity. However, even this may change as the social atomization induced by global market penetration becomes increasingly dysfunctional. With the decline of socially integrating institutions and the consequent atrophy of collective social ties, education may soon again be called upon to stitch together the fraying social fabric. There are already signs that this is happening both in the UK and within the European Union with the burgeoning debate about the 'learning society' (EU Commission, 1996; Ranson, 1994). After many years of neglect the question of education and citizenship is coming back onto the agenda.

The major dilemmas for governments and educationalists in the coming decade will revolve around how to reconstruct cultures of citizenship and nationhood in ways which are appropriate to modern conditions and yet conducive both to a deepening of democracy and to a strengthening social solidarity. The question poses many difficult problems about the competing claims to loyalty of the local community, the region, the nation and the supra-national world. At the national level it requires the forging of notions of civic national identity which are both inclusive and mobilizing, which reconstitute the legitimacy of the public domain and the primacy of the public good. For the individual it means constructing identities and negotiating loyalties within the complex constellation of collectivities defined by geography, ethnicity, age and nationality as well as cultivating the skills and predispositions which enable active and conscious participation in democratic society at community and national levels.

Education has a major role to play in all this. 'The challenge of the modern era', as Stewart Ranson has written, is 'the creation of a moral and political order that expresses and enables an active citizenship ... to regenerate and constitute more effectively than ever before a public – an educated public – that has the capacity to participate actively as citizens in the shaping of a learning society and polity' (1994, p. 102). Education must remain the public arena where tolerance, mutual respect and understanding and the ability to cooperate are cultivated. Just as it offers opportunities for individual development and advancement, it must also strive to promote civic identity and civic competence and to make possible a democratic and cohesive society. Education cannot ignore the realities of the global market. But nor can it surrender to global commodification.

# Notes

## CHAPTER 1   POSTMODERNISM AND STATE EDUCATION

1.  Fukuyama seems now to have moved away from this position. In his latest
    book (*Trust*, 1995), he appears to have discovered that there are other
    models of successful capitalism other than the American *laissez-faire*, free-
    market variety, and now extols the virtues of 'trust-based' capitalism as
    found, he claims, in Asian capitalism.

## CHAPTER 2   EDUCATION AND STATE FORMATION IN EUROPE AND ASIA

1.  In *Education and State Formation* (1990) I almost invariably used the word
    state for nation state to avoid implying a cultural nationalist understanding
    of the nature of statehood. However, this, in a way, simply sidesteps the
    problem.

## CHAPTER 3   TECHNICAL EDUCATION AND STATE FORMATION IN NINETEENTH-CENTURY ENGLAND AND FRANCE

1.  For economic historians see, for example: E.J. Hobsbawm, *Industry and
    Empire*, Harmondsworth, 1968; D. Landes, *The Unbound Prometheus*,
    London, 1969. For education historians see, for instance: E. Ashby,
    'Technology and the Academies. An Essay on Universities and the
    Scientific Revolution', in A.H. Halsey et al., *Education, Economy and
    Society*, London, 1961; S. Cotgrove, *Technical Education and Social
    Change*, 1958; A. Green, *Education and State Formation*, London, 1990;
    G. Roderick and M. Stephens, *Education and Industry in the Nineteenth
    Century*, London, 1978; H. Silver and J. Brennan, *A Liberal Vocationalism*,
    London, 1988; M. Sanderson, *The Missing Stratum: Technical School
    Education in England, 1900–1990s*, Athlone, 1994. A rare recent dissenter
    from this view is W.D. Rubenstein in *Capitalism, Culture and Decline in
    Britain, 1750–1990*, London, 1993.
2.  See: T. Huxley, 'Technical Education', in C. Bibby (ed.), *T.H. Huxley on
    Education*, Cambridge, 1971; L. Playfair, *Industrial Education on the
    Continent*, lecture at the Government School of Mines, Science and Applied
    Arts, London, 1852; J. Scott Russell, *Systematic Technical Education for
    the English People*, London, 1869; S.P. Thompson, op. cit.

3.  Quoted in C. Barnett, 'Technology, Education and Industrial and Economic Strength', in A. Finch and P. Scrimshaw (eds), *Standards, Schooling and Education*, London, 1980, p. 67.
4.  Royal Commission on Technical Instruction, Second Report, 1884, p. 508
5.  See G.C. Allen, *The British Disease*, Hobart Paper, London, 1967; P. Anderson, 'The Origins of the Present Crisis', *New Left Review*, 23, 1964 and 'Figures of Descent', *New Left Review*, 161, 1987; C. Barnett, *The Audit of War: The Illusion and Reality of Britain as a Great Nation*, London, 1986; A. Sampson, *The Changing Anatomy of Britain*, London, 1983; M. Sanderson, op. cit.; M.J. Wiener, *English Culture and the Decline of the Industrial Spirit, 1850–1980*, Harmondsworth, 1981.
6.  The classic statement of this case can be found in the polemical open letters written by Edward Baines Junior, the leading Dissenter and editor of the *Leeds Mercury*, to Lord John Russell: Letters to the Right Honourable John Russell *On State Education*, London, 1946.
7.  Royal Commission on Technical Instruction, Sixth Report, 1884, p. 1.
8.  Royal Commission on Technical Instruction, Second Report, 1884, Vol. 1, Part 1, p. 23.
9.  Select Committee, *On the Provision for Giving Instruction in Theoretical and Applied Science to the Industrial Class*, 1867–8, p. 130.

## CHAPTER 5   EDUCATION AND CULTURAL IDENTITY IN THE UNITED KINGDOM

1.  From an original article written with Richard Aldrich.

## CHAPTER 6   EDUCATIONAL ACHIEVEMENT IN CENTRALIZED AND DECENTRALIZED SYSTEMS

1.  Current research conducted by Hilary Steedman and Andy Green for the UK Department for Education and Training project: 'International Comparisons of Skills Supply and Demand'. To be published by the Centre for Economic Performance, London School of Economics.
2.  Canada Statistics/OECD, *Literacy, Economy and Society, Results of the First International Survey*, 1995, p. 84.
3.  The report from OFSTED, written by Professor David Reynolds, compares primary teaching in Taiwan and the UK and ascribes the allegedly higher standards in maths among Taiwanese pupils to the prevalence of orderly and structured whole-class teaching in that country.
4.  The education system in Scotland is considerably different from that in England and Wales and is not discussed here.

## CHAPTER 7 EDUCATION, GLOBALIZATION AND THE NATION STATE

1.  The Chinese form the dominant ethnic group with 76.7 per cent of the population, but there are sizeable minorities of Malays (14.7 per cent), Indians (6.4 per cent) and others (2.2 per cent) (1983 figures; Quah, 1984, p. 110). While English is the dominant language for public purposes, there are three other official languages including Malay, Mandarin Chinese and Tamil and these are spoken at home by the majority of the population. The society is also pluri-religious with 29 per cent in 1983 reporting to be Taoist, 26 per cent Bhuddist, 16 per cent Muslim and 10 per cent Christian (Quah, 1984, p. 110).
2.  As the 1959 MOE report put it: 'To act as a bridge to span simultaneously the four streams of education and to unify a community composed of different races, the setting up of one national language is vital. A common link for undivided loyalty to one another and to the state is provided in the national language.' Quoted in W.O. Lee, *Social Change and Educational Problems in Japan, Singapore and Hong Kong*, 1991, p. 58.
3.  The diploma qualifications have been evaluated as being at a level equivalent to the Higher National diploma in the UK. See Green and Steedman (1996).
4.  Reich (1991) argues to the contrary that increasing proportions of R&D activity for the MNCs is located abroad. He quotes National Science Foundation data which show American-owned corporations increased their overseas spending on R&D by 33 per cent between 1986 and 1987, compared to a 6 per cent increase in R&D spending in the USA. Beginning in 1987 Eastman Kodak, W.R. Grace, Du Pont, Mark, Procter & Gamble and Upjohn all opened R&D facilities in Japan (see Reich, 1991, p. 123).
5.  See *The Observer*, 23 April 1996.
6.  *Kyoiku, Gabujyutu, Bunka niokeru Koryu* was published by Monbusho, the National Ministry of Education (Tokyo: Okurasho, 1994). The Ad Council published four reports: National Council on Educational Reform, *Reports on Educational Reform* (Government of Japan, Tokyo: Okurasho, 1987). I owe these references, and the translation, to Keiko Yokoyama.
7.  David Phillips of the New Zealand Ministry of Education and Victoria University in Wellington is currently engaged on research into the history of this symbiosis in Anglo-New Zealand policy borrowing.

# Bibliography

Adams, D. and Gottlieb, E.E. (1993) *Education and Social Change in Korea*, New York: Garland.

Adler, M.E., Petch, A.J. and Tweedie, J.W. (1986) *Parental Choice in Education Policy*, Edinburgh University Press.

Ainley, P. (1993) *Class and Skill: Changing Divisions of Knowledge and Labour*, London: Cassell.

Ainley, P. and Corney, M. (1990) *Training for the Future: the Rise and Fall of the Manpower Services Commission*, London: Cassell.

Ainley, P. and Vickerstaff, S. (1993) 'Transitions from Corporatism: The Privatisation of Policy Failure', *Contemporary Record*, Vol. 7, No. 3.

Ainley, P., Gokulsing, M. and Tysome, T. (1996) *Beyond Competence: The NCVQ Framework and the Challenge to Higher Education in the New Millennium*, Aldershot: Avebury.

Albisetti, J. (1983) *Secondary School Reform in Imperial Germany*, Princeton University Press.

Aldrich, R. and Dean, D. (1991) 'The Historical Dimension', in R. Aldrich (ed.), *History in the National Curriculum*, London: Kogan Page.

Allen, G.C. (1967) *The British Disease*, London: Hobart Paper.

Amsden, A. (1992) *Asia's Next Giant. South Korea and Late Industrialization*, Oxford University Press.

Anderson, B. (1983) *Imagined Communities*, London: Verso.

Anderson, P. (1964) 'The Origins of the Present Crisis', *New Left Review*, No. 23.

Anderson, P. (1974), *Lineages of the Absolutist State*, London: Verso.

Anderson, P. (1984) 'Modernity and Revolution', *New Left Review*, No. 144.

Anderson, P. (1987) 'Figures of Descent', *New Left Review*, No. 161.

Anderson, R.D. (1875) *Education in France, 1848–1870*, Oxford University Press.

Appelbaum, R. and Henderson, J. (eds) (1992) *States and Development in the Asia Pacific Rim*, London: Sage.

Archer, M. (1979) *The Social Origins of Education Systems*, London: Sage.

Archer, M. and Vaughan, M. (1971) *Social Conflict and Educational Change in England and France, 1789–1848*, London: Cambridge University Press.

Arnold M. (1882) *Higher Schools in Universities in Germany*, London: Macmillan.

Aronowitz, S. and Giroux, H. (1991) *Post-Modern Education: Politics, Culture and Social Criticism*, Minneapolis: University of Minnesota Press.

Artz, F.D. (1966) *The Development of Technical Education in France, 1848–1870*, Cleveland: Society for the History of Technology.

Ashby, A. (1961) 'Technology and the Academies. An Essay on Universities and the Scientific Revolution', in A.H. Halsey, I.J. Floud, C.A. Anderson (eds), *Education, Economy and Society*, New York: Free Press of Glencoe.

Ashton, D. and Green, F. (1996) *Education, Training and the Global Economy*, London: Elgar.

Ashton, D.N. and Sung, J. (1994) *The State, Economic Development and Skill Formation: A New Asian Model*, Centre for Labour Market Studies, University of Leicester.

Avis, J., Bloomer, M., Esland, G., Gleeson, D. and Hodkinson, P. (1996) *Knowledge and Nationhood: Education, Politics and Work*, London: Cassell.

Bailey, B. (1990) 'Technical Education and Secondary Schooling, 1905–1945', in P. Summerfield and E. Evans (eds), *Technical Education and the State Since 1950*, Manchester University Press.

Baines, E. (1946) 'On State Education', *Letters to the Right Honourable John Russell*, London.

Bairoch, P. (1993) *Economics and World History*, London: Harvester Wheatsheaf.

Ball, C. (1991) *Learning Pays*, London: Royal Society of Arts.

Ball, S.J. (1990a) *Politics and Policy Making in Education: Explorations in Policy Sociology*, London: Routledge.

Ball, S.J. (1990b) *Education, Inequality and School Reform: Values in Crisis*, Kings' College Memorial Lecture.

Barnett, C. (1980) 'Technology, Education and Industrial and Economic Strength', in A. Finch and P. Scrimshaw (eds), *Standards, Schooling and Education*, Sevenoaks: Hodder and Stoughton.

Barnett, C. (1986) *The Audit of War: The Illusion and Reality of Britain as a Great Nation*, London: Macmillan.

Baudrillard, J. (1986) *L'Amérique*, Paris.

Bell, D. (1974) *The Coming Post-Industrial Society*, London: Heinemann

Benavot, A., Cha, Y.-K., Kamens, D., Meyer, J. and Wong, S.-K. (1991) 'Knowledge for the Masses: World Models and National Curricula, 1920–1986', *American Sociological Review*, Vol. 6, pp. 85–100.

Bendix, R. (1964) *Nation-Building and Citizenship*, University of California Press.

Bennett, R.J., Wicks, P. and McCoshan, A. (1994) *Local Empowerment and Business Services: Britain's Experiment with Training and Enterprise Councils*, London: UCL Press.

Berman, M. (1982) *All That Is Solid Melts Into Air*, London: Pluto.

Bishop, A. S. (1971) *The Rise of a Central Authority in English Education*, Cambridge University Press.

Blackstone, T., Cornford, J. and Hewitt, P. (1992) *Next Left: An Agenda for the 1990s*, London: IPPR.

Boli, J. (1989) *New Citizens for a New Society. The Institutional Origins of Mass Schooling in Sweden*. Oxford: Pergamon.

Bondi, L. (1991) 'Choice and Diversity in School Education: Comparing Developments in the United Kingdom and the USA', *Comparative Education*, Vol. 27, No. 2.

Boucher, L (1982) *Tradition and Change in Swedish Education*, Oxford: Pergamon.

Bowles, S. and Gintis, H. (1976) *Schooling in Capitalist America*, London: Routledge & Keegan Paul.

Boyne, B. and Rattansi, A. (eds) (1990) *Post-Modernism and Society*, London: Macmillan.

Breton, R. (1984) 'The Production and Allocation of Symbolic Resources: An Analysis of the Linguistic and Ethnocultural Fields in Canada', *Canadian Review of Sociology and Anthropology*, Vol. 21, No. 2, pp. 123–44.

Brown, P. and Lauder, H. (1992) 'Education, Economy and Society: An Introduction to a New Agenda', in P. Brown and H. Lauder (eds), *Education for Economic Survival: From Fordism to Post-Fordism?*, London: Routledge.

Brown, P. and Lauder, H. (1996) 'Education, Globalization and Economic Development', *Journal of Education Policy*, Vol. 11, No. 1.

Brubaker, R. (1992), *Citizenship and Nationhood in France and Germany*, Cambridge, Mass.: Harvard University Press.

Burke, A.W. (ed.) (1985) *The Modernizers: Overseas Students, Foreign Employees, and Meiji Japan*, Boulder, Col.: Westview Press.

Burnham, J. (1945) *The Managerial Revolution, or What is Happening in the World Now?*, Harmondsworth: Penguin.

Callinicos, A. (1987) *Against Postmodernism: A Marxist Critique*, Cambridge: Polity Press.

Carnoy, M. (1993) 'School Improvement: Is Privatization the Answer', in J. Hannaway and M. Carnoy (eds), *Decentralization and School Improvement*, San Francisco: Jossey-Bass.

Carr, W. and Hartnett, A. (1996) *Education and the Struggle for Democracy: The Politics of Educational Ideas*, Buckingham: Open University Press.

Casey, B. (1990) *Recent Developments in West Germany's Apprenticeship System*, London: Policy Studies Institute.

Castells, M. (1992) 'Four Asian Tigers with a Dragon's Head: A Comparative Analysis of the State, Economy and Society in the Asian Pacific Rim', in R. Appelbaum and J. Henderson (eds), *States and Development in the Asia Pacific Rim*, London: Sage.

CBI (1989) *Towards a Skills Revolution*, London: CBI.

CEDEFOP (1987a) *The Role of the Social Partners in Vocational Training and Further Training in the Federal Republic of Germany*, Berlin: CEDEFOP.

CEDEFOP (1992) 'The Role of the State and the Social Partners; Mechanisms and Spheres of Influence', *Vocational Training*, No. 1, Berlin.

Centre for Contemporary Cultural Studies: Education Group 11 (1981) *Unpopular Education*, London: Hutchinson.

Chancellor, V. (1970) *History for their Masters*, Bath: Adams & Dart.

Chitty, C. (1989) *Towards a New Education System*, Brighton: Falmer Press.

Chitty, C. (1991) Introduction, in C. Chitty (ed.), *Post-sixteen Education: Studies in Access and Achievement*, London: Kogan Page.

Chomsky, N. (1969) *American Power and the New Mandarins*, New York: Pantheon Books.

Chubb, J. and Moe, T. (1990) *Politics, Markets and America's Schools*, Washington DC: Brookings Institute.

Cipolla, C. M. (1969) *Literacy and Development in the West*, Harmondsworth: Penguin.

Clammer, J. (1993) 'The Establishment of a National Ideology', in G. Rodan (ed.), *Singapore Changes Guard: Social, Political and Economic Directions in the 1990s*, Cheshire, Melbourne: Longman.

Coffield, F. (1992) 'Training and Enterprise Councils: The Last Throw of Voluntarism', *Policy Studies*, Vol. 13, No. 4.

Colley, L. (1994) *Britons: Forging the Nation*, 1707–1837, London: Pimlico.

Cooper, R. (1996) *The Post-Modern State and the World Order*, London: Demos.

Corrigan, P. and Sayer, D. (1985) *The Great Arch: English State Formation as Cultural Revolution*, London: Blackwell.

Cotgrove, S. (1958) *Technical Education and Social Change*, London: Allen & Unwin.

Cowen, R. (1996) 'Last Past the Post: Comparative Education, Modernity and Perhaps Postmodernity', *Comparative Education*, Vol. 3, No. 2.

Cummings, W.K. (1980) *Education and Equality in Japan*, Princeton University Press.

Curtis, B. (1988) *Building the Educational State: Canada West, 1836–1837*, London, Ontario: Falmer Press.

Davey, I. and Miller, P. (1990) 'Family Formation, Schooling and the Patriarchal State', in M. Theobald and D. Selleck (eds), *Family, School and State in Australian History*, London: Allen & Unwin.

Davey, I. and Miller, P. (1991) *Patriarchal Transformations, Schooling and State Formation*, Paper for Social Science History Association Conference, New Orleans.

Davies, C. (1993) 'Concentric, Overlapping and Competing Loyalties and Identities', in K. Schleicher (ed.), *Nationalism in Education*, Frankfurt: Peter Lang.

Day, C.R. (1987) *Education and the Industrial World: The École d'Arts et Métiers and the Rise of French Industrial Engineering*, Cambridge, Mass.: MIT Press.

Department for Education White Paper (1992) *Diversity and Choice*, London: HMSO.

Derouet, J.L. (1991) 'Lower Secondary Education in France: From Uniformity to Institutional Autonomy', *European Journal of Education*, Vol. 26, No. 2.

de Tocqueville, A. (1955) *The Old Regime and the French Revolution*, trans. Stuart Gilbert, New York: Doubleday Anchor Books.

Deyo, F. (1992) 'The Political Economy of Social Policy Formation: East Asia's Newly Industrialized Countries', in R. Appelbaum and J. Henderson (eds), *States and Development in the Asia Pacific Rim*, London: Sage.

Dicey, A. V. (1914) *Lectures on the Relation between Law and Public Opinion in England during the Nineteenth Century*, London: Macmillan.

Donald, J. (1992) *Sentimental Education*, London: Verso.

Dore, R. (1984) *Education in Tokugawa Japan*, London: Athlone.

Dore, R. and Sako, M. (1989) *How the Japanese Learn to Work*, London: Routledge.

Dunning, J.H. (1993) *Multinational Enterprises and the Global Economy*, Wokingham: Addison-Wesley.

Durkheim, E. (1956) *Education and Sociology*, trans. S.D. Fox, New York: Free Press.

Durkheim, E. (1977) *The Evolution of Educational Thought*, London: RKP.

Edwards, R. (1994) 'From a Distance? Globalization, Space-Time Compression and Distance Education', *Journal of Open Learning*, Vol. 9, No. 3.

Edwards, T. and Whitty, G. (1992) 'Parental Choice and Educational Reform in Britain and the United States', *British Journal of Educational Studies*, Vol. 40, No. 2.

Employment Department (1988) *Employment for the 1990s*, London: HMSO.

Employment Department (1992) *People, Jobs and Opportunity*, London: HMSO.

Erault, M. (ed.) (1991) *Education and the Information Society*, London: Cassell.

European Union Commission for Research on Education and Training (1996) *White Paper on Education and Training: Teaching and Learning; Towards the Learning Society*, European Commission, Brussels.

Featherstone, M., Lash, S. and Robertson, R. (eds) (1995) *Global Modernities*, London: Sage.

Felstead, A. (1993) *Putting Individuals in Charge, Leaving Skills Behind? UK Training Policy in the 1990s*, Discussion Paper in Sociology S93 (7), University of Leicester.

Finegold, D. and Soskice, S. (1988) 'The Failure of Training in Britain: Analysis and Prescription', Oxford Review of Economic Policy, Vol. 4, No. 3.

Fukuyama, F. (1992) *The End of History and the Last Man*, London: H. Hamilton.

Fukuyama, F. (1995) *Trust*, London: H. Hamilton.

Fuller, B. and Robinson, R. (eds) (1992) *The Political Construction of Education*, New York: Praeger.

Gaill, Mairtin mac an (1993) 'The National Curriculum and Equal Opportunities', in C. Chitty (ed.), *The National Curriculum: Is It Working?*, London: Longman.

Gamble, A. (1981) *Britain in Decline*, London: Macmillan.

Garnier, M., Hage, J. and Fuller, B. (1989) 'The Strong State, Social Class and Controlled School Expansion in France, 1881–1975', *American Journal of Sociology*, Vol. 45, No. 2.

Gellner, E. (1983) *Nations and Nationalism*, Oxford: Blackwell.

Gellner, E. (1992) *Postmodernism, Reason and Religion*, London: Routledge.

Giddens, A. (1985) *The National-State and Violence*, Cambridge: Polity Press.

Gilbert, R. (1984) *The Impotent Image. Reflections of Ideology in the Secondary School Curriculum*. London: Falmer.

Gildea, T. (1988) *The Third Republic from 1870–1914*, New York: Longman.

Gintis, H. and Bowles, S. (1981) 'Contradiction and Reproduction in Education Theory', in R. Dale et al. (eds), *Education and the State*, Vol. 1, Milton Keynes: Open University Press.

Giroux, H. (1992) *Border Crossings*, London: Routledge.

Glendenning, F. (1973) 'School History Textbooks and Racial Attitudes', *Journal of Educational Administration and History*, Vol. 2.

Glowka, D. (1989) 'Anglo-German Perception of Education', *Comparative Education*, Vol. 25, No. 3.

Gopinathan, S. (1994) *Educational Development in a Strong-Developmentalist State: The Singapore Experience*, Paper presented at the Australian Association for Research in Education Annual Conference.

Gramsci, A. (1972) *Selections from the Prison Notebooks*, London: Lawrence & Wishart.

Green, A. (1990) *Education and State Formation: The Rise of Education Systems in England, France and the USA*, London: Macmillan.

Green, A. (1994) 'Postmodernism and State Education', *Journal of Education Policy*, Vol. 9, No. 1.

Green, A. (1995a) 'The Role of the State and the Social Partners in VET Systems', in L. Bash and A. Green (eds), *Youth, Education and Work: World Yearbook of Education 1995*, London: Kogan Page.

Green, A. (1995b) 'The European Challenge to British Vocational Education and Training', in P. Hodkinson and Issit, M. (eds), *The Challenge of Competence: Professionalism through Vocational Education and Training*, London: Cassell.

Green, A. and Mace, J. (1994) *Funding Training Outcomes*, Post-16 Education Centre Working Paper, London Institute of Education.

Green, A. and Steedman, H. (1993) *Educational Provision, Educational Attainment and the Needs of Industry: A Review of the Research for Germany, France, Japan, the USA and Britain*, Report Series 5, London: National Institute of Economic and Social Research.

Green, A. and Steedman, H. (1996) *International Comparisons of Skills Supply and Demand*, Report to DFEE, London School of Economics.

Grew, R. and Harrigan, P. (1991) *Schools, State and Society: The Growth of Elementary Schooling in the Nineteenth Century*, University of Michigan Press.

Gundara, J. and Jones, C. (1990) 'Nation States, Diversity and Interculturalism: Issues for British Education', in D. Ray and D. Poonwassie (eds), *Education and Cultural Differences*, New York: Garland.

Habermas, J. (1995) 'Modernity – an Incomplete Project', in H. Foster (ed.), *Postmodern Culture*, London: Pluto.

Hall, S. and Gieben, B (1992) *Formations of Modernity*, Cambridge: Open University Press/Polity Press.

Hall, S., Held, D. and McGrew, T. (eds) (1992) *Modernity and its Futures*, Cambridge: Open University Press/Polity Press.

Hampden-Turner, C. and Trompenaars, F. (1993) *The Seven Cultures of Capitalism*, London: Piatkus.

Hanson, E. (1990) 'School-Based Management in the United States and Spain', *Comparative Education Review*, Vol. 34, No. 4.

Harvey, D. (1990) *The Condition of Post-Modernity*, Oxford: Blackwell.

Havel, V. (1994) 'The New Measure of Man', *New York Times*, 8 July.

Hayes, C. (1984) *Competence and Competition*, London, IMS/NEDO.

Held, D. (1989) *Political Theory and the Modern State*, Cambridge: Polity.

Hill, D. and Cole, M. (1993) 'Postmodernism, Education and the Road to Nowhere: A Materialist Critique', unpublished paper.

Hill, M. and Lian Kwen Fee (1995) *The Politics of Nation-Building and Citizenship in Singapore*, London: Routledge.

Hillgate Group (1987) *The Reform of British Education*, London: Hillgate.

Hirst, P. and Thompson, G. (1992) 'The Problems of "Globalization": International Economic Relations, National Economic Management and the Formation of Trading Blocs', *Economy and Society*, Vol. 21, No. 4.

Hirst, P. and Thompson, G. (1995) 'Globalization and the Future of the National State', *Economy and Society*, Vol. 24, No. 3.

Hirst, P. and Thompson, G. (1996) *Globalization in Question: The International Economy and Possibilities of Governance*, Cambridge: Polity.

HM Government (1994), *Competitiveness: Helping Business to Win*, Cm 2563, London: HMSO.

HMI (Her Majesty's Inspectorate) (1986) *Education in the Federal Republic of Germany: Aspects of Curriculum and Assessment*, London: HMSO.

HMI (1990) *Aspects of Education in the USA: Teaching and Learning in New York Schools*, London: HMSO.

HMI (1991) *Aspects of Primary Education in France*, London: HMSO.

HMI (1992) *Teaching and Learning in Japanese Elementary Schools*, London: HMSO.

Hobsbawm, E.J. (1969) *Industry and Empire*, Harmondsworth: Penguin.

Hobsbawm, E.J. (1977) *The Age of Capital, 1848–1875*, London: Abacus.

Hobsbawm, E.J. (1989) *The Age of Empire, 1875–1914*, London: Weidenfeld & Nicholson.

Hobsbawm, E.J. (1990) *Nations and Nationalism since 1780: Programme, Myth, Reality*. Cambridge: Cambridge University Press.

Hobsbawm, E.J. (1994) *The Age of Extremes: The Short Twentieth Century, 1914–1991*, London: Michael Joseph.

Horio, T. (1988) *Educational Thought in Modern Japan*, ed. and trans. S. Platzer, University of Tokyo Press.

Horn, P. (1988) 'English Elementary Education and the Growth of the Imperial Ideal: 1880–1914', in J. Mangan (ed.), *'Benefits Bestowed'? Education and British Imperialism*, Manchester University Press.

Hutton, W. (1995) *The State We're In*, Chatham, Kent: Mackays.

Huxley, T. (1971) 'Technical Education', in C. Bibby (ed.), *T.H. Huxley on Education*, London: Cambridge University Press.

Illich, I. (1971) *Deschooling Society*, New York: Harper & Row.

Inkeles, A. (1982) 'National Differences in Scholastic Performance', in P. Altback, R. Arnove and G. Kelly (eds), *Comparative Education*, New York: Macmillan.

Inkeles, A. and Sirowy, L. (1983) 'Convergent and Divergent Trends in National Education Systems', *Social Forces*, Vol. 62, No. 2.

International Assessment of Achievement (IEA) (1988) *Science Achievement in Seventeen Countries*, London: Pergamon Press.

International Assessment of Educational Progress (IAEP) (1992) *Learning Mathematics*, New Jersey: Educational Testing Service.

IPPR (1991) *A British Baccalauréat*, London: Institute for Public Policy Research.

Jameson, F. (1984) 'Postmodernism, or the Cultural Logic of Capital', *New Left Review*, No. 149.

Jensen, J. (1989) 'The Talents of Women, the Skills of Men: Flexible Specialization and Women', in S. Wood (ed.), *The Transformation of Work*, London: Unwin Hyman.

Johnson, C. (1982) *MITI and the Japanese Miracle*, Stanford University Press.

Johnson, C. (1995) *Japan Who Governs? The Rise of the Developmental State*, New York: W.W. Norton.

Jones, K. (1989) *Right Turn: the Conservative Revolution in Education*, London: Radius.

Jones, K. (ed.) (1992) English and the National Curriculum; *Cox's Revolution?*, London: Kogan Page.

Kaestle, C.F. (1983) *Pillars of the Republic: Common Schools and American Society, 1780–1860*, Toronto: Hill & Wang.

Katz, M. (1971) *Class, Bureaucracy and Schools*, New York: Praeger.

Katz, M. (1976) 'The Origins of Public Education: A Reassessment', *History of Education Quarterly*, Winter.

Keep, E. (1991) 'The Grass Looked Greener: Some Thoughts on the Influence of Comparative Vocational Training Research on the UK Policy Debate', in P. Ryan (ed.), *International Comparisons of Vocational Education and Training for Intermediate Skills*, Lewes: Falmer Press.

Keep, W. and Mayhew, K. (1993) *UK Training Policy: Assumptions and Reality*, ESRC Seminar Paper, December.

Kennedy, P. (1989) *The Rise and Fall of the Great Powers. Economic Change and Military Conflict from 1500 to 2000*, London: Fontana Press.

Kenway, J. (1992) *Marketing Education in the Post-Modern Age*, Paper to the AARE Conference San Francisco.

Kermode, F. (1973) *Lawrence*, London: Fontana.

Koike, K. and Inoki, T. (eds) (1990) *Skill Formation in Japan and South East Asia*, University of Tokyo Press.

Korean Education Development Institute (1984) *Schooling and Social Achievement*, Seoul: KEDI.

Korean Education Development Institute (1985) *Korean Education 2000*, Seoul: KEDI.

Kumar, K. (1992) 'New Theories of Industrial Society', in P. Brown and H. Lauder (eds), *Education for Economic Survival*, London: Routledge.

Landes, D. (1969) *The Unbound Prometheus: Technological Change and Industrial Development in Western Europe from 1750 to the Present*, London: Cambridge University Press.

Lauglo, J. (1995) 'Forms of Decentralization and the Implications for Education', *Comparative Education*, Vol. 31, No. 1.

Lauglo, J. and McLean, M. (eds) (1985) *The Control of Education*, London: Kogan Page.

Lee, W.O. (1991) *Social Change and Educational Problems in Japan, Singapore and Hong Kong*, London: Macmillan.

Low, G. (1988) 'The MSC: A Failure of Democracy', in M. Morris and C. Griggs (eds), *Education – The Wasted Years? 1973–1986*, Lewes: Falmer Press.

Lynn, R. (1988) *Educational Achievement in Japan: Lessons for the West*, London: Macmillan.

Lyotard, J.-F. (1984) *The Postmodern Condition*, Manchester University Press.

McCullough, G. (1989) *The Secondary Technical School: A Usable Past?*, London: Falmer.

Macfarlane, A. (1978) *Origins of English Individualism*, Oxford: Blackwell.

McGrew, A. and Lewis, P.G. et al. (1992) *Global Politics: Globalization and the Nation State*, Cambridge: Polity.

McLean, M. (1990) *Britain and the Single Market Europe*, London: Kogan Page.

McLean, M. (1995) 'Education and Training in the New Europe: Economic and Political Contexts', in L. Bash and A. Green (eds) *Youth, Education and Work: World Yearbook of Education*, London: Kogan Page.

Mangan, J. (ed.) (1988) *Benefits Bestowed? Education and British Imperialism*, Manchester University Press.

Mangan, J. A. (ed.) (1993) *The Imperial Curriculum: Racial Images in Education in the British Colonial Experience*, London: RKP.

Manpower Services Commission (MSC) (1985) *Competence and Competition*, Sheffield: MSC.

Marsden, D. and Ryan, P. (1985) 'Work, Labour Markets and Vocational Preparation: Anglo-German Comparisons of Training in Intermediate Skills', in L. Bash and A. Green (eds), *World Yearbook of Education: Youth, Education and Work*, London: Kogan Page.

Marquand, D. (1988) *The Unprincipled Society. New Demands and Old Politics*, London: Cape.

Marshall, T.H. and Bottomore, T. (1992) *Citizenship and Social Class*, London: Pluto Press.

Marx, K. (1993) 'Review of Guizot', in J. Fernbach (ed.). *Surveys from Exile*, London: Penguin.

Mathews, J. (1989) *Tools of Change: New Technology and the Democratization of Work*, London: Pluto.

Mayer, A. (1981) *The Persistance of the Old Regime*, New York: Pantheon Books.

Meager, N. (1990) 'TECs: A Revolution in Training and Enterprise, or Old Wine in New Bottles?', *Local Economy*, Vol. 6, May.

Melton, J. Van Horn. (1988) *Absolutism and the 18th-Century Origins of Compulsory Schooling in Prussia and Austria*, Cambridge University Press.

Meyer, J. et al. (1985) 'Public Education as Nation-building in America: Enrolments and Bureaucratization in the American States, 1870–1930', *American Journal of the Sociology of Education*, Vol. 3.

Mill, J.S. (1871) *Autobiography*, ed. J. Stillinger, London: Oxford University Press.

Miller, P. (1986) *Long Division: Schooling in South Australian Society*, Netley, S. Australia: Wakefield Press.

Milward, A.S. (1992) *The European Rescue of the Nation State*, London: Routledge.

Mitter, W. (1992a) 'Educational Adjustments and Perspectives in a United Germany', *Comparative Education*, vol. 28, No. 1.

Mitter, W. (1992a) 'Education in Eastern Europe and the Former Soviet Union in a Period of Revolutionary Change', *Oxford Studies in Comparative Education*, Vol. 2, No. 1.

Mitter, W. (1994) 'Nationalism, Regionalism, and Internationalism in Europe: An East–West Comparison of Educational Development', in K. Schleicher (ed.), *Nationalism in Education*, Frankfurt: Peter Lang.

Moore, B. Jnr (1967) *Social Origins of Dictatorship and Democracy*, Boston: Beacon Press.

Moore, D. (1990) 'Voice and Choice in Chicago', in W. Clune and J. Witte (eds), *Choice and Control in American Education*, Vol. 2, London: Falmer Press.

Morris, P. (1995) Introduction in P. Morris and A. Sweeting (eds), *Education and Development in East Asia*, New York: Garland Press.

Morris, P. and Sweeting, A. (1991) 'Education and Politics; the Case of Hong Kong from an Historical Perspective', *Oxford Review of Education*, Vol. 17, No. 3.

Murray, R. (1988) 'Life After Henry', *Marxism Today*, October.

Nairn, T. (1981) *The Break-up of Britain: Crisis and Neo-Nationalism*, London: Verso.

National Commission on Education (1993) *Learning to Succeed*, London: Heinneman.

National Commission on Excellence in Education (1984) *A Nation at Risk: The Imperative for Educational Reform*, Washington, US Congress.

Nietzsche, F. (1968) *The Will to Power*, New York: Vintage Books.

OECD (1985) *Education and Training Beyond Basic Schooling*, Paris: OECD.

OECD (1990) *Pathways to Learning*, Paris: OECD.

OECD (1995) *Education at a Glance*, Paris: OECD.

OECD/Statistics Canada (1995) *Literacy, Economy and Society*, Paris: OECD

Ohmae, K. (1990) *The Borderless World*, London: Collins.

Ohmae, K. (1996) *The End of the Nation State: The Rise of Regional Economies*, London: Harper-Collins.

Olson, M. (1982) *The Rise and Decline of Nations*, New Haven, Conn.: Yale University Press.

Passin, H. (1965) *Society and Education in Japan*, New York: Teachers' College Press.

Perkin, H. (1985) *Origins of English Society*, London: Ark.

Perkin, H. (1989) *The Rise of Professional Society: England Since 1880*, London.

Perry, P.J.C. (1976) *The Evolution of British Manpower Policy*, London: BACIE.

Pieterse, J.N. (1995) 'Globalization as Hybridization', in M. Featherstone, S. Lash and R Robertson (eds), *Global Modernities*, London: Sage.

Piore, M. and Sabel, C. (1984) *The Second Industrial Divide*, New York: Basic Books.

Playfair, L. (1852) *Industrial Education on the Continent*, Lecture at the Government School of Mines, Science and Applied Arts, London.

Pollert, A. (1988) 'The Flexible Firm: Fixation or Fact', *Work, Employment and Society*, Vol. 2, No. 3.

Polanyi, K. (1957) *The Great Transformation*, Boston, Mass.: Beacon Press.

Porter, M.E. (1990) *The Competitive Advantage of Nations*, London: Macmillan.

Postlethwaite, N. (1982) 'Success and Failure in Schools', in P. Altback, R. Arnove and G. Kelly (eds), *Comparative Education*, New York: Macmillan.

Prais, S.J. (1987) 'Education for Productivity: Comparisons of Japanese and English Schooling and Vocational Preparation', *National Institute Economic Review*, February.

Prost, A. (1968) *Histoire de l'Enseignement en France*, 1800–1967, Paris: Armand Colin.

Prost, D. (1995) Review Essay: 'Education and the National Question Today', *Comparative Education Review*, Vol. 39, No. 2.

Quah, J.S.T. (1984) 'The Public Policy-Making Process in Singapore', *Asian Journal of Public Administration*, Vol. 6, No. 2.

Raffe, D. (1993) *Tracks and Pathways: Differentiation in Education and Training Systems and their Relation to the Labour Market*, Paper given to the Conference of the European Research Network on Transitions in Youth, Universidad Autónoma de Barcelona.

Rainbird, H. (1990) *Training Matters: Union Perspectives on Industrial Restructuring and Training*, Oxford: Blackwell.

Ramirez, F. and Boli, J. (1987) 'The Political Construction of Mass Schooling: European Origins and Worldwide Institutionalization', *Sociology of Education*, Vol. 60.

Ranson, S. (1993) *Reviewing Education for Democracy*, Paper delivered to IPPR/Goldsmiths' Seminar on Alternative Education Policies, London, March.

Ranson, S. (1994) *Towards a Learning Society*, London: Cassell.

Ratansi, A. and Reeder, D. (1992) *Essays in Honour of Brian Simon,* London: Lawrence & Wishart.

Reich, R. (1991) *The Work of Nations: A Blueprint for the Future*, New York: Vintage.

Reisner, E. (1922) *Nationalism and Education since 1789*, New York: Macmillan.

Reynolds, D. and Farrell, S. (1996), *Worlds Apart? A Reviews of International Surveys of Educational Achievement Involving England*, London: OFSTED/HMSO.

Rhee, Jong-Chan (1994) *The State and Industry in South Korea*, London: Routledge.

Ringer, F. (1979) *Education and Society in Modern Europe*, Bloomington: Indiana University Press.

Robertson, R. (1995) 'Globalization: Time-Space and Homogeneity-Heterogeneity' in M. Featherstone, S. Lash and R. Robertson (eds) *Global Modernities*, London: Sage.

Robinson, W. P. and Taylor, C. A. (1989) 'Correlates of Low Academic Attainment in Three Countries: England, France and Japan', *International Journal of Educational Research*, Vol. 13.

Robinson, W. P., Taylor, C.A. and Piolat, M. (1992) '*Redoublement in Relation* to Self Perception and Self Evaluation: France', *Research in Education*, Vol. 47, May.

Rodan, G. (1993) 'Preserving the One-Party State in Contemporary Singapore', in K. Hewison, R. Robinson and G. Rodan (eds), *Southeast Asia in the 1990s: Authoritarianism, Democracy and Capitalism*, St Leonards, NSW: Allen & Unwin.

Roderick, G. and Stephens, M. (1978) *Education and Industry in the Nineteenth Century*, London: Longman.

Royal Commission on Technical Instruction (Samuelson Commission) (1884) *Second and Sixth Reports*, London.

Royal Society (1991) *Beyond GCSE*, London: Royal Society.

Rubinstein, W. D. (1993) *Capitalism, Culture and Decline in Britain*, 1750–1990, London: Routledge.

Ruberti, A. (1993) 'Guidelines for Community Action in the Field of Education and Training', unpublished European Commission working paper.

Rust, V. (1991) 'Post-modernism and its Comparative Education Implications', *Comparative Education Review*, Vol. 35, No. 4.

Sadler, M. (1979) *Selections from Sadler: Studies in World Citizenship*, compiled by J. Higginson, Liverpool: Dejall & Meyorre.

Sampson, A. (1983) *The Changing Anatomy of Britain*, London.

Samuel, R.H. and Thomas, R. (1949) *Education and Society in Modern Germany*, London: Routledge and Kegan Paul.

Sanderson, M. (1994) *The Missing Stratum: Technical School Education in England, 1900–1990s*, London: Athlone Press.

Schleicher, K. (ed.) (1993), *Nationalism in Education*, Frankfurt: Peter Lang.

Schoppa, J. (1991) *Education Reform in Japan: A Case of Immobilist Politics*, London: Routledge.

Scott Russell, J. (1869) *Systematic Technical Education for the English People*, London: Bradbury Evans.

Scruton, R. (1980) *The Meaning of Conservatism*, Harmondsworth: Penguin.

Select Committee (1867–8) *On the Provision of Giving Instruction in Theoretical and Applied Science to the Industrial Class*, London.

Seton-Watson, H. (1977) *Nations and States. An Enquiry into the Origins of Nations and the Politics of Nationalism*. London: Methuen.

Sexton, S. (1987) *Our Schools: A Radical Policy*, London: Institute of Economic Affairs.

Sheldrake, J. and Vickerstaff, S. (1987) *The History of Industrial Training in Britain*, Aldershot: Avebury.

Shephard, J. (1992) Speech to TEC Conference, Birmingham, 2 July.

Silver, H. and Brennan, J. (1988) *A Liberal Vocationalism*, London: Methuen.

Simon, B. (1965) *Education and the Labour Movement, 1870–1920*, London: Lawrence & Wishart.

Simon, B. (1969) *The Two Nations and the Educational Structure*, 1780–1870, London: Lawrence & Wishart.

Simon, B. (1988) *Bending the Rules*, London: Lawrence & Wishart.

Singapore Government (1991) *The Next Lap, Singapore*: Times Editions Pte Ltd.

Smiles, S. (1859) *Self Help*, London: John Murray.

Smith, A.D. (1995) *Nations and Nationalism in the Global Era*, Cambridge: Polity Press.

Soon Teck Wong (1992) *Development of Human Resources and Technological Capability in Singapore*, Working Paper, Economic Development Institute of the World Bank.

Spencer, H. (1851), *State Education Self-Defeating*, London: John Chapman.

Stephens, M. (1991) *Education and the Future of Japan*, Sandgate, UK: Japan Library.

Stone, H. (1969), 'The Educational Revolution in England, 1600–1900', *Past and Present*, No. 42.

Streeck, W. (1987) 'Skills and the Limits of Neo-liberalism: The Enterprise of the Future as a Place of Learning,' *Work, Employment and Society*, Vol. 3, No. 1.

Streeck, W. and Schmitter, P. (1991) 'From National Corporatism to Transnational Pluralism: Organized Interests in the Single European Market', *Politics and Society*, Vol. 19, No. 2.

Sultana, R. (1995) 'A Uniting Europe, a Dividing Education? Supra-nationalism, Euro-centrism and the Curriculum', *International Studies in the Sociology of Education*, Vol. 5, No. 2.

Swedish Ministry of Education and Science (1993) *Strategies for Education and Research*, Stockholm.

Szebeny, P. (1992) 'State Centralization and School Autonomy: Process of Educational Change in Hungary', *Oxford Studies in Comparative Education*, Vol. 2, No. 1.

Tanguy, L. (1991) *Quelle Formation Pour Les Ouvriers et Les Employés de France*, Paris: La Documentation Français.

Thompson, S.P. (1879) *Apprentice Schools in France*, London .

Tilly, C. (1990) *Coercion, Capital and European States*, AD 990–1992, Oxford: Blackwell.

Turner, P. (1991) *Capital Flows in the 1980s: A Survey of Major Trends*, BIS Economic Papers Number 30, April, Bank for International Settlements, Geneva.

Tyack, D. (1966) 'Forming the National Character: Paradox in the Educational Thought of the Revolutionary Generation', *Harvard Educational Review*, Vol. 36, No 1.

Tyack, D. and James, T. (1986) 'State Government and American Public Education: Exploring the Primeval "Forest"', *History of American Education Quarterly*, Vol. 26, No. 1.

Usher, R. and Edwards R. (1994) *Postmodernism and Education: Different Voices, Different Worlds*, London: Routledge.

Vickerstaff, S. (1992) 'Training for Economic Survival', in P. Brown, and H. Lauder (eds), *Education for Economic Survival*, London: Routledge.

Wade, R. (1990) *Governing the Market: Economic Theory and the Role of Government in East Asian Industrialization*, Princeton University Press.

Waters, M. (1995) *Globalization*, London: Routledge.

Weber, E. (1979) *Peasants into Frenchmen: The Modernization of Rural France, 1870–1914*, London: Chatto.

Webster, R. (1990) 'Education in Wales and the Rebirth of a Nation', *History of Education*, Vol. 19, No 3.

Weiss, J.H. (1982) *The Making of Technological Man: The Social Origins of French Engineering Education*, Cambridge, Mass.: MIT Press.

White, M. (1987) *The Japanese Educational Challenge*, London: Macmillan.

Whitty, G. (1992) 'Education, Economy and National Culture', in R. Bocock and K. Thompson (eds), *Social and Cultural Forms of Modernity*, Buckingham: Open University Press.

Wielemans, W. and Choi-Ping Chan, P. (eds) (1994) *Education and Culture in Industrializing Asia. The Interaction between Industrialization, Cultural Identity and Education*, Leuven University Press.

Wiener, M.J. (1981) *English Culture and the Decline of the Industrial Spirit, 1850–1980*, Harmondsworth: Penguin.

Winkler, D. (1993) 'Fiscal Decentralization and Accountability: Experience in Four Countries', in J. Hannaway and M. Carnoy (eds), *Decentralization and School Improvement*, San Francisco: Jossey-Bass.

Winterton, J. and Winterton, R. (1994) *Collective Bargaining and Consultation over Continuing Vocational Training*, London: Employment Department.

Wolf, A. (1992) *Mathematics for Vocational Students in France and England: Contrasting Provision and Consequences*, Paper No. 23, London: National Institute of Economic and Social Research.

Wolf, A. (1995) *Competence-Based Assessment*, Buckingham: Open University Press.

Wolf, A. (1996) 'Vocational Qualifications in Europe: The Emergence of Common Assessment', in L. Bash and A. Green (eds), *Youth Education and Work: World YearBook of Education, 1995*, London: Kogan Page.

World Bank (1984) *East Asian Economic Miracle*, Geneva: World Bank.

Young, Yi-rong (1994) *Education and Social Change in Taiwan*, Paper to 16th Congress of the Comparative Education Society in Europe, Copenhagen, June.

# Index